CONTENTS

Dedication

For my children Bethan, Catrin and Danny.

Thanks

I would like to thank the staff at Oxford Study Courses, who have made me feel so welcome on countless Easter and Summer Revision courses.

How to use this guide

Each section contains detailed notes on the four single party states of China, Russia, Italy and Germany. In addition, I have provided practice essay questions, partially completed by me but with space for you to have a go at too.

Annotating this guide will help you reflect on its contents and improve your recall.

Tackling Paper 2

What do you need to know about Paper 2?

• The examination lasts **one and a half hours**

• There are **FIVE** sections, each on a different 20th century world history topic. 'The origins and development of authoritarian and single-party states' is **Topic 3**.

• Six essay questions will be set on each topic, so 30 in total

• Candidates have to answer **two** questions each chosen from **different** topics

• The maximum mark for each question is 20

• Paper 2 is worth 25% of the Higher Level assessment and 45% of the Standard Level assessment.

• The structure of each section is:

  - Three questions will refer to either events or people named in the IBO syllabus:

    Hitler, Stalin, Nasser, Kenyatta, Nyerere, Peron, Castro, Sukarno and Mao

  - Two questions will be open (you can use your own examples, rather than just those named in the IBO syllabus, so, for example, you could use Mussolini). So the section in my guide on Mussolini and Fascist Italy can be used in any question on Topic 3 that is open and does not specify one of the 9 named single party or authoritarian rulers.

  - At least one question will be on social, economic or gender issues.

  - At least one question on each topic will demand examples from two regions. When the question refers to 'region', it means one of the 4 regional options (Africa; Americas; Asia and Oceania; Europe and the Middle East) defined by the world map in the introduction to 20th century world history topics. Any one of the questions may be a comparative question.

Advice on tackling Essays

• You must spend a few minutes carefully looking at the paper and weighing up the choice of questions, before you make up your mind on which two questions to answer.

• Look very closely at the wording of the questions, making sure that you understand their implications and what you need to address in your answer.

• Pay particular attention to 'command' words such as: 'to what extent', 'analyse', 'compare and contrast'. In the case of 'To what extent was Nazi Germany a totalitarian state?' you must weigh up the ways in which it was and the ways in which it was not totalitarian, reaching a conclusion about whether it was totally, largely, partly, or not at all, totalitarian. 'Compare and contrast the methods by which Hitler and Mao came to power' would require you to examine the similarities and the differences between their methods. 'Analyse' means examine or scrutinise, so 'analyse the conditions which gave rise to the single party state in China' would require you to examine the circumstances which made possible the Chinese Communist Party's success, explaining which conditions (social, political, economic, military) benefited the CCP and evaluating which were most important.

• Always plan your answer, spending at least 2 or 3 minutes doing this for each essay, if not longer (but no more than 5 to 6).

• Give equal time to each essay you write. Do not be tempted to spend much longer on one at the expense of the other.

• Answer the question. Keep your approach analytical, do not drift in to a description of events. Focus tightly on the question; do not deviate.

• Perhaps the best way of ensuring that each paragraph is linked to the title, is to check that your first sentence (the 'key' sentence) is making a statement that directly answers the question.

• For each point that you make, provide an explanation of what light that point sheds on the question/why it is significant and also present evidence or a precise example to support it. So the drill should be **'Statement, Explanation, Example'.**

• Always write in complete sentences and be as clear as you can in your use of English. The clearer your English, the more effectively you will communicate your points to the examiner.

• Always write a proper introduction. This must identify the key issues raised by the question. You should also outline your thesis, the line of argument that your answer will take.

• Make sure that you leave time for a proper conclusion. The main purpose of this is to restate your key arguments.

• Do not feel that you have to pack your answer with references to differing schools of historical interpretation and named historians. You will get credit for such historiographical references, where used appropriately, but you could reach the top mark band without any such references. Certainly do not insert them just for the sake of displaying your knowledge if they do not contribute to answering the question.

• Whatever information you insert in to your answer, whether in the form of a fact, a statistic or a quotation, do make sure that you explain its significance and how it answers the question. If you do that, your essay should remain focused.

THE RISE AND RULE OF THE SINGLE PARTY STATE IN RUSSIA: 1900-41

The Origins of the Single Party State

In October 1917 Lenin's Bolsheviks seized power in Petrograd, Russia's capital, and after a vicious Civil War, created the USSR (the Union of the Soviet Socialist Republics), a single party state which was to endure until 1991. In order to explain the success of the Bolsheviks in establishing the first socialist state in history, it is necessary to examine both the failings of the Russian monarchy, which collapsed in February 1917, and also of the short-lived Provisional Government, which filled the void left by the abdication of the last tsar (emperor), Nicholas II. In addition, the Bolsheviks' strengths must be analysed, to determine how they successfully exploited conditions in order to overthrow the Provisional Government.

Background

When Winston Churchill greeted Josef Stalin at the Yalta Conference in 1945, towards the end of the Second World War, he congratulated Stalin on Russian troops reaching Berlin. Stalin's reply was that those of Tsar Alexander I had got as far as Paris!

The Russian Empire had been ruled by the Romanov dynasty since the 17th century and was a huge land mass, comprising about 50 different nationalities. By the 19th century several fundamental weaknesses became apparent.

Q. **What long-term weaknesses of the Russian monarchy led to its collapse in 1917?**

1. A failure to match the military strength of European great powers such as Germany and France.
2. A failure to address widespread peasant poverty.
3. A failure to achieve the levels of industrialisation reached by western European governments, notably those of Britain and Germany.
4. An inability to broaden its political support through a programme of constitutional reform; Russia's monarchy was almost unique among the Great Powers in refusing (up to 1905) to share any of its power with its subjects.

Q. **What were the long-term military causes of the 1917 Revolutions?**

At the beginning of the 19th century Russia had been one of the great military powers of Europe, which, under Tsar Alexander, had defeated Napoleon. However, over the course of the 19th century Russia fell far behind the other Great Powers, such as Britain and France, as the latter underwent profound economic and social changes as they rapidly industrialised. Russia's backwardness was cruelly exposed during the Crimean War (1854-56) in which Tsar Nicholas I (1825-55), and his son, Alexander II (1855-81), saw Russia's armed forces humiliated on home soil by the British and French. Alexander II's reforming Minister of War, Dimtri Miliutin, did introduce universal military service (1874) and the Russian

Army performed rather better against Turkey in 1877-78. However, Russia's lack of industrialisation meant that Russia was not in the same league in terms of military power as countries like Germany. This was highlighted by Russia's humiliating defeat by Japan in 1904-5. A series of military reforms was instituted after this but they were not due for completion until 1917 and the outbreak of the First World War in 1914 caught Russia unprepared for a major conflict.

Q. What were the long-term socio-economic causes of the 1917 Revolutions?

1.   Agricultural backwardness

Until the middle of the century, the bulk of the population comprised millions of serfs (peasants) who were tied to the land belonging to noble landlords and the Russian crown. In spite of Alexander II, the "Tsar-liberator" granting them personal freedom in 1861, rural poverty remained a huge cause of social tension and peasant unrest grew in the last quarter of the 19th century and the opening years of the 20th. The causes were:

- Chronic land shortage
- A rapidly growing peasant population
- Very low levels of literacy
- The burden of redemption payments that peasants were required to make in order to pay for the land they purchased from the landlords.

Peasant uprisings would play a major role in both the 1905 Revolution and the October 1917 Revolution.

2.   Late but very rapid industrialisation

As noted above, little industrialisation took place in Russia before the 1890s. Although, the total number of industrial workers in Russia grew from 800,000 (1855) to about 1.3 million (1887), this was still only 1% of Russia's population (113 million) and Russia continued to fall further and further behind rapidly industrialising countries, notably the USA, Britain and Germany. It was not until the 1890s that the Russian government initiated a programme of rapid industrialisation in an attempt to catch up with the West and retain Russia's status as a great military power.

Coal production increased 500% in the years 1880 to 1900 to 16 million tons p.a. Russian industry grew at 8% p.a. in 1890s and by 1900 had become world's fifth industrial power, though still a long way behind GB, France, Germany and the USA. However, industrial growth was highly dependent on foreign investment and a world recession from 1900 hit Russia hard, which was one of the causes of 1905 Revolution.

Furthermore, both before and after the 1905 Revolution, the rapid pace of industrialisation caused huge strain on Russia as industrial workers crowded into the rapidly growing cities of St Petersburg and Moscow. The population of St Petersburg and Moscow more than doubled in the period 1881-1914 (to 2.2 million and 1.3 million respectively).

The raid pace of industrialisation did not just create immense social tensions in the towns, it also worsened the condition of the peasants because the peasants were being squeezed by high taxes which the government used to fund industrialisation. Higher levels of taxation meant that the peasants were obliged to sell more grain, therefore making them more vulnerable to famine. A series of bad harvests in the 1890s led to growing rural unrest.

Q. What were the long-term political causes of the 1917 Revolutions?

The Tsarist monarchy was, until the 1905 Revolution, an autocracy in which all political power was vested in the ruler and under which political parties and organisation were illegal. As the 19th century wore on, it became apparent that growing sections of the educated classes felt alienated from the monarchy because of its refusal to share power with them. In this respect, Russia's political system failed to change when most other European monarchies were granting elected assemblies or devolving power more widely. Alexander II (1855-1881) did try to modernise Russia in certain respects; in addition to emancipation, he pushed through a whole series of educational, judicial, administrative and military reforms. However, he was intent on maintaining his autocratic powers.

The development of Political Opposition

1.   The Liberals

Paradoxically, opposition to the Tsarist system actually increased massively under the "Tsar-liberator"; firstly, many of the educated classes had their hopes of fundamental change raised by Alexander's announcement that serfdom would be abolished, only to have them dashed by what they saw as a flawed reform which did not radically improve the lives of the peasantry. Moreover, the zemstva reform (1864), which introduced local self-government aroused hopes of an elected duma (national assembly), which Alexander II then dashed. Historians see this as a tragedy since, after the assassination of Alexander II in 1881 by terrorists committed to a peasant revolution, it meant there was no chance for constitutional government to develop. Under Alexander II's son and grandson, Alexander III (1881-94) and Nicholas II (1894-1917), the Russian monarchy followed a reactionary political course, resolutely opposed to sharing its power even with the educated classes. Instead political reform was thrust upon an unwilling Nicholas II as a result of the 1905 revolution and so, arguably, was doomed to fail.

2.   The Revolutionaries

From Alexander II's reign onwards two distinct types of revolutionary movement emerged in Russia. Whereas the liberals sought to pressurise the monarchy into conceding an elected assembly, revolutionaries sought the overthrow of the monarchy.

a) **Populists** in the late 19th century and the **Social Revolutionaries** (SRs) in the early 20th century, aimed at a peasant revolution, which would see a huge transfer of land from the monarchy and nobility to the peasant masses. The Social Revolutionary Party was founded in 1901 and was led by Victor Chernov. The SRs campaigned for universal suffrage and a peasant revolution. They were involved in peasant risings in 1902 and their Combat Organisation organised terrorist attacks.

b) **The Marxists**. From 1883 onwards, the ideas of the German communist writer, Karl Marx, began to attract growing numbers of Russian intellectuals who sought to transform Russia by means of a revolution of the industrial proletariat (factory workers). In 1898, the Russian Social Democratic Labour Party was established; Lenin was a founding member. However, the Russian Marxists proved very argumentative and remained divided throughout the period up to the 1917 Revolution, e.g. between the "economists" who advocated pushing for better conditions for the industrial workers and those who argued for socialist revolution. In 1902, Lenin wrote *"What is to be done?"* in which he argued for the need for a disciplined, elite party of full-time revolutionaries to act as the 'vanguard' of a proletarian revolution. The following year, the Social Democrats split over this issue when its leaders gathered for a congress at Brussels and London. Lenin's ideas were opposed by Julius Martov, who argued for a broad, less exclusive party; Lenin's faction became known as the **Bolsheviks** and Martov's as the **Mensheviks**. Before the outbreak of the First World War, both Marxist factions remained tiny in terms of membership and support.

Long-term weaknesses of Tsarism highlighted: The1905 Revolution

The 1905 Revolution has often been presented as a dress rehearsal for the 1917 revolutions because the long-term structural problems indicated above contributed to both the 1905 and 1917 revolutions.

Its causes

1. **Growing peasant unrest**. This was the result of:

    • High taxes (to pay for industrialisation)
    • Redemption dues (to pay for the land they acquired when they had been emancipated (1861)
    • Overpopulation
    • Bad harvests from the late 1890s
    • Growing peasant literacy, partly the result of the 1874 military reform, meant peasant risings were more co-ordinated

1902 onwards saw large-scale peasant revolts in the Ukraine; by 1904 there were risings across much of Russia. Peasants sought to increase their landholdings and lower their taxes, especially redemption dues.

2. **Industrial unrest**

    • Rapid industrial growth ended abruptly in 1899, largely because of an international financial crisis, which meant foreign investment dried up, but also because of bad harvests in 1897-1901, which led to a fall in government tax revenue.
    • The 1900-1905 recession resulted in high unemployment and wage cuts.
    • There had been increasing numbers of strikes in the 1890s due to the terrible living and working conditions of the growing industrial proletariat. From the mid-1890s Marxist revolutionaries played a significant role in organising strikes.
    • Zubatov, Chief of Police in Moscow, organised official trade unions to try to channel working class discontent. This scheme backfired as the Zubatov unions organised large-scale strikes. In 1903 Father Gapon took up Zubatov's idea and in 1905 organised the "Bloody Sunday" protest.

3. **Growing political opposition**

    • The Social Democratic Party was set up in 1898. This was a Marxist organisation.
    • The Social Revolutionary Party was set up in 1901, and aimed at peasant revolution.
    • The liberals were angered by military failures against Japan and formed the Union of Liberation which organised a series of reform banquets in 1904 but the Tsar only made vague promises of reform.

All of the above groups drew the majority of their leaders from the professional middle-classes who grew rapidly in numbers in the second half of the 19th century following Alexander II's reforms. The 1890s saw a revival of revolutionary and liberal opposition to the autocracy.

4. Growing unrest among many of the non-Russian peoples

This was in response to the Russification policies of Alexander III (1881-94) and Nicholas II (1894-1917), which involved imposing the Russian language and the Russian Orthodox Church on the Tsar's non-Russian subjects. Resentment was particularly great in Finland, which led to an upsurge in Finnish nationalism, including the assassination of Finland's governor-general, Bobrikov, in 1904.

5. Military disaster: the Russo-Japanese War (1904-5)

Towards the end of the 19th century, Russia turned its attention to the Far East, encouraged by the weakness of the Chinese Empire. In 1898 the Chinese government allowed Russia the right to build a railway across Manchuria and a 25 year lease on the Liaotung Peninsula. Nicholas II's ministers looked to expand into Korea too, which brought Russia into conflict with Japan, which regarded Korea as its sphere of influence. Japan attacked Russia's naval base in Manchuria, Port Arthur, in 1904.

- Port Arthur surrendered to the Japanese (December 1904)
- The Russian army was defeated at Mukden (February 1905)
- Russia's Baltic fleet was destroyed in the Tsushima Straits (May 1905)
- Russia agreed peace terms with Japan in the Treaty of Portsmouth (September 1905); Russia had to withdraw from Manchuria

News of each defeat provoked protests in Russia, e.g. the political banquets of November-December 1904 organised by the liberals of the Union of Liberation.

6. Bloody Sunday - the trigger for revolution

In January 1905 demonstrators, led by Father Gapon, marched on the Winter Palace, carrying a petition. Troops killed probably 1000+. This sparked off a wave of strikes across Russia.

In July 1905, liberals set up the Cadet (Kadet) Party, which was led by Paul Miliukov. They demanded an elected Duma (parliament). By September the country was in the grips of a General Strike, there were widespread peasant rebellions and there were risings among some of the non-Russian nationalities. In October, the St Petersburg Soviet was set up to represent the interests of the workers. Trotsky was its chairman. It looked as if the monarchy might be overthrown. However, this was not to be the case.

Q. How did the Russian monarchy survive the 1905 Revolution?

• Nicholas II reluctantly made concessions in the October Manifesto: he granted a State Duma (parliament), elected on a wide franchise and cancelled redemption payments. Middle and upper class liberals were bought off by the manifesto. The October Manifesto also ensured the loyalty of the officer class and gave rise to a second liberal party, the Octobrists, who were committed to making the new parliamentary system work.

• The liberals were also prepared to support the government because they were worried by the establishment of the St Petersburg Soviet in October and the General Strike it organised. The working-class and peasant revolutionaries were still dissatisfied as they had not won their demands for an 8-hour working day or for land redistribution.

• In September, the Treaty of Portsmouth ended the war with Japan. Russian troops could now be moved back to western Russia to restore order.

• December 1905 saw the arrest of leading members of the St Petersburg Soviet and the ruthless suppression of a workers' rising in Moscow.

• In April 1906, Sergei Witte, the Prime Minister, negotiated a large loan from France, so the Nicholas II's government was now financially more secure.

• 1906 saw an upturn in world trade and so the recovery of Russian industry. In 1906 Russian industry grew at a rate of 6%.

Q. Was Tsarism doomed to fail by 1905 and its survival until 1917 merely the postponement of the inevitable?

The Russian monarchy was lucky to survive the 1905 Revolution. It was weakened by terrible problems: rural unrest; backward agriculture; a discontented proletariat; alienated educated classes; restless nationalities.

The First World War destroyed the Russian monarchy but historians are divided over whether, if war had been avoided, reforms carried out in 1905-14 might have provided the basis for its long-term survival. However, on balance, the evidence suggests that the monarchy was not adapting sufficiently to survive, particularly given Nicholas II's limitations.

Q. What reforms were carried out?

• The October Manifesto (1905) created the Duma
• Peter Stolypin's land reforms (1906-11) permitted peasants to leave the mir (village communes)
• Military reforms (1906 onwards) – the establishment of a High Command; mobile artillery, the abolition of election of NCOs; more trains

Constitutional reform

The October Manifesto provided Nicholas II with a great opportunity to win over the moderate educated classes, for so long alienated by the government's refusal to allow its participation in politics. The 1905 Revolution had demonstrated the disunity of the revolutionaries. The revolutionary movement was in decline after 1905; this was partly the result of 2000 executions in 1906-7.

However, Nicholas II almost immediately undermined the October Manifesto with the Fundamental Law (April 1906), under which Nicholas retained the right of veto over legislation and ministers were responsible to him, not the Duma. The Tsar closed the first two dumas abruptly and then rigged the electoral system in 1907. Nicholas refused to work with the Duma, even in the case of the Third and Fourth Dumas where the more conservative Octobrists were the largest party. By 1914 the Duma parties were allying themselves with the growing strike movement. Nicholas' political incompetence undermined the monarchy's chances of survival, particularly once he became increasingly reliant on the self-styled holy man, Rasputin, whose unsavoury reputation undermined respect for the royal family.

Agricultural Reform

Peter Stolypin (Prime Minister, 1906-11) was banking on the *"sober and the strong"*; he sought to encourage a prosperous peasant class by allowing peasants to consolidate their strips and leave the village commune. However,

• Only 20% of peasants broke away from the communes and agricultural productivity remained low.

- Only 5% of Russia's peasants were making a profit by 1914.
- Stolypin's reforms did not tackle the problem of rural overpopulation; Russia's population grew from 125 million in 1900 to 159 million by 1913. Even if the nobles' 140 million acres of land had been distributed among the peasantry, there would still have been land hunger.

Peasant unrest was a major factor in both the 1905 and 1917 revolutions. Stolypin had said that 20 years of peace were needed if Russia was to be stabilised; his reforms only had 7 years of peace, but even before war broke out the numbers of peasants leaving the communes had decreased.

Military reforms

Significant progress was made after the disastrous defeat against Japan in 1904-5. This was shown by the relatively quick mobilisation at the start of the First World War, in August 1914, which surprised the Germans. However, the military reforms were not due for completion until 1917. With Russia's army still far behind that of Germany, Nicholas II had to avoid war. Humiliating diplomatic defeats in 1908-9 and 1912-13 during the crises over Austria-Hungary's annexation of Bosnia-Herzegovina and the Balkan Wars meant that the Russian government felt obliged to mobilise when Austria-Hungary attacked Serbia in July 1914. The First World War fatally undermined the loyalty of the Russian army and made revolution possible.

Industrialisation

- Russia's industrial proletariat (4.5 million by 1914) was concentrated in Kiev, Moscow and St Petersburg, living in awful conditions.
- Health Insurance, introduced in 1912, made little difference.

- 1906-14 saw renewed industrial growth at a slightly less rapid rate than before 1900 (1906-14 = average of 6% p.a.)
- There were relatively few strikes until 1912 when the Lena Massacre occurred; from then onwards, there was a growing strike movement; 4000 in the first 6 months of 1914.
- In spite of renewed industrialisation, Russia was still way behind the West; in 1914 Germany's coal production was 5 times that of Russia, its steel production 4 times that of Russia. Therefore, Russia faced a technologically superior Germany at the start of the First World War.

Q. Why did the reforms of 1905-14 prove 'too little and too late' to save the Russian monarchy?

- The Russian monarchy's problems proved too great to survive the immense strains imposed by the First World War.
- Rapid industrialisation and a backward agricultural system created huge tensions within Russia
- Nicholas II's refusal to honour the spirit of the October Manifesto meant political support for the monarchy did not broaden.
- Amongst Nicholas II's ministers, only Stolypin and Witte grasped the need for fundamental reform; Nicholas II dismissed Witte in 1905 and seemed to be on the point of dismissing Stolypin when he was assassinated in 1911.

Q. What were the short-term causes of the 1917 Revolutions?

Answer: all of the long-term problems facing Tsarism were worsened by the impact of the First World War.

'War is the locomotive of history' (Leon Trotsky).

1.   Military disaster in the First World War

Russia's war effort got off to a promising start, with rapid mobilisation and Russian troops crossing into East Prussia (eastern Germany) within a few days of the outbreak of war. However, the Germans crushed the Russians at the Battles of Tannenburg and the Masurian Lakes. The Russian General Staff had only planned for a 3 month campaign and the War Ministry had no plans for wartime munitions production because it was assumed the reserve of 7 million shells was adequate.

Russia proved incapable of competing with Germany's armed forces because of the gulf between the two countries' industrial bases; Russia had only 4.5 million industrial workers out of a total population of 159 million. The Government did recruit more men into the factories but many of the new workers were untrained former peasants and therefore output actually fell at first. At the outbreak of war the Russian government failed to establish a Ministry of Supply. The generals, the Duma and industrial leaders had to put huge pressure on the government before it tackled the shell-shortage, and then this was not achieved until 1916.

The war transformed an army of well-trained professional officers, commanding three year trained recruits into a colossal body of poorly trained conscripts; 9 million men were called up in the first 12 months. The Army expanded too quickly for sufficient numbers of officers to be trained and commissioned, so it was quite common for a regiment of 3000 men to have no more than 12 officers. Therefore, there was a great reliance on non-commissioned officers who were largely drawn from the ranks of the peasantry. They became a radical group and were to lead the garrison mutinies of February 1917 and set up the military soviets.

In May 1915 the Germans launched an offensive against Russia's North-West Front; this resulted in the Germans occupying large amounts of western Russia. Consequently, General Brusilov withdrew Russian troops on the South-West Front. 1 million Russians surrendered during 1915.

In August 1915 Nicholas II appointed himself commander-in-chief, in spite of his ministers' please for him not to. This proved disastrous as government became increasingly chaotic with the Tsar, based at Mogilev, hundreds of miles away from his ministers and the Duma, in Petrograd (formerly St Petersburg). Furthermore, it gave greater authority to the Tsarina Alexandra, who was widely unpopular because of her arrogance and German background, and to Rasputin, who exerted a sinister influence over her and who now had a major say in ministerial appointments. Also, although Nicholas did not make key military decisions, now that he was commander-in-chief, further defeats were blamed on him personally.

In June 1916 General Brusilov launched a massive Russian offensive against the Austrians in Galicia. Initially, it was a brilliant success but a German counter-offensive led to a major Russian retreat and a serious decline in morale among Russian troops.

By 1917, 1.7 million Russians had been killed, 8 million wounded and 2.5 million were prisoners. Norman Stone has shown that the Russian Army was not on the point of collapse in 1917 but morale was poor, the Germans had advanced deep in to western Russia and the loss of many of the pre-war professional officers meant that discipline in the army was beginning to break down.

2.   Economic Problems

(a)   Inflation: Government spending increased by 800% between 1914 and 1916. The Government printed more paper money and abandoned the gold standard. Prices increased by 400% between August 1914 and March 1917. The government made the sale of alcohol illegal and so lost much tax revenue (as the Government had had a monopoly on the sale of vodka).

(b)   Food shortages: 15 million peasants were called up to the armed forces. Horses were requisitioned. Food shortages became very serious from 1916 when peasants started hoarding grain because they could not afford to buy scarce manufactured goods (at the now inflated prices). The transport network focused on supplying the army's needs.

(c)   Crisis in the cities:
The war exacerbated the problems already being caused by rapid industrialisation. Petrograd's population increased from 2.1 million to 2.65 million and Moscow's from 1.6 million to 2 million, leading to severe overcrowding. By 1917 state-owned factories were employing four times as many workers as in 1914 and 33% of these were in Petrograd. In 1917 less than 10% of factory workers received what was regarded as the minimum living wage of 200 roubles a month. Food shortages were worst in the cities. One million workers went on strike in 1916.

3.   Political problems

Nicholas II continued to display a reluctance to work with the Duma, which particularly angered its members given the huge challenges that the war posed for Russia. In August 1914, the Duma voted money for the war, with only the Bolshevik deputies voting against. The Tsar then adjourned it and called the Duma back only for brief sessions in the following two and a half years.

The Duma politicians and other leading members of the middle and upper classes then proceeded to take their own measures to help the war effort as they became increasingly alarmed at the incompetence and lethargy of the Tsar's government. So essentially, an alternative government was evolving in Russia during the war years:

- In 1914, the Union of Zemstva, led by Prince Lvov, took over organising supplies and medical care; by 1916 it had 8000 associated institutions. At first its work was supported by donations but eventually the Government provided money.

- In 1915, the Central War Industries Committee was set up by leading industrialists in order to tackle the army's supply problems.

In August 1915 Nicholas recalled the Duma and most of the deputies (236/421) united to form the Progressive Bloc which demanded a "government of public confidence." By this, they meant that the Tsar should choose his ministers from the leading members of the largest parties in the Duma. It appears that a majority of the Tsar's ministers advised him to make concessions to the Duma but Nicholas II did not and instead adjourned it again.

In November 1916, Nicholas summoned another session of the Duma. The leader of the Kadets, Paul Miliukov, attacked government incompetence and posed the question whether this was the result of was *'stupidity or treachery?'* In December, Rasputin was murdered by Prince Yusupov but, even with Rasputin's malign influence removed, Nicholas II still opposed making political concessions. It is at this point that a group of Duma politicians, including the Octobrist and Kadet leaders, Miliukov and Guchkov, and the generals, Brusilov and Alexeyev, began to plot to remove the Tsar.

The February Revolution

February	23	Riots and strikes in Petrograd
	25	Mutiny of troops in Petrograd
	26	The Tsar ordered the Duma to adjourn but it refused
	27	Petrograd Soviet set up
March	1	Duma set up the Provisional Government under Prince Lvov
	2	Nicholas II abdicated

(Old Style Dates – Russia was using a calendar 13 days behind that in use in Western Europe)

The downfall of the Russian monarchy was not planned and took everyone by surprise, including revolutionary groups like the Bolsheviks. There were 400,000 workers in Petrograd and by February 23rd there were only nine days supply of flour left. Demonstrations over bread shortages led to riots, which merged with a strike at the Putilov armaments factory. Unlike the 1905 Revolution, much of the Petrograd garrison openly sided with the rioters (the first mutinies occurred on February 25th) and the situation became serious.

→ The Tsar's response was feeble, he was warned by both the military commander in Petrograd, General Khabalov, and by Rodzianko, the President of the Duma, but he did nothing. Worse still, on February 26th, Nicholas II dismissed the Duma.

→ The Duma decided to continue to meet and on February 27th workers and soldiers marched on the Tauride Palace where the Duma was meeting.

→ The Duma was unsure whether to support the rioters or not but one Socialist Revolutionary deputy, Alexander Kerensky, helped persuade them to do so. Rodzianko announced that the Duma was taking control of the capital.

→ At the same time the workers and soldiers in Petrograd elected a Soviet as they had done during the 1905 Revolution.

→ By February 28th, most of the 160,000 soldiers in Petrograd had either mutinied or given up trying to restore order. There were about 1,300 casualties in the fighting in Petrograd (half civilians, half soldiers and police).

→ Rodzianko contacted General Alexeyev, Chief of the General Staff. They agreed that the immediate abdication of the tsar and the establishment of a new government were essential if order were to be restored.

→ On March 2nd, Nicholas II, at Pskov, on his way back to the capital, was informed by his generals and a delegation of Duma deputies that they would no longer support him. Nicholas agreed to abdicate in favour of his son, Alexis, but later decided that he was too ill and so decided on his own younger brother, the Grand Duke Michael. Michael refused and so Russia became a Republic.

The Duma leaders and generals had hoped to use the disturbances in Petrograd to force a change of tsar, but had not intended to establish a republic. They had reached the conclusion that Nicholas II had to be removed if Russia were to stand any chance of winning the war and of avoiding a social revolution.

The Duma (March 1st) chose ten of its members to serve as a Provisional Government; this was dominated by the liberal parties (Kadets and Octobrists). The Prime Minister was Prince Lvov, and the Provisional Government included one Socialist Revolutionary, Alexander Kerensky. Paul Miliukov was the Foreign Minister and Alexander Guchkov was Minister of War.

Whilst all of this was happening most of the leading Bolsheviks and Mensheviks were still in exile.

The Second Revolution: October 1917

The Failure of the Provisional Government March-October 1917

The simple answer to the question of why the Provisional Government fell after just 8 months is that it was unable to resolve the problems that had caused the collapse of the monarchy.

Q. What was the Provisional Government weakened by?

(i)   Its own reforms

The Provisional Government (from now on PG) issued a series of liberal reforms, including freedom of the press, the release of political prisoners, and the abolition of the death penalty. It abolished the Okhrana (tsarist secret police). This reduced the government's coercive capabilities at a time of crisis, a dangerous move.

(ii)   The Soviets: 'Dual Authority'

The PG intended to introduce a new, democratic system of local government but took until August to create a scheme. In the meantime soviets (elected councils of workers, soldiers and peasants) had been set up across Russia to take charge of the localities; therefore, the PG did not have effective control of Russia.

It used to be thought that the PG had responsibility but no power because of the existence of the Petrograd Soviet (PS from now on) but historians now think that the PG had a "window of opportunity" in March-April when fear of a counter-revolution by conservative army officers bound the PS and PG together. However, it is difficult to see how the PG, which essentially represented the propertied classes and was chosen by the Duma, and the PS, which primarily represented the working classes, could continue to work together in the long run.

On March 1st, the PS issued Order Number 1, which required all army units to elect soldiers' committees and said that soldiers should only obey the PG if its orders had been approved by the PS.

(iii)   By continuing defeats in the war

The PG and PS were both in favour of continuing the war but had different attitudes to it. Miliukov and the PG were strongly committed to the war, the propertied classes were, largely, very nationalistic and sought territorial gains from the war (e.g. Constantinople from Turkey). The PG was also heavily dependent on loans from its allies. The Soviets argued in favour of "revolutionary defencism", that is a war of self-defence or a war against German imperialism.

In April Miliukov sent a secret note to the Allies saying that the PG did not agree with the Soviets' call for the rejection of imperialist war aims by all the warring nations. This note was made public and provoked riots in Petrograd. Miliukov and Guchkov resigned and 6 socialists joined the PG in May.

Alexander Kerensky now became War Minister and organised a massive offensive in June 1917, by the first week in July this had failed disastrously, with 1 million casualties. News of this provoked serious disturbances in Petrograd known as the July Days. During the late summer and autumn of 1917, desertion became widespread among soldiers and military discipline began to breakdown.

(iv)   By peasant land seizures

The PG accepted the need for land redistribution but insisted this could only be carried out with compensation to the nobles (the PG represented the propertied classes) and would have to wait until a Constituent Assembly met (and it kept on postponing elections for the Constituent Assembly). The peasants were not prepared to wait and by September there were increasing land seizures, with the peasant soviets deciding on how the land should be redistributed. These seizures provoked desertions among the soldiers and further reduced food supplies as the estates being seized and broken up were often the most efficient ones.

Q. Why were the Bolsheviks able to seize power in October 1917?

(i)   Because Lenin persuaded the Bolshevik Party that a second revolution was possible

When Nicholas II abdicated, Lenin was in Switzerland. The German government, intent on destabilising Russia, arranged for Lenin's return to Russia in a sealed train in April 1917. On April 4, Lenin delivered his April Theses in which he argued that the soviets had the sole right to govern. Lenin said that the task of the Bolsheviks was not to extend freedom to all classes but to transfer power to the working classes. Most Bolsheviks had, like the Mensheviks and Socialist Revolutionaries, believed that they should support the PG in order to prevent a right-wing counter-revolution, convinced that a proletarian revolution was impossible in Russia given the small size of its industrial working class. It took several weeks before Lenin was able to win over the rest of his party to the idea of a second revolution.

In the April Theses, Lenin coined the slogan - "Peace, Bread, Land, all power to the Soviets." This proved in the long-term very attractive to ordinary Russians, particularly urban workers and garrison soldiers, who became desperate to see an end to the war, high inflation and food shortages.

However, until autumn 1917 it was the Mensheviks and Socialist Revolutionaries who dominated the soviets and not the Bolsheviks.

In June 1917, when the First All-Russian Congress of Soviets met, the Bolsheviks won only 12% of the seats.

Distribution of seats in the First All-Russian Congress of Soviets

SRs	285
Mensheviks	245
Bolsheviks	105

(ii)   Because Lenin's policy of opposing the PG meant that as the latter became more unpopular, the Bolsheviks increased their support

All of the other major parties, including the Social Revolutionaries and the Mensheviks, supported and indeed participated in the PG. As the PG grew increasingly unpopular, the Bolsheviks, who alone unreservedly opposed the PG, picked up more support. In February 1917, the Bolsheviks probably had in the region of 10,000 members; by October, this had grown to around 300,000 and most of them were concentrated in Petrograd and Moscow.

(iii)   Because the Bolsheviks were able to survive the setback they suffered during the July Days

News of the failure of Kerensky's Offensive sparked a rebellion in Petrograd, known as the July Days. It is difficult to know who was responsible for the July Days (3-6 July). Afterwards the Bolsheviks said the SRs and Mensheviks had begun the rising, whereas the SRs and Mensheviks blamed the Bolsheviks. It is probable that the workers of Petrograd and sailors from the nearby Kronstadt naval base started the rising and then called on the Bolsheviks to take a lead. At this stage the PG still had sufficient military support and was able to restore order by bringing up loyal troops from the front.

Kerensky now became Prime Minister and arrested a number of leading Bolsheviks, branding them as German agents. Lenin went into hiding. Kerensky brought in more socialists as members of the PG but the PG was still dominated by its four Kadet members.

(iv)   Lenin revised Karl Marx's line on the peasants

Marx had dismissed the peasants as incapable of acting as a revolutionary class. Lenin adjusted this view as the peasants made up 80% of the Russian population and were war weary and already seizing land. Lenin argued that Russian circumstances were such that the peasants could be a genuinely revolutionary force. The Bolsheviks did not have their own land policy so they simply adopted that of the SRs and accepted peasant land seizures. This won some peasant support for the Bolsheviks and led to some SRs being prepared to support the Bolsheviks (they became known as the **Left SRs**).

(v)   The Kornilov Affair (August 1917) boosted support for the Bolsheviks

This episode enabled the Bolsheviks to recover from their setback in the July Days. General Kornilov was the commander of the Russian forces on the South-West Front. He believed that it was necessary to destroy revolutionary forces in Russia before Russia could defeat Germany - *"It's time to hang the German supporters and spies, with Lenin at their head, and to disperse the Soviet."*

Kornilov told Kerensky that he intended to bring loyal troops to Petrograd to restore order. It is not clear whether Kerensky first approved of this but then changed his mind when he suspected Kornilov intended to set up a dictatorship or whether it was just Kornilov's plan. Kerensky, short of loyal troops in the capital, released Bolsheviks from prison and armed the Petrograd workers, many of them Bolshevik supporters. These militias were known as the *"Red Guards."* In the end Kornilov's advance did not reach Petrograd as railway workers sabotaged the railway tracks and some of Kornilov's troops mutinied. Kornilov was arrested. The Kornilov affair exposed the weakness of the PG and bolstered support for the Bolsheviks in Petrograd.

(vi)   Because the Bolsheviks gained majorities in the Petrograd and Moscow Soviets (September 1917)

In mid-September the Bolsheviks achieved majorities in the Petrograd and Moscow Soviets. This was to some extent because the other parties were less committed than the Bolsheviks at attending meetings of the soviets and their sub-committees. In March 1917 3000 deputies had gathered for the first meeting of the PS, by autumn 1917 attendance was just a few hundred.

More importantly, as the authority of the PG crumbled, it was the Bolsheviks who benefited most in terms of increased support, as it was they who were implacably opposed to it and appeared to offer to the workers and garrison soldiers a genuine alternative to the PG's policies. The spread of the soviets, the increasing number of factory committees, elected by the workers to run the factories, growing land seizures by the peasants and the creation of independent national governments, e.g. in the Ukraine, all undermined the PG's authority.

After the Kornilov Affair the Soviets moved increasingly to the Left and the PG increasingly to the Right. A clash, therefore, was increasingly likely. As Lenin put it, *"Either a soviet government or Kornilovism. There is no middle course."* On September 12th Lenin urged the Bolsheviks to prepare for immediate revolution. He was worried about the elections to the Second All-Russian Congress of Soviets, due to meet late October, and the elections for the Constituent Assembly due in November. He was convinced that the Bolsheviks had to seize control before these elections because both might go against the Bolsheviks.

(vii)   Because Lenin was able to persuade doubters among the Bolshevik leadership that the time was right to stage a second revolution

The Central Committee of the Bolshevik Party remained dubious about an immediate revolution, and some leading Bolsheviks opposed the idea of a Bolshevik takeover, preferring to see a coalition of socialist parties (Bolsheviks, Mensheviks, SRs) taking power. On October 7th Lenin slipped back into Petrograd and, on 10th October, the Central Committee agreed in principle for revolution but it did not decide on a date. Ironically it was the PG which determined the date of the Bolshevik revolution as Kerensky, fearing a rising, ordered the arrest of leading Bolsheviks and the closing down of their newspapers on October 23rd. Lenin ordered an immediate rising.

(viii)   Because Trotsky used the Bosheviks' control of the Petrograd Soviet to plan and stage the seizure of Petrograd

Leon Trotsky, who had joined the Bolsheviks in July 1917, having previously been a Menshevik, organised the Bolshevik rising, using his positions as Chairman of the Petrograd Soviet and Chairman of the Soviet's Military Revolutionary Committee.

The October Revolution (Old Style dates)

August		The Kornilov Affair
September		Trotsky elected Chairman of the Petrograd Soviet
October	7	Lenin returned to Petrograd
	10	Bolshevik Central Committee voted for a rising
	16	Military Revolutionary Committee was set up by the Petrograd Soviet
	23	Kerensky closed down Bolshevik newspapers
	24	The Military Revolutionary Committee took defensive measures to secure key positions in Petrograd
	25	Bolsheviks seized control of Petrograd Second All-Russia Congress of Soviets met; approved new Sovnarkom government under Lenin as president
	26	Fall of the Winter Palace

The October Revolution

The revolution took place between late on October 24th and October 26th. Trotsky called on the garrison of the Peter and Paul fortress to take control of the city in the name of the Soviets. There was little fighting and perhaps only 5 people were killed. The PG had very few loyal troops left: a few officer cadets, a women's battalion and a bicycle regiment. Most of the soldiers in Petrograd and the sailors from the nearby naval base at Kronstadt supported the Bolshevik rising. Kerensky managed to escape, the rest of the PG was arrested when the Winter Palace was taken early on 26th October.

On the evening of October 25th the Second All-Russian Congress of Soviets met. Despite Lenin's earlier misgivings, the Bolsheviks had over 300 delegates out of a total of 649 and Lenin informed the delegates that the PS had seized power in their name. The Right SRs and Mensheviks walked out but the Left SRs were prepared to support the Bolsheviks.

The October Revolution: Some Historical Interpretations

The Communist Party's view	» The October Revolution was the inevitable result of class struggle. » Stresses the brilliance of Lenin's leadership. » It was a popular revolution, inspired and organised by the Bolshevik Party
The Liberal view (e.g. Robert Conquest, Richard Pipes)	» Ruthless Bolsheviks took advantage of the collapse of government authority to seize power. » The October Revolution was a coup d'etat by the Bolsheviks who had only limited popular support. » The Bolsheviks were successful because of their organisational skills and the leadership of Lenin and Trotsky.
Revisionist views (e.g. Orlando Figes)	» Emphasise the importance of revolution from below. Revisionists argue that there was a growing popular movement, characterised by the growing influence of the soviets, in Russia that would have overthrown the Provisional without the Bolsheviks' intervention. » The Bolsheviks exploited this popular revolution to their advantage and betrayed the people by imposing a brutal single-party dictatorship, suppressing the workers' movement.

The Consolidation of Power

The Bolsheviks were in control of Petrograd as a result of their insurrection on October 24th but elsewhere the take-over was not so smooth. Fighting lasted a week in Moscow between Officer Cadets and Red Guards, with 500 killed. It was the end of November before other cities were won over. Rural areas were much more difficult to deal with and few peasants were Bolshevik supporters. Civil war did not break out at this stage, partly because the Bolsheviks' opponents were waiting to see what would happen when elections to the Constituent Assembly were held (November 12th). Most people did not expect the new government to last long because of the scale of the problems facing it:

1.   Economic crisis; by November 1917 prices were 1000% higher than they had been in 1914.
2.   Opposition from other political groups.
3.   The War; by late 1917, the Germans had advanced closer to Petrograd.

Lenin was more realistic than many of the Bolsheviks: he realised that the Bolsheviks would have to fight a civil war to gain control of the rest of Russia, and that this would involve ignoring many of the principles of communism and creating a ruthless, dictatorial government. In December 1917 Lenin set up the Cheka, the Bolshevik secret police. Lenin also believed that the communist revolution could not survive in Russia alone, but must be spread to other countries.

Given its limited power, Sovnarkom's first steps did not strictly reflect Bolshevik ideology but were an attempt to satisfy the aspirations of the Russian masses. At the end of October, Sovnarkom published a series of decrees and measures:

1.   The Decree on Land

This decree handed over the estates of the crown, church and aristocracy to the peasants. This simply legalised what the peasants had already done. Some Bolsheviks were very angry about this because they believed that since land was part of the means of production it should now belong to the state, not to individual peasants. However, Lenin's pragmatic view was accepted as 300,000 Bolsheviks could not deprive 125 million peasants of their land. In February 1918 the Bolshevik government passed a decree declaring that all land belonged to the state, but they did not attempt to implement it.

2.   The Decree on Workers' Control of the Factories

Again the Bolsheviks simply recognised what had already happened, that the industrial workers had seized control of the factories, even though many of the factory committees were controlled by the Mensheviks.

3.   State Capitalism

This is the term used to describe the economic policy of the Bolsheviks from October 1917 to June 1918 (when War Communism replaced it). Bolshevik economic policy during this period, and through the Civil War, was improvised. Lenin's economic writings before 1917 had been very theoretical, he had given little thought to economic planning. Therefore, from 1917 to summer 1918 the Bolsheviks had to use existing structures; in December, they did establish Vesenkha (the Supreme Council of the National Economy) to regulate the national economy, but its control was limited at first. However, it did nationalise banks and the railways and cancelled debts owed to foreign governments.

4.   The Decree on Nationalities

The Bolsheviks declared that the non-Russian peoples had the right to break away from the former Russian Empire. Independence movements had already sprung up in a number of areas, notably the Ukraine, Georgia and in the Baltic region. The Bolsheviks would later use the Red Army to force the Ukraine and Georgia into the USSR (formally set up in 1922).

5.   The Decree on Peace

On October 25th (November 8th NS), the Bolsheviks published a decree calling for a *"just, democratic peace"* between all countries involved in the war. Lenin's call for a peace settlement without land transfers and financial indemnities (reparations), was a public relations' exercise, because he knew that the priority was to achieve a quick peace settlement if the Bolsheviks were to consolidate their power and that would mean accepting harsh terms from the German government. Trotsky, the Commissar for Foreign Affairs, favoured trying to spin the peace talks out in the hope that when the German workers saw how greedy their government was for land - and given the growing burdens imposed by the war on the German population - they would revolt and Germany would have its own communist revolution. Peace talks opened at Brest-Litovsk in December 1917.

An armistice (ceasefire) was agreed for November 22nd and peace talks began at Brest-Litovsk in December 1917. Trotsky's delaying tactics - *"neither peace, nor war"* - only irritated the Germans who launched a new offensive against the Russians in February 1918. Lenin insisted a treaty be signed and, in spite of opposition from several leading Bolsheviks, including Trotsky and Bukharin, the Bolshevik government agreed. Trotsky resigned as Commissar for Foreign Affairs and became Commissar for War.

6.   The Treaty of Brest-Litovsk (March 1918)

The main terms of the treaty that Germany imposed on Russia were:

o   Russia lost Poland, Estonia, Latvia, Lithuania, Finland, the Ukraine and Georgia
o   33% of its population
o   33% of its arable land
o   Russia had to pay an indemnity of 6000 million marks

Russia regained the Ukraine and Georgia in 1921 and, after Germany's defeat in 1918, the Baltic states and Poland were given their independence.

Lenin favoured accepting the German demands because Russia was too weak to continue the war and only by making peace could the Bolsheviks concentrate on consolidating and extending their control within Russia and sorting out the economic problems that had brought about the downfall of the Tsar and of the Provisional Government. In any case, Lenin believed that ultimately workers revolutions would break out in Germany and other European countries. His perspective therefore was not that of a Russian nationalist but of an international socialist.

The Left Social Revolutionaries, who had supported the Bolsheviks since the October Revolution, now resigned in protest from Sovnarkom, meaning that the Bolshevike held every position in it. On March 8th, the Seventh Congress of the Bolshevik Party changed the name of the party to the Communist Party and, on March 10th, Lenin moved the capital from Petrograd to Moscow.

7.   Elections to the Constituent Assembly (November 1917)

The Bolsheviks had criticised the Provisional Government for delaying elections to the Constituent Assembly and some Bolsheviks favoured a broad coalition of socialist parties, so Lenin felt he had to allow elections to go ahead on November 12th. He correctly anticipated that the Bolsheviks would not do well.

Results of the Constituent Assembly Elections

Party	Number of seats
Bolsheviks	175 (24%)
Left SRs	40
Right SRs	370 (52%)
Mensheviks	16
Kadets	17
National parties	86

8.   Lenin's closure of the Constituent Assembly (January 1918)

On January 5th, the Constituent Assembly met and elected the leader of the Right SRs, Victor Chernov, its President. The Bolsheviks, who were in the minority, withdrew and Lenin sent in the Red Guards to close down the Assembly. On January 6th, Lenin declared that the Assembly was permanently dissolved. Lenin was opposed to western ideas of democracy, believing in the need for a dictatorship of the Bolshevik Party to rule on behalf of the working classes.

Trotsky remarked that, *"We have trampled under foot the principles of democracy for the sake of the loftier principles of a social revolution."* Lenin's actions were criticised by foreign communists likes the German leaders Rosa Luxemburg and Karl Liebknecht. In Russia it led to a civil war that would last until late 1920, ending in Bolshevik victory and transforming the Communist (Bolshevik) Party itself.

9.   The establishment of a secret police

The Bolsheviks set up the Cheka, a secret police force in December 1917. The Cheka was led by Felix Dzerzhinsky.

The Civil War (1918-20)

By spring 1918 armed opposition to the Bolsheviks was developing in many parts of Russia. Many army commanders were anti-communist who, now Russia had pulled out of the war, could attempt to overthrow the Bolsheviks. General Kornilov and General Denikin led an anti-Bolshevik army in the south; Admiral Kolchak commanded anti-Bolshevik forces in western Siberia and became the most important White leader; and General Yudenich led a White army in Estonia.

The anti-Bolsheviks, known as the 'Whites', consisted of very diverse groups; including ex-tsarist commanders, Kadets and right-wing political organisations. In addition, for much of 1918 the Social Revolutionaries fought against the Communists (Reds). In June 1918 the Executive Committee of the Soviets expelled all Right Social Revolutionaries and Mensheviks from the Soviets for openly attacking the Communist (Bolshevik) dictatorship and the Treaty of Brest-Litovsk. The Left Social Revolutionaries had already resigned from Sovnarkom over the Treaty of Brest-Litovsk (March). In July the SRs unsuccessfully attempted to seize power in Moscow. The Communists (Bolsheviks) now expelled the Left SRs from the Soviets. In August an SR assassin, Fanny Kaplan, seriously wounded Lenin. In June 1918, Victor Chernov set up an SR government in Samara. However, Admiral Kolchak, the White leader in the area east of the Urals, soon clashed with the SRs.

The Communists relaxed their persecution of the SRs and Mensheviks in November 1918 and many SRs and Mensheviks then fought for the Communists.

Also fighting in the Civil War, against both the Communists (Reds) and the Whites, were the Greens. These were peasant forces, the largest of which was in the Ukraine led by the anarchist Nestor Makhno. In addition, nationalist movements in the Baltic, Ukraine and Georgia were trying to break away from Russian control during this period. In the case of Georgia, a popular Menshevik government remained in power until the Red Army overthrew it in 1921.

Both Reds and Whites used Terror as a means of destroying opposition and intimidating the population into obedience. The Red Terror formally began in September 1918, but had unofficially existed since July. During the Civil War, the Cheka (the Communist secret police) executed at least 50,000 people.

The start of the Civil War is difficult to date exactly but is often identified with the revolt of the Czech Legion in May 1918. The Czech Legion consisted of Austro-Hungarian prisoners of war who were returning, via the Trans-Siberian Railway, to Western Europe to fight against the Central Powers in the hope of setting up an independent Czech state. They clashed with Bolshevik troops in May and decided to join with the Whites to overthrow the Bolsheviks. The Civil War lasted until the end of 1920.

Foreign intervention

The Whites received help from the USA, Britain, France, Italy and Japan. However, this help was half-hearted and soon withdrawn. The interventionist powers were:

- worried about the possibility of a communist revolution spreading to their own countries
- angry that the Bolsheviks refused to pay back foreign loans
- initially hopeful that, if they helped overthrow the Bolsheviks, Russia might rejoin the war against Germany.

British intervention did help ensure that the Baltic states were able to break away from Russia and become independent.

The Course of the Civil War

May–August 1918	The initial phase was marked by gains for the Whites. The Czech Legion attacked the Bolsheviks. Foreign powers began to send troops to Russia in June.
September–November 1918	The Bolsheviks counter-attacked against the Czechs and recaptured Kazan (about 300 miles east of Moscow). In November Admiral Kolchak took control of the White forces in the East.
1919	This was the most dangerous period for the Bolsheviks because they faced several White offensives, launched by Kolchak in March, Denikin in August–October and Yudenich in September–October. By October, the situation looked very threatening for the Bolsheviks and Lenin proposed withdrawing from Petrograd (Trotsky persuaded the Central Committee against this). However, the White offensives were not co-coordinated and Trotsky, as War Commissar, was able to deal with them separately. The foreign powers began to withdraw their forces, so that most were gone by December.
1920	Admiral Kolchak was captured and executed. The last White army was evacuated from the Crimea in December 1920.

War with Poland, 1920-21

In January 1920 the Reds recaptured the Ukraine but Poland then invaded the Ukraine in an attempt to expand its borders. In July the Red commander, General Tukhachevsky, forced the Poles out of the Ukraine and invaded Poland. Lenin expected the Polish workers to rise in revolt against the Polish government but they did not and the Red army was driven back into Russia. In October an armistice was signed, leading to the Treaty of Riga (March 1921).

Q. Why did the Communists (Reds) win the Russian Civil War?

1.   The Whites lacked political unity or unified leadership
They were weakened by the fact that they had diverse aims; some wanted to restore the tsar, others to set up a moderate republic or a military dictatorship. The murder of the royal family at Ekaterinburg in July 1918 removed the possibility that the Whites might rally around them.

2.   The Whites never co-ordinated their attacks
The White commanders, their forces spread out over thousands of miles, failed to link up, the nearer to Moscow they got, the more strained their lines of communication became.

3.   The Communists were more united and had better leadership
In contrast to the Whites, the Communist Party was united behind Lenin and had a shared ideology (Marxism). Lenin and Trotsky were very effective leaders; they were ruthless and pragmatic. Lenin was able to push through controversial yet necessary policies such as reintroducing one-man management into the factories and employing ex-tsarist officers in the Red Army.

4.   The Communists controlled a more coherent and compact area
The Communists were defending a central region well served by railways and their lines of communication were much shorter than those of the Whites. The Reds controlled the great industrial centres of Moscow and Petrograd.

5.   Trotsky, as War Commissar, formed the Red Army into a disciplined force.

Q. What were the key features of the Red Army?

» Trotsky and Lenin rejected the demands of some leading Communists that the Party adopt Revolutionary Warfare. Lenin and Trotsky resorted to conscription (May 1918), instead of relying on the ill-disciplined but enthusiastic Red Guard militias that had been formed in 1917. By the end of 1918 the Red Army was 100,000 strong; by April 1919, 500,000; and by June 1920, 5 million. By contrast, the Whites never managed to raise more than 650,000 soldiers.

» In the face of bitter opposition from other leading Communists, Trotsky recruited 50,000 former tsarist officers. Trotsky said that the officers were *"to be squeezed like lemons and discarded later."* Former officers who refused to serve were put into concentration camps and their families were held hostage to ensure the officers' loyalty.

» The Communist Party appointed political commissars to every army unit; Trotsky described the commissars as the *"iron corset"*. Trotsky toured the fronts in an armoured train and dealt ruthlessly with deserters and incompetents.

» Trotsky restored the practice of appointing (rather than electing) officers.

6.   Lenin presented the Bolsheviks as a patriotic force

The Whites were unpopular because of their foreign support and their brutality (though the Bolsheviks were as brutal).

7.   Foreign support for the Whites was limited and was withdrawn by the end of 1920.

8.   The peasants hated the Whites

This was because the Whites were committed to restoring land to the nobility.

9.   From May 1918, Lenin took measures to control the economy, which were known as War Communism

These were only partly successful.

Q. What were the key features of War Communism?

○   All factories of any size were nationalised and military discipline was applied to the factories.

○   Middle class managers, accountants and engineers were brought back to run the factories, most of which had been placed under workers' control in the months after the revolution, usually with disastrous results.

○   Food and grain were seized from the peasants by Red Guards in order to feed the workers and the troops.

○   The old inflation-ridden currency was abandoned. Instead wages were paid in food and fuel and trade was by barter.

Q. What were War Communism's results?

○   The peasants decided it was not worth growing food for the Communists to steal and so reduced their sowing. The result was a terrible food shortage, leading to possibly 7,500,000 deaths.

○   Food shortages in the towns led to large-scale migration from the cities; between 1917 and 1920 the urban population fell by 33%.

○   War Communism did not prevent a continuing fall in industrial and agricultural output; by 1921 the grain harvest was only 50% of the 1913 level and industrial production had fallen to just 20% of the 1913 level. However, the economic crisis was as bad in the areas controlled by the Whites.

○   War Communism ensured that the Red Army was fed and equipped. It took the majority of resources: e.g. 60% of food, and 70% of shoes.

The Consequences of the Civil War and of the Communists' Victory

The Communist government had survived the Civil War but its ruthless methods had made it deeply unpopular. When Lenin had been planning the 1917 Revolution, he believed that it would not be possible to create a socialist state in Russia, given its lack of industrialisation, unless help from more advanced countries was forthcoming. He had assumed that revolution would spread to other parts of Europe, but by 1921 Lenin realised that Russia would be the only country with a communist government for some time. Communist revolutions had failed in Germany and Hungary in 1919-20. Lenin knew that a strong army and secret police would be needed to defend his government from external and internal threats. The *"dictatorship of the proletariat"*, or more accurately the dictatorship of the Communist Party, would have to continue indefinitely.

Crises facing the Communist Party in 1921:

(i)   The Krondstadt Rebellion (February-March 1921)

In February-March 1921 sailors at the naval base at Kronstadt, near Petrograd, revolted against the Communist Party. They protested that the Communists had broken all the promises that they had made to the Russian people; that the Cheka was arresting members of other socialist parties and stealing food from the peasants. Eventually the rising was brutally crushed by the Red Army. The Krondstadt Rebellion alarmed the Communist leadership because the Kronstadt sailors had been among their most committed supporters in 1917 and during the Civil War.

(ii)   Rebellion in Tambov Province

Peasants in Tambov also rebelled against the government; they attacked and robbed grain convoys.

(iii)   Widespread strikes

Strikes occurred in 77% of Russia's large and medium-sized factories during 1920.

(iv)   Economic chaos and famine

Agricultural and industrial output had fallen drastically as a result of the Civil War and the Treaty of Brest-Litovsk. In excess of 7 million Russians died of famine and disease in 1921, leading Lenin to call on the International Red Cross for help.

The Establishment of Single Party Rule

Ever since the closure of the Constituent Assembly in January 1918, it had been apparent that Lenin had no intention of sharing power with any other parties. For the majority of the Civil War many Mensheviks and Socialist Revolutionaries had fought in the Red Army but, in 1921, with the Communists victorious, Lenin banned the Menshevik and Socialist Revolutionary parties. The Communist Party was the sole legal party in the Soviet Union. In the same year, Lenin expelled 150,000 members of the Communist Party, mostly former Mensheviks and Socialist Revolutionaries.

The Creation of the Union of Soviet Socialist Republics (USSR)

Lenin had promised that the various nationalities of the tsar's former empire would be allowed to choose whether they wished to be part of Russia or to be independent. Once Lenin was assured of victory in the Civil War, he reneged on this promise; as the Red Army captured areas during the Civil War, they imposed Communist governments on them and turned them into Soviet Socialist Republics. In 1923 a new constitution created the Union of Soviet Socialist Republics (USSR). Each Republic had its own government, which, in theory, could make decisions in certain areas of policy, such as health and education, without reference to Moscow. In economic policy, the Republics acted under the instructions of local Commissars who followed orders from a Union Commissar in Moscow. Foreign and Defence policy were entirely directed from Moscow by all Union-Commissars.

The Structure of the Government	The Structure of the Communist Party

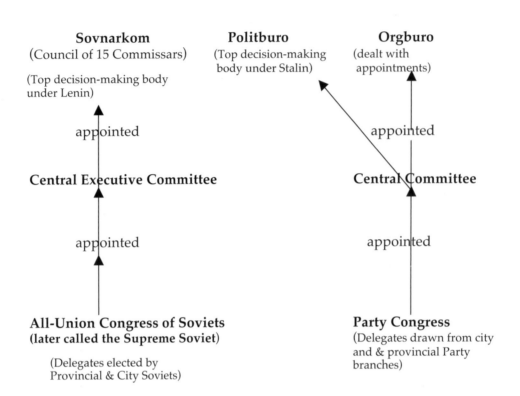

Sovnarkom
(Council of 15 Commissars)

(Top decision-making body under Lenin)

Politburo
(Top decision-making body under Stalin)

Orgburo
(dealt with appointments)

↑ appointed

↑ appointed

Central Executive Committee

Central Committee

↑ appointed

↑ appointed

**All-Union Congress of Soviets
(later called the Supreme Soviet)**

(Delegates elected by
Provincial & City Soviets)

Party Congress
(Delegates drawn from city
and & provincial Party
branches)

The Nature of the Party and the State in the USSR

1. Hierarchical pyramids *(see diagram above)*

Both the Party and State organisations were organised in a hierarchical pyramid (see diagram above). In theory, power flowed from the base (local Party branches and local Soviets) but in practice power flowed from the top downwards. The Party followed the principle of 'Democratic Centralism' which meant that the leadership was elected but once policy-decisions had been made they were binding on the Party members. Increasingly, decision-making was monopolised at the top of the state and party structures.

2. The Party was the principal organisation in the USSR, dominating state institutions

Membership of Sovnarkom (the cabinet), the highest state institution, was monopolised by the Communist Party leadership. In turn, local state institutions, the Soviets, met less and less frequently and became agents of Sovnarkom (and therefore the Party leadership). Elections to the soviets became less frequent and more subject to Party control and the All-Union Congress of Soviets and the Central Executive Committee (Vtsik) lost control over Sovnarkom. The Congress of Soviets had little power and met for only a few days each year. The Party apparatus, not the state apparatus, is where real power resided.

a) Centralisation of power within the Party leadership

During the Civil War, there was a growing trend for orders to be sent down from above and important posts, especially local Party secretaryships, were filled by appointment from above and not by election from below. However, until 1921 there was still considerable freedom of debate within the Party, for example, at the 9th Party Congress (1920), the Workers' Opposition, a faction within the Party, criticised the domination of the Party by the Central Committee and also the policy of War Communism.

However, because of the economic and political crises facing the Party in 1921, the 10th Party Congress passed the "Resolution on Party Unity", which banned factions within the Party and made debate within the Party less open and public. The Workers' Opposition was banned and 150,000 Party members were purged.

b) Party membership expanded rapidly

The Civil War saw both a major expansion in Party membership and a growing bureaucratisation of the Party; growing numbers of Party members held administrative posts. By 1921 there were 732,000 members; by 1933 Party membership had risen to over 3.5 million. Most of the new recruits were drawn from the working class whereas many of the old Bolsheviks had educated backgrounds. Historians tend to agree that this growth in the size and bureaucratisation of the Party facilitated Stalin's rise to power as he held the key positions within the Party administration.

The Stalin Constitution of 1936

In 1936 a new constitution, drafted by Bukharin, replaced the original constitution of the USSR. The main differences were that there were now more republics (11 rather than the 7 when the USSR was set up in 1923) and that the All-Union Congress was replaced by the Soviet of the Union and the Soviet of the Nationalities, which together made up the new Supreme Soviet. However, only candidates approved by the Communist Party could stand for election and the Supreme Soviet had no real power, meeting for just a few days each year.

The new 'Stalin Constitution' on paper granted Soviet citizens a range of democratic freedoms, including freedom of speech and liberty of conscience. However, this was just a façade, intended largely to impress foreign socialists; the reality was the Great Terror: mass arrests, executions without trial and the proliferation of prison camps, administered by the Gulag.

Economic policy 1921-28

The New Economic Policy 1921

Facing economic collapse, famine and widespread revolts, Lenin decided that War Communism had to be abandoned. In March 1921, at the Tenth Congress of the Communist Party, Lenin introduced his new economic policy (NEP). Many members of the Party were horrified by what they regarded as a retreat towards capitalism but Lenin demonstrated his leadership qualities by winning over the Congress.

Q. What were NEP's main features?

(i) Capitalism was restored to the countryside in the sense that free trade in grain was reinstated. Grain requisitioning was ended. The peasants had to hand over 10% of their grain to the government, as a tax in kind, but were allowed to sell any surplus grain to private traders who became known as *Nepmen*.

(ii) The old devalued rouble was replaced by a new currency.

(iii) A mixture of socialism and capitalism prevailed in the urban economy. Larger factories and industrial concerns, such as steel plants and coal mines, the *"commanding heights of the economy"*, as Lenin called them, were to remain under state control. This meant that the state employed about 75% of the industrial workforce. NEP led to the reintroduction of private ownership of small and medium sized factories.

Q. How successful was NEP?

NEP made possible a gradual recovery from the economic crisis of 1920-21. By 1928, Russian industrial output had reached the 1914 level; agriculture recovered faster. In 1923 this led to what Trotsky dubbed the "scissors crisis," where food prices were falling while the price of scarce manufactured goods remained high. Peasants could not afford the tools, pots and other manufactured goods that they needed.

Stalin's Rise to Power

The struggle to succeed Lenin originated not with his death in 1924 but from 1922 when he suffered the first of a succession of strokes and was increasingly incapacitated. By 1929, Josef Stalin had emerged as the sole leader of the Communist Party but back in the early 1920s few Russians would have predicted his rise to power.

Q. How was Stalin able to secure the Party leadership?

i.   Stalin was a member of the Politburo and Orgburo, the top committees within the Party and **he held several powerful positions within the Party apparatus**; in particular, Lenin appointed him General Secretary in 1922. He was able to use this to develop a power base within the Party, as he could promote and dismiss influential Party officials, particularly local Party secretaries. Stalin realised that the key to power lay in control over the Party organisation, rather than within state institutions. The Party grew rapidly, numbering 800,000 by 1925 and over 1.5 million by 1929. As its membership expanded, control over it became increasingly centralised, concentrating enormous power in Stalin's hands. Trotsky, Stalin's main rival for the leadership, held no significant position within the Party apparatus and so was unable to develop his own power base to compete with Stalin.

ii.   **Stalin's rivals underestimated him.** Lacking the charisma or the oratorical brilliance of Trotsky, the other leading figures in the Party ignored the 'grey blur', as Stalin was once dubbed, and concentrated their efforts on preventing Trotsky from gaining control over the Party.

iii.   **Stalin was a very skilful political operator** and was able to play off different factions within the Party leadership against each other.

These divisions were partly the result of:

• **Personal rivalries**, for example, Kamenev and Zinoviev resented Trotsky's arrogance and were prepared to work with Stalin against Trotsky in the period 1922-25. During this period, Stalin, Kamenev and Zinoviev formed a three-man leadership team, known as the 'triumvirate' or 'troika'. They combined to force Trotsky's resignation as Commissar for War in 1925. Only in 1926 did Zinoviev and Kamenev decide to work with Trotsky in the so-called 'United Opposition'; but by then it was too late to prevent Stalin removing them from the Politburo.

• **Major policy disagreements** within the Party. The Party was split over whether to continue with NEP or not. From 1923, those on the Left of the Party (e.g. Trotsky and Zinoviev) believed NEP should be replaced by rapid industrialisation and a move towards collectivisation of agriculture, whereas those on the Right (chiefly Bukharin) argued that NEP was working and should be maintained.

The other key policy dispute was over the issue of promoting worldwide revolution. The Left, particularly Trotsky, favoured 'Permanent Revolution', seeing international revolution as essential to the survival of socialism in Russia. By contrast, the Right adopted the slogan 'Socialism in One Country', arguing that, having witnessed the suppression of communist revolutions in Germany and Hungary, international revolution was not possible for the foreseeable future and so the Russian Communist Party must focus on establishing a socialist economy at home.

Stalin began by supporting the Right against the Left on the question of NEP and he used the support of the Right to remove the Left from the Politburo in 1926. Then from 1928, Stalin turned on the Right and attacked NEP, urging the Party to adopt rapid industrialisation and forced collectivisation. In 1929-30, the Right (Bukharin, Rykov and Tomsky) were removed from the Politburo and replaced by supporters of Stalin.

iv. **Stalin was also much better than his rivals at gauging the mood of the ordinary Party members**. He realised that in the mid-1920s the Party had little interest in exporting revolution abroad, weary as it was after the upheavals of 1917-21, and that most of the Party thought that NEP was a success in permitting economic recovery. Equally, Stalin judged correctly that most Communists had, by 1928-29, began to have serious reservations about NEP because economic growth was slowing down and the peasants were withholding grain from the markets in an attempt to force prices up. By the late 1920s, many in the Party were impatient to launch more socialist economic policies, such as collectivisation of agriculture, and wanted to transform the USSR into a modern industrial state.

v. **Stalin was able to outmanoeuvre Trotsky** by appearing as the chief mourner at Lenin's funeral (having misled Trotsky about its date) and then by promoting himself as the true heir of Lenin.

vi. **Trotsky's health was poor** in 1924-25, just when he needed to be at his strongest as the power struggle developed.

vii. **Stalin was fortunate** in that, following Lenin's death in January 1924, the **Central Committee decided not to publish Lenin's *Political Testament*** in which Lenin had been deeply critical of Stalin (and somewhat less so of other leading Communists) and had recommended Stalin's dismissal as General Secretary.

viii. **Stalin was able to use the Resolution on Party Unity (1921) to silence his opponents** within the top echelons of the Party, by branding them as factions seeking to undermine Party unity. So first Trotsky, Zinoviev and Kamenev were branded the 'Left Opposition' and later Bukharin, Tomsky and Rykov were labelled the 'Right Opposition'.

The Politburo 1924-26

'Left Communists'	'Right Communists'
Trotsky Zinoviev Kamenev	Bukharin Rykov Tomsky

◄───────────────────────────►

Stalin moves his position between the Right and Left factions

The Struggle to Succeed Lenin

1922	• Stalin appointed General Secretary of the Party • Lenin suffered two strokes • Triumvirate of Stalin, Zinoviev and Kamenev formed collective leadership • Lenin wrote his Political Testament
1923	• Lenin added postscript to Political Testament, calling for Stalin's removal as General Secretary • 'Scissors Crisis' led Trotsky and others on the Left to question NEP
1924	• Lenin's death • Central Committee suppressed Lenin's Political Testament
1925	• Trotsky resigned as War Commissar • Party Congress endorsed NEP and Socialism in One Country • Zinoviev and Kamenev began to oppose Stalin
1926	• United Opposition of Trotsky, Zinoviev and Kamenev • United Opposition removed from the Politburo • Voroshilov and other allies of Stalin joined the Politburo
1927	• Zinoviev, Kamenev and Trotsky were expelled from the Party • Grain procurement crisis began as peasants withheld grain
1928	• Grain procurement crisis continued • Stalin responded by requisitioning grain in the so-called 'Urals-Siberia method' • Bread rationing introduced in Moscow and Leningrad • First Five Year Plan introduced; NEP abandoned
1929/30	• Party Congress set ambitious targets for First Five Year Plan • Right Opposition (Tomsky, Rykov and Bukharin) removed from Politburo • Trotsky expelled from the USSR • Collectivisation introduced; the 'liquidation of the kulaks'

Stalin and the Historians

Historians see Stalin's rise to power and the relationship between Stalinism and Leninism in a variety of different ways. Some argue that Stalin's rule represented a major deviation from that of Lenin, whilst others see a basic continuity in their methods. Some of the key interpretations are summarised below.

Structuralist approach (e.g. Richard Pipes)	Regard Stalin as a product of Russia's circumstances. A strong ruler was required because the country was just emerging from nearly a decade of war and civil war. Stalin was the natural successor to Lenin because of the way the Party had become increasingly bureaucratised.
Continuity between Leninism and Stalinism (e.g. Robert Conquest)	Lenin created the single party dictatorship and system of terror, which Stalin continued. So Stalin was the heir to the Leninist tradition.
Stalinism viewed as a deviation from Leninism (e.g. Stephen Cohen)	Stalin distorted Lenin's legacy. Lenin used terror during the Civil War only as a temporary, emergency measure; Lenin allowed dissent within the Party; Lenin was hostile to a cult of the leader. Stalin, by contrast, used terror as a normal feature of government when the USSR was at peace; he suppressed debate within the Party; he created a monstrous personality cult. Historians like Cohen argue that Communism could have developed in a very different, less brutal way if another leader, such as Bukharin, had succeeded Lenin.

Stalin's Economic Policies: 'The Revolution From Above'

Historians often use the phrase 'the Revolution from above' to characterise Stalin's economic policies in the 1930s. They argue that the economic changes brought about by Stalin and imposed on the Russian people represented much more of a transformation of society than the Bolsheviks' seizure of power in 1917. Stalin abandoned Lenin's New Economic Policy (NEP) and introduced rapid industrialisation in the guise of his Five Year Plans (1928 onwards) and forced collectivisation (from 1929).

Q. Why did Stalin end NEP and instead introduce Collectivisation and the Five Year Plans?

→ NEP had enabled the economy to recover, by 1926, from the effects of the First World War and Civil War, but economic growth slowed down thereafter.

→ Lenin had presented NEP as a temporary retreat from socialism. By the late 1920s, many Communists were impatient to get on and build a modern, socialist economy; they wanted to pursue a more heroic vision than the tired compromise with capitalism that NEP represented.

→ By 1927, several international developments seemed to threaten the USSR's security, e.g. the coming to power in Poland of Pilsudski (1926), who was aggressively anti-communist; the breaking off of Russian-British diplomatic relations; and the brutal massacre of Chinese communists by Chiang Kaishek's Nationalists. This 'war scare' appeared to highlight the need for Russia to catch up in industrial terms with the West; and, for that to happen, Stalin argued that the modernisation of agriculture, by means of collectivisation, was also essential.

As Stalin later put it in a speech of 1931, *"We are fifty or a hundred years behind the advanced countries. We must make good this distance in ten years. Either we do it, or we shall be crushed. This is what our obligations to the workers and peasants of the USSR dictate to us"*.

→ There were serious food shortages in 1927-28 because the peasants and the state were at loggerheads. The government had cut the price they paid for the peasants' grain in order to find the resources to invest in industrial expansion. The peasants retaliated by marketing less grain.

→ Stalin responded to this 'grain procurement crisis' by reviving forced grain requisitioning when he visited Siberia in 1927. Stalin judged his '*Urals-Siberia method*' a success and this seems to have prompted him to turn to collectivisation as a means of achieving greater state control over the grain supply.

→ Stalin and many others in the Party saw collectivisation as a means of eliminating class enemies, the 'kulaks' or rich, 'exploiting' peasants, who could be presented as 'petty capitalists'. Collectivisation was consistent with Marxist-Leninist principles: collective ownership would replace private ownership. All factions within the Communist Party had agreed that the peasantry should be encouraged to join collectives but Right Communists like Bukharin argued against forced collectivisation. However, on the eve of collectivisation less than 3% of Russia's agricultural land was collectivised.

→ Stalin viewed forced collectivisation as the way to provide the surplus manpower, food and money required for rapid industrialisation. Stalin and his supporters believed that larger farm units (the collectives) would be more efficient than the old small peasant farms. Current Russian grain yields were only half of those in Germany. Stalin assumed that more grain would be grown, which could be used to feed an enlarged industrial workforce and for export abroad to earn the foreign currency to buy foreign machinery needed to equip Russia's factories.

→ Stalin's motivation for collectivisation was also political. The peasants had never been enthusiastic supporters of the Communist Party and the Party had only achieved limited control over the countryside. The new collectives were to be run by a Party-appointed chairman and the new Motor Tractor Stations each had an NKVD (secret police) unit attached. Thus the peasants would be much more firmly under the Party's control.

Collectivisation: The Process

Stalin's policy of collectivisation constituted a revolution in the countryside, forcing 25 million peasant households into 240,000 collective farms. In the process, the peasants' traditional way of life based on the village commune and attachment to the Orthodox Church was destroyed. Millions died in the process and millions more fled from the villages into the growing industrial cities. Collectivisation and rapid industrialisation were inextricably linked.

'Dekulakisation'

The forced collectivisation programme of 1929-30 was in effect a declaration of war against the peasants by the Party. Stalin launched collectivisation by attacking the kulaks or richer peasants. In practice the term 'kulak' was applied to any peasant who resisted forced collectivisation. In December 1929 Stalin announced that the Party aimed at 'liquidating the kulak as a class'. The Party recruited 25,000 urban activists and sent them, supported by the Red Army and NKVD, into the countryside to implement collectivisation.

Q. Why did Stalin start by attacking the kulaks?

→   Because the kulaks were viewed as petty bourgeoisie since they owned and often rented out land. Their elimination was therefore a further to step towards the creation of a 'classless' society.

→   Dekulakisation served as a warning to the peasantry of the consequences of not co-operating with the Party.

In the winter of 1929-30, in the region of 1.5 million 'kulaks' were dispossessed of their land. Many were forcibly deported to Siberia or Central Asia or were killed while many others fled to the towns. There was widespread peasant resistance to collectivisation and not just by the richer peasants. Party activists responded savagely but peasants continued to defy them by slaughtering their livestock rather than handing it over to the collectives.

Q. Why did Stalin call a temporary halt to collectivisation in 1930?

By 1930, 55% of farmland had been collectivised but in March Stalin announced that collectivisation had to be voluntary and, in an article in *Pravda* (the Party newspaper) entitled 'Dizzy with Success', accused Party officials of excessive force.

• Some historians interpret this as a cynical ploy by Stalin to encourage the peasants to co-operate so that the success of the 1930 harvest would not be compromised by the upheavals.

• Other historians, such as Lynne Viola, argue that collectivisation did get out of control and that Stalin was genuinely trying to reassert central government's control over local officials and activists in order to end the chaotic conditions prevailing in the countryside.

Forced collectivisation reinstated: 1931

From the beginning of 1931 the Party reverted to forced requisitioning. This time it was accompanied by limited concessions to the peasants: they were permitted to retain small private plots of land (averaging 0.3 hectare) and some livestock. By 1935, over 90% of farmland had been collectivised. The Party set up a small number of state farms (Sovkhoz) in which the peasants worked for a wage but the majority of families in each collective and the peasants had to deliver to the state a fixed quota of produce at prices set by the state. The peasants were allowed to retain any surplus grain (after the state quota was delivered) but they also had to pay the Motor Tractor Stations, set up in the 1930s, from which they rented tractors. However, tractors were in short supply in the early 1930s.

The Famine of 1932-33

In this period millions of peasants died in a man-made famine. Estimates range from 4 to 6.5 million deaths. The disruption caused by collectivisation and by peasant resistance to it, resulted in falling grain output but what transformed that into a famine was the fact that the state took a far higher percentage of the harvest, leaving the peasants to starve. Non-Russian areas, particularly the Ukraine, suffered most. In Kazakhstan, the population fell by 20% in the 1930s.

Q. **Did Stalin achieve his aims in collectivising agriculture?**

✔ The Party now had much greater control over the peasants and the countryside. Collectivisation has often been termed by historians as a new form of 'serfdom' for the peasants.

✔ More importantly for Stalin, the state now had much greater control over the grain supply. Whereas in 1928 the state procured (obtained) 15% of the harvest; by 1935, this had risen to 35%. In 1933 grain procurements had peaked at 40%.

✔ The increased grain procurements enabled the state to feed an expanded industrial workforce, although this was only true after 1935 because the chaos of the early stages of collectivisation resulted in food rationing for the towns. Higher grain procurements also meant more could be exported abroad in order to purchase machinery to equip Russia's new factories. Russia exported 5 million tons of grain a year in 1931-32 and even during the terrible famine 2 million tons of grain a year were sold abroad.

✔ Collectivisation led to a massive increase in the urban population, which grew by 12 million in the first 5 years of collectivisation. This provided the workforce for Russia's developing industries under the Five Year Plans.

✖   Grain production and overall agricultural productivity increased only marginally. In 1913 Russia's population produced 0.5 tons of grain per head; by 1937, this had increased fractionally to 0.57 tons per head. Collectivisation did not lead to greater efficiency because the peasants lacked the incentives to work hard on the land belonging to the collectives.

✖   The collectives remained inefficient in the long-term too. By the 1960s, the USSR was obliged to purchase large amounts of grain from Canada and the USA. By contrast, the peasants did work hard on their small private plots, which, though only constituting 5% of the USSR's arable land, produced 25% of its fruit and vegetables.

✖   Livestock levels in the USSR fell massively and did not fully recover until the 1950s. By the early 1930s, the peasants had slaughtered 65% of their sheep and 46% of their cattle.

Rapid Industrialisation (1928-41)

The First Five Year Plan (1928-32)

Three years after the First Five Year Plan (FFYP from here on) was launched, Stalin made it clear in a speech referred to above that the tempo of industrialisation could not be lessened because Russia was behind its capitalist enemies. The USSR was the world's sole socialist state, with the exception of Outer Mongolia, and Stalin therefore saw rapid industrialisation as essential to safeguard Russia from attack. This motivation was similar to that of Tsar Alexander III and Tsar Nicholas II when they initiated industrialisation programmes in the 1890s in an attempt to revive Russia's status as a great power.

At the 15th Party Congress in December 1927, several possible sets of targets for industrial expansion were debated. The Central State Planning Commission in Moscow, known as Gosplan, drew up a range of possible targets for industrial expansion. Towards the end of 1928 the Central Committee adopted the most ambitious of the targets but it was not until the 16th Party Congress, held in April 1929, that the targets for the FFYP were officially fixed. The FFYP ended private ownership in industry, thereby abandoning Lenin's New Economic Policy. The FFYP aimed at a massive 236% increase in total industrial output. The 'command economy' was born, with targets set by Gosplan for factories all over the USSR.

Stalin saw the whole enterprise in heroic and military terms and used military language in exhorting the population to smash targets and create a modern socialist economy in the process. Stalin declared that *'there are no fortresses that Bolsheviks cannot storm.'* The FFYP was chaotically managed, with targets being constantly revised upwards and Stalin deciding to complete the plan in four years. Centralised planning led to many mistakes being made, as did the fact that 9 million of the workers recently recruited in to the new factories were unskilled peasants. 1500 new factories were constructed by the end of 1932, many of them in previously undeveloped areas east of the Ural Mountains, e.g. Magnitogorsk was built from scratch as a vast steel-producing centre. The prestigious Moscow Metro (underground) project was begun along with the Volga-White Sea Canal.

The Second Five Year Plan (1933-37)

To some extent in drawing up the Second Five Year Plan, the Communist leadership learnt from its mistakes in the FFYP and set lower targets for industrial expansion. The period 1934-35 saw great success as many of the factories built under the FFYP were now up and running. Food rationing was ended in 1935. However, from 1936 the Second Plan was disrupted by the Stakhanovite movement, which sought to encourage the workers to emulate the record-breaking exploits of the coal-miner, Alexi Stakhanov, and led to 'storming' methods where factories worked round the clock to maximise production. However, this approach led to machinery being broken and industrial workers becoming exhausted. Stalin's Purges, from 1936 onwards, led to hundreds of thousands of skilled workers, engineers and managers being sent to the labour camps or executed.

The Third Five Year Plan (1938-41)

The main focus was on industries linked to rearmament because Stalin became increasingly fearful of an attack by Hitler's Germany. The Third Five Year Plan was cut short by the Nazi invasion of June 1941.

'Carrot and Stick' Methods

Stalin used a range of methods to try to achieve his goal of transforming the USSR into an industrial superpower.

'Stick'

✘	'Iron discipline' in the factories. Workers were threatened by harsh punishments for absenteeism or for not meeting quotas.
✘	The reintroduction of internal passports (1932) made it difficult for workers to switch jobs or move from town to town.
✘	Prison camp (Gulag) labour was widely used, e.g. 70,000 prisoners died constructing the Belomor Canal.
✘	'Show Trials' of managers and engineers, who were accused of 'wrecking' and industrial sabotage on behalf of capitalist powers, terrorising the workforce into compliance with the state's demands on them. The first such trial was the Shakhty Trial (1928) of 53 engineers, 5 of whom were executed.

'Carrot'

✔	Higher wages were introduced for skilled workers and for exceeding targets (1931). Both practices ran counter to Marxist principles.
✔	Propaganda. The Stakhanovite movement encouraged workers to smash targets and those who did were rewarded with medals and dubbed 'heroes of socialist labour', feted in the Soviet press. Also Socialist Realist Art celebrated the achievements of the Five Year Plans.
✔	Komsomol (Young Communist League) activists voluntarily contributed to some key projects such as building Magnitogorsk.

Q. How did Stalin find the resources to industrialise?

→ By taking more grain from the peasants and then using it to feed the growing towns and to export it in order to buy foreign machinery.

→ By heavy taxation.

→ By driving down living standards; the historian, Leonard Schapiro, calculated that Russian living standards by 1940 were half of those in 1928.

→ By massively increasing the industrial workforce (Russia's urban population practically doubled to 56 million in the 1930s), recruiting peasants who were fleeing from collectivisation and greater numbers of women factory workers.

Q. How successful were Stalin's Five Year Plans?

Official Soviet statistics, produced during and after Stalin's rule, about the increases in industrial production achieved during the 1930s are very suspect not just because they were inflated for propaganda purposes, but also because of the falsification of figures by managers desperate to avoid punishment for non-fulfilment of targets. Nonetheless, Western historians agree that the 1930s saw a huge expansion of Soviet industry.

	1927	1939
Coal (millions of tons)	35	145
Pig iron (millions of tons)	12	40

Some figures relating to industrial output in Russia, 1927-39

The 'upside"

↑	The USSR's Gross National Product (GDP) tripled during 1928-40, whereas no other major economy came close to even doubling output. For much of the 1930s the major capitalist countries were still in the throes of the Great Depression.
↑	The USSR in 1928 had been behind the USA, Britain, Germany and France in terms of industrial output and only just ahead of Japan; by 1940 Soviet output was bettered only by the USA. Arguably without this expansion the USSR's victory over Nazi Germany in 1941-45 would not have been possible.
↑	Comparing production figures for 1927/8 and 1940, western historians estimate a fourfold increase in coal and electricity production between 1927 and 1940, and a sixfold increase in steel. Oil production "only" doubled in this period, but this was one area of industry where Russia was already a world leader in 1927.

↑	Huge projects like the Dneiper Dam and the Moscow Metro, were completed. 8,000 new industrial enterprises were built.
↑	The USSR was transformed into an industrial society in terms of the increase in urban population, from 26 million (1926) to 56 million by 1939.
↑	The literacy rate increased from 51% to 81% of the population, as the Party recognised the need for a more educated workforce. 70,000 libraries were built. Technical colleges turned out 300,000 engineering graduates in the 1930s.

The 'downside'

↓	Although GOSPLAN's centralised planning proved successful in expanding the volume of industrial output, it was far from successful in ensuring quality. The USSR still lagged behind the West in this respect. This is illustrated by the huge difference in the durability of Soviet duplication of certain machine parts and a lack of others. John Scott, in his book "Behind the Urals", provides an explanation for why many Soviet projects ran into difficulties and why much of what was produced was poor quality; many of the industrial workers were recently recruited peasants, who *"were completely unfamiliar with industrial tools and processes."*
↓	The FYPs suffered from the effects of 'gigantomania': Stalin was obsessed with huge projects. Some of them were totally misconceived, e.g. the Belomor Canal, which was too shallow to take the warships for which it was designed.
↓	Although the USSR had risen to the rank of the world's second industrial power by 1940, this expansion had been very largely focussed on heavy industry. Consumer good production rose during the 1930s but by only a third of the increase in iron output. In this respect the USSR did not catch up with the West.
↓	In the long-term, the 'Command Economy' did not work; after World War Two, Soviet industry stagnated and the technological gap (except in certain defence industries) with the West widened. The collapse of Soviet Communism at the end of the 1980s owed much to the inefficiency and lack of incentives that characterised both collectivised agriculture and the state-owned and directed industrial sector.

Q. Could industrialisation have been achieved without Stalin's methods?

Answer: 'No'

Some historians argue that without Stalin's brutal methods and unslackening pace Russia would not have caught up with the West and would not have been able to survive Hitler's invasion in 1941. They argue that Stalin made a unique contribution to industrialisation in accelerating the whole process, abandoning the cautious approach of Bukharin and other leading Communists, and by finding the resources to transform Russia without the foreign investment that had characterised rapid industrialisation under the last two tsars. Left Communists like Trotsky and Preobrazhensky had, in the 1920s, attacked NEP because they believed it would not permit large-scale industrial expansion.

Answer: 'Yes'

Other historians claim that similar industrial growth rates to those of the 1930s could have been achieved by continuing NEP. They point out that Stalin's methods were often counter-productive, for example over-centralised planning stifled local initiative and 'storming' caused accidents and often led to a drop in productivity as workers became exhausted. As importantly, they rightly emphasise the fact that Stalin's other policies undermined the FYPs. The purges of 1936-38 destroyed many talented managers and engineers; collectivisation led to food shortages in the towns until 1935.

Stalin consolidates his power: The Great Terror (1936-38)

'Terror' and 'Purges' were regular features of the USSR in the 1920s and 1930s. Even in the relatively calm years of NEP (1921-28), 450,000 people had been arrested for 'counter-revolutionary activities'. Lenin had set up a secret police and prison camp system as a means of eliminating class enemies and suppressing political opposition. He had purged the Communist Party of 150,000 members in 1921, expelling them from the Party. This was in order to eliminate those who were not committed to the Party but had joined simply to further their careers; Trotsky termed them 'radishes' – red on the outside but white inside.

In a sense the Great Terror (1936-38) was simply a continuation of the dictatorial methods employed by Lenin. The continuity between Lenin's policies and those of Stalin seemed to be confirmed by a mass reform campaign in 1933-34 when a Party Control Commission expelled 20% of the Party membership. However, what Stalin did next was quantitatively and qualitatively different from anything seen before. Stalin purged over one third of the entire membership and executed about 600,000 of them. This was accompanied by sweeping purges of the armed forces and the imprisonment of millions of ordinary Soviet citizens. The prison camps mushroomed all over the country, under the control of the Gulag, which administered the camp system.

Prominent Old Bolsheviks and senior military commanders were convicted at much-publicised Show Trials but the fates of the mass of ordinary victims went unreported. Not until Gorbachev in the late 1980s did the Party openly reveal and discuss the Terror of the 1930s. Foreign historians have only gained access to Soviet archives since the collapse of Communism but that access has already led historians to revise their thinking on the scale and causes of the Great Terror.

A Timeline of Terror

1928	Shakty Trial: 55 engineers in the Donbass region charged with sabotage.
1930	Trial of the "Industrial Party': Show trial of leading figures in state industrial research and planning institutions, including Gosplan.
1932	Riutin, former Moscow Party Secretary, circulated a document attacking Stalin as 'the evil genius of the Revolution'. Riutin was expelled from the Party, though Stalin had demanded his execution.
1933-34	20% of Communist Party members were expelled.
1934	Seventeenth Party Congress; Sergei Kirov gained more votes than Stalin in the elections to the Central Committee.
1934	Murder of Kirov, Secretary of the Leningrad Party (December). Historians are divided over whether Stalin was responsible. Robert Conquest argues Stalin was; Isaac Deutscher believes Stalin was not behind the murder but decided to use it to justify the purges that followed. Stalin immediately issued a decree giving increased powers to the NKVD in dealing with terrorist suspects. Thousands of Party members in Leningrad were arrested, accused of involvement in Kirov's murder.
1936	'Trial of the 16': Kamenev, Zinoviev and 14 other 'Old Bolsheviks' were put on show trial, convicted and executed for alleged involvement in Kirov's murder and in a 'Trotskyite' conspiracy. Yagoda, NKVD chief, was arrested and replaced by Yezhov.
1937	'Trial of the 17': the 'Anti-Soviet Trotskyist Centre' were tried for plotting with Germany. Those executed included Radek. Torture was officially legalised. The Decree on 'Anti-Soviet Elements' led to regional arrest quotas for the NKVD, which was instructed to execute 28% of those arrested. Official Soviet figures record 353,000 executions in 1937 but this is probably an under-reporting.

	Marshal Tukhachevsky (commander-in-chief) and 7 other generals were convicted and executed after show trials. Arrest of over 35,000 army officers in the period 1937-38
1938	'Trial of the 21': the 'Trotskyite-Rightists' were put on show trial. Most prominent victims were Bukharin and Rykov. NKVD records report 328,000 people executed (again probably an under-estimate).
1939	The Terror was scaled down. Yezhov had been arrested in 1938 and was replaced by Beria. The NKVD itself was now purged; the Soviet historian Dimitri Volkogonov estimates that 23,000 NKVD agents were executed.
1940	Trotsky was assassinated in Mexico by a Stalinist agent.

Q. Why did the Great Terror happen?

To an extent Stalin's purges were, like those of Lenin, motivated by a desire to keep the Party pure and committed, particularly as it had grown so enormously by 1933. However, Stalin's Purges were on a totally different scale both in terms of the numbers of victims and the savagery of the process. Stalin's Terror was driven by certain motives which did not underlie Lenin's repression.

→ Stalin was intent on building up and retaining his own personal power. He used the purges to remove Old Bolshevik rivals like Zinoviev and Kamenev. Stalin had defeated these Old Bolsheviks in the 1920s but they still had some influence within the Party; for example, Rykov, Tomsky and Bukharin had been reinstated on the Central Committee in 1929. Stalin used the Show Trials to not just eliminate his former rivals but also to destroy their reputation, so he alone could take the credit for the Party's achievements.

→ Stalin's personality undoubtedly played a key part: he was vain, mistrustful, and unforgiving and took a pleasure in humiliating rivals and opponents. The historian Robert Conquest in particular has presented Stalin as the architect and driving force behind the Terror. There is plenty of evidence of Stalin's personal involvement, for example, his signature on many lists of those to be arrested and executed.

→ Stalin seems to have had genuine cause for concern about opposition to his economic policies within the Party. Certainly Riutin and, to a lesser extent, Kirov had voiced serious doubts about forced collectivisation. It seems likely that Stalin was responsible for Kirov's murder in 1934, which he then used as an excuse to embark on a series of purges on an unprecedented scale.

→ Revisionist historians, e.g. J. Arch Getty and Sheila Fitzpatrick, argue that it is wrong simply to blame Stalin's paranoia for the purges; though he did see enemies everywhere, other members of the Party either supported the purges because they could thereby eliminate their rivals and win promotion or because they saw it as a necessary part of the battle to build socialism.

Revisionist historians have challenged the traditional view of the all-powerful Stalin and the all-powerful Communist Party; they argue that the central leadership's control over the localities was never complete and that key policies such as dekulakisation and the purges generated a dynamic of their own, with the leadership in Moscow losing control to some extent of the processes they had unleashed.

The context for the Purges must be considered; they followed the violent campaign to enforce collectivisation and the USSR appeared threatened by the rise of Nazi Germany and Japanese expansionism.

→ Certainly Yezhov, the NKVD chief, was a powerful force behind the purges and the NKVD undoubtedly saw the Purges as an opportunity to increase their own power and influence within the USSR.

Q. What were the effects of the Great Terror?

- 600,000 Party members lost their lives in the 1930s.

- Starting with the Commander-in-Chief, Tukhachevsky, Stalin removed almost half of the Red Army senior officers. This greatly weakened the Red Army, as shown in the Finnish War in 1939-40 and encouraged Hitler's invasion, with nearly fatal consequences.

- Millions of ordinary, innocent, Russians ended up in the Gulag. They endured terrible conditions, particularly in the freezing conditions of the camps in the East. At least 70,000 prisoners died constructing the Belomor Canal. Historians have reached differing conclusions about the number of victims of the Terror. Robert Conquest estimates that between 7 and 8 million people were sent to the camps, of whom about 2 million died. Dimitri Volkogonov has suggested the much higher figures of 16 million prison camp inmates and 7 million deaths.

- A climate of fear gripped the Soviet people as no one knew who might or might not be an informer. Stalin intended thereby to terrorise the population into obedience.

- The Purges' disruptive effects were felt in industry where the arrest of large numbers of engineers and managers seriously undermined the Second Five Year Plan and accounts for Stalin's reduction in the scale of the purges in 1939. Nonetheless the purges had the permanent effect of stifling initiative.

- Stalin's domination over the Party was now complete. To a large extent, Stalin had created a new Party, by means of the purges, who owed unswerving loyalty to Stalin. Stalin did not call a Party Congress, supposed to meet every three years, between 1939 and 1952.

- The cult of Stalin, underway since Stalin's 50th birthday celebrations in 1929, expanded hugely. Stalin even supplanted Lenin as the most important symbol of the Party. Stalin's image was ubiquitous, appearing on posters or in the form of statues and paintings. In a way, Stalin's icon took the place of the religious imagery swept away by the Bolshevik Revolution. The personality cult encouraged ordinary Russians to regard Stalin as a father-figure, the genius who guided every aspect of national life.

Society and Culture in the USSR

Religion

Karl Marx was an atheist who famously wrote that '*Religion is the opium of the people*', meaning that the ruling classes used it to ensure obedience from the exploited working classes. In October 1917 the Bolsheviks confiscated all church lands. During the Russian Civil War (1918-20), the Bolsheviks killed many Orthodox Christian priests because the Orthodox clergy tended to support the Whites. Most Orthodox bishops were arrested in the 1920s.

The Communist Party sought to eradicate religious belief by organising anti-religious propaganda; in 1926 the Party created the League of Militant Atheists to carry out that function. Persecution of Orthodox Christians increased after 1929 as part of Stalin's attack on the peasants' traditional way of life during Collectivisation. A decree of 1929 barred churches from participating in any activities other than church services. Stalin did allow a small number of churches to remain open, so that he could claim that the freedom of worship enshrined in the 1936 Stalin Constitution was being observed. By the end of the 1930s only 2% of Orthodox churches were still operating. However, that does not mean that the Party had eliminated religious belief; in the 1937 Census, 57% of Russians said that they were believers. Probably as a consequence of this, the leaders of the League of Militant Atheists were purged.

In the 1920s, the Soviet state had persecuted Muslims less than the Orthodox Church. However, in the 1930s this changed dramatically and 95% of mosques were closed down.

Education

The Party made tackling illiteracy a major priority right from the start. Only 40% of adult males were literate in 1913; by 1926, this had risen to 70% and, by 1939, to 94%. The People's Commissariat for Enlightenment, led by Anatoly Lunarcharsky, sought to increase educational opportunities for the working classes. In the 1920s progressive educational reforms were introduced in the USSR; examinations and uniforms were abolished. From 1928, it became increasingly difficult for anyone with a bourgeois background to gain access to higher education.

During the 1930s, the state, responding to the needs of the Five Year Plans, expanded technical and vocational training at the expense of more academic courses. Stalin did reverse some of the more progressive elements of Soviet educational policy; in the 1930s, uniforms and exams were reintroduced and it was no longer a requirement to be of working class background to be admitted to higher education.

The Party placed a great emphasis on expanding educational provision during the 1930s, in order to provide the educated workforce required in the newly industrialised USSR. In 1930, all children were obliged to have a minimum of 4 years primary education. By 1939, it was compulsory for children to have 7 years schooling.

Youth Movements

The Communist Party sought to mobilise young people and mould their developing minds so that they became committed Communists. Young people aged 14-28 were recruited into Komsomol (Young Communist League); between the ages of 9 and 14, children joined the All-Union Lenin Pioneer Organisation; younger children belonged to the Little Octobrists.

The Arts

In the 1920s artists, e.g. Vladimir Tatlin, and writers had considerable freedom to experiment with new genres like Futurism and Modernism. However, Stalin disapproved of more abstract art forms and saw art solely in propaganda terms.

In the 1930s artists had to conform to 'Socialist Realism'; art, music and writing were required to glorify the achievements of the Five Year Plans and Stalin's genius. Nikolai Ostrovsky's novel, *How the Steel was tempered'* in which the hero is a zealous member of Komsomol is typical of Socialist Realist art. In 1932 Andrei Zhdanov was put in charge of the newly created Union of Soviet Writers. Zhdanov attacked bourgeois individualism', that is art which explored the individual's feelings and art that was not accessible to ordinary people. Typical of the atmosphere that prevailed in the 1930s was Pravda's condemnation of Dimitri Shostakovitch's opera, *Lady Macbeth*, as *"Muddle instead of music'*.

Family Life

Following the Bolshevik Revolution, divorce was made easier and abortion was legalised. By contrast, Stalin adopted a more traditional approach to family life, partly because he sought to increase Russia's population, and in 1936 he made abortion illegal and divorce harder to get. However, in the 1930s Stalin could be seen to undermine traditional family life by encouraging women to work in factories, for example by providing crèche and canteen facilities.

Soviet Foreign Policy 1918-41

Worldwide Revolution and Isolation

Lenin and Trotsky saw revolution in international terms. When the Bolsheviks came to power in 1917, Lenin assumed that communist revolutions would soon break out in other parts of the world. Indeed, Lenin was banking on revolutions in more advanced capitalist countries as a solution to the problem of how to create socialism in backward Russia.

In October 1917 the Bolsheviks confiscated all foreign assets in Russia. This, combined with Russia's withdrawal from the First World War following the conclusion of the Treaty of Brest-Litovsk (1918), and the apparent threat of Bolshevik ideology contaminating other countries, led to foreign intervention in the Russian Civil War on the Whites' side. As Winston Churchill put it, Britain, France, the USA, Italy and Japan were seeking to 'strangle Bolshevism in its cradle'. Russia's diplomatic isolation was emphasised by its absence from the Paris Peace Conference (1919) at the end of the First World War and by its initial exclusion from the League of Nations (1920). Foreign backing could not prevent the Whites' defeat in the

Civil War by 1921; however, it confirmed the USSR's suspicions of the West, which characterised Soviet foreign policy throughout the interwar years.

The Failure of Worldwide Revolution

In 1919, in order to facilitate worldwide revolution and to ensure their own ascendancy over foreign communist parties, the Bolsheviks created an international organisation of Communist parties called the Third International or Comintern.

As predicted by Lenin, communist revolutions broke out in Berlin, Bavaria and Hungary in 1919. However, contrary to Lenin's expectations, all of these risings failed even though Bela Kun was in power in Hungary for over 4 months. Moreover, Lenin's assumption that Polish workers would rise up when the Red Army invaded Poland was proved unfounded and the ensuing Russo-Polish War (1920-21) ended in retreat and humiliation for the Bolsheviks.

Permanent Revolution versus *Socialism in One Country*

With no prospect of communist revolutions occurring elsewhere for the foreseeable future, the Russian leadership argued furiously about the direction of Soviet foreign policy. Trotsky was still passionately committed to organising worldwide revolution and became the main spokesman for the policy of 'Permanent Revolution'. Stalin. However, promoted an alternative strategy, known as 'Socialism in One Country' which argued that international revolution must be postponed and in the meantime the USSR had to be modernised and a socialist economy created before the USSR could seek to export socialist revolution abroad. The majority of the Party backed Stalin's policy at the Party Congress in 1925.

Trade Agreements

As early as 1921, Lenin recognised the need to develop commercial links with the West in order to help rebuild Russia's shattered economy after nearly a decade of war and civil war. The search for more foreign trade was an important element in Lenin's New Economic Policy (1921). The Russian Foreign Ministry was successful in brokering trade agreements with Great Britain, Poland, Finland, Germany and Turkey in 1921.

Isolation in the 1920s

In spite of signing trade agreements with many European countries, the USSR remained diplomatically isolated. It was not until 1924 that Great Britain officially recognised the USSR and not until 1933 that the USA did so. The USSR did not join the League of Nations until 1934.

The two 'pariah' states come together: Russo-German relations in the 1920s

It was perhaps unsurprising that the country with which the USSR developed its closest links in the 1920s was Germany; both countries were 'outcasts'; the USSR because of its Communist ideology and commitment to promoting worldwide revolution and Germany because of its alleged responsibility for starting the First World War. Neither was invited to join the League of Nations in 1920.

In 1922 the USSR and Germany signed the Treaty of Rapallo, which restored normal diplomatic relations and made provision for extensive commercial links between the two countries. In addition, the USSR secretly agreed that the German armed forces could train on Russian soil and that German industrialists could establish armaments factories in Russia in order to circumvent the military restrictions imposed by the Treaty of Versailles (1919). The USSR maintained close relations with Germany by signing the Treaty of Berlin in 1926, which was renewed in 1931. German engineers provided technical advice on Russian industrial projects in the 1920s.

Soviet policy towards China

Since the mid-19th century China had been increasingly weak and prey to foreign intervention and exploitation. Russia had joined in the attempt to further its influence in China and had established a protectorate over Outer Mongolia. Russo-Japanese rivalry over Manchuria and Korea had led to the Russo-Japanese War (1904-5). The Chinese Empire had collapsed in 1911, resulting in the country being carved up by a series of warlords. By 1921 two Chinese political parties had emerged, dedicated to reunifying China and making it a great power: the Nationalists (Guomindang or GMD) and the Chinese Communist Party (CCP).

The Russian leadership saw an opportunity to promote Soviet influence in China by helping one or both of these Chinese parties to overthrow the weak Beijing government which the western governments recognised. However, there was a major dispute between Stalin and Trotsky on this issue; Trotsky favoured backing the CCP whilst Stalin believed that the CCP was too small and so argued for pressing the CCP into an alliance with the much bigger GMD.

It was Stalin's view that prevailed; Comintern provided advice, training and money to the GMD-CCP alliance and helped broker the First United Front (1923) between them. However, Stalin's strategy proved disastrous when, in 1927, Chiang Kaishek, the GMD leader, turned on the CCP and massacred thousands of them Chiang then established himself as President of China, with the decimated remnant of the CCP licking its wounds in remote Jiangxi province. When Mao Zedong emerged in the mid-1930s as CCP leader, he developed his own brand of communism and kept the CCP largely independent of Russian influence.

Stalin's Foreign Policy

By the early 1930s Stalin had become increasingly anxious about the possibility of facing a war on two fronts, with Germany in the West and Japan in the East.

Stalin had totally underestimated the threat of the anti-Russian and anti-Communist Nazi Party in Germany until Hitler came to power in 1933. Until then, Comintern had ordered the German Communist Party to concentrate its attack on the Socialist Democratic Party, its main rival for working class support. This made it easier for Hitler to come to power.

Q. Why did Stalin believe the USSR was under threat?

The Japanese threat	From 1931 onwards, Japan pursued an aggressive foreign policy. Having occupied Manchuria in 1931-32, Japan invaded Jehol province in China in 1933 and then launched a full-scale invasion of China in 1937. Japan signed the Anti-Comintern Pact with Nazi Germany in 1936. In 1939 Russian and Japanese forces engaged each other at Khalkin-Gol on the Mongolian-Manchurian border, resulting in tens of thousands of casualties. This proved a decisive moment in easing Stalin's concerns about a war on two fronts, because it led to the Japanese government favouring the strategy of the South Strike Group within the Japanese armed forces who advocated an attack on the European powers' colonies in South-East Asia. The strategy of the North Strike Group, which consisted of a plan to seize Siberia from the USSR, was now dropped.
The Nazi threat	From 1933, the USSR was confronted with the prospect of an increasingly aggressive and powerful Germany, under a regime that was extremely hostile to Communism. Hitler's ultimate goal was to achieve 'lebensraum' (living-space) in the East at the expense of the USSR. From 1935 onwards, Hitler rapidly built up Germany's armed forces and began to undermine the restrictions placed on Germany by the Versailles Treaty. In 1938 Hitler annexed Austria and absorbed Czechoslovakia in two stages in 1938-39.

Stalin's search for security in the 1930s

Faced by growing threats to the USSR, at a time when it was still far behind the West in terms of industrialisation, Stalin sought to increase Soviet security by ending the USSR's diplomatic isolation. For much of the 1930s, Stalin looked to the West for 'collective security' against the threat posed by Hitler but eventually in 1939 Stalin did a complete about-turn and signed the Nazi-Soviet Pact.

Underlying the twists and turns of Soviet foreign policy in the 1930s is a consistent search for security, with Stalin looking to play off the western democracies against Germany and vice-versa. Up to 1939, Maxim Litinov was the Soviet Commissar for Foreign Affairs and he favoured closer links with the West. In 1939, Stalin replaced Litinov with Vyacheslav Molotov, who preferred a deal with Nazi Germany.

Phase One: Stalin looks to the West (1934-39)

1934	The USSR was admitted to the League of Nations, with a permanent seat on the League's Council. The USSR signed a Non-Aggression Pact with the Baltic States
1935	The USSR signed pacts with France and Czechoslovakia, committing itself to defend the latter against attack. However, the French government never ratified this agreement. At the 7th Congress of the Communist International, Stalin's new strategy of organising an Ant-Fascist Popular Front was announced; this involved encouraging alliances of Communists and other left-wing parties throughout Europe to fight against Fascism. Before this, Comintern had worked to undermine other socialist parties, notably in Germany. In 1936-38 a Popular Front government was in power in France and in 1936-39 Spain was governed by a Popular Front coalition.
1936	Stalin sent aid to the Republicans in the Spanish Civil War (1936-39). Stalin was concerned by German and Italian intervention on General Franco's side, so from October 1936 USSR provided the Republicans with tanks and planes and military advisers. Franco's Nationalists won in 1939.

Phase Two: Stalin wavers between the Western democracies and Hitler (1938-39)

1938	The Sudeten Crisis: in the autumn of 1938 Hitler looked poised to attack Czecholslovakia in a dispute over the German-speaking area called the Sudetenland. However, Great Britain and France were desperate to appease Hitler and avoid war, so, at the Munich Conference (September-October 1938), they agreed to hand over the Sudetenland to Germany. The USSR was an ally of Czechoslovakia but was not invited to the Munich Conference. It is difficult to know whether Stalin would have honoured the 1935 Czech Pact if France had been willing to fight too but, what is clear, is that Stalin's suspicions of Britain and France were deepened by the Sudeten Crisis. Stalin suspected that Britain and France were seeking to encourage Hitler to expand eastwards at Russia's expense, so that western Europe would be left in peace.
1939	In the spring/summer of 1939, as Hitler prepared to invade Poland, Stalin considered competing diplomatic overtures from the British and French on the one hand and the Nazis on the other. Anglo-French-Soviet talks foundered on mutual suspicions. A particular sticking-point was Stalin's insistence that the Red Army be able to send troops into Poland and Rumania in the event of a German attack. Britain and France suspected that this request was designed to bring about Soviet domination of the East. In August 1939, Stalin rejected the French-British offer of a military pact and shocked the world by getting his new Commissar for Foreign Affairs, Molotov, to conclude a Non-Aggression Pact with Nazi Germany.

Phase Three: Stalin seeks security in a Pact with Hitler (1939)

1939	The Nazi-Soviet Pact (Molotov-Ribbentrop Pact): in public it pledged both sides to friendly relations but there were secret protocols attached to it. In the secret protocols, Stalin and Hitler agreed to partition Poland. In addition, Hitler consented to Soviet expansion at the expense of Latvia, Lithuania, Estonia and Finland.

Q. **What were Stalin's motives in concluding the Nazi-Soviet Pact?**

At first sight, a pact between Communist Russia and Fascist Germany appears surprising and might suggest a lack of consistency on Stalin's part. However, from Stalin's perspective this represented merely a tactical shift; his objective all along had been Soviet security, but his methods of achieving that had changed.

✔ The Non-Aggression Pact won the USSR a breathing-space; it bought time in which Soviet rearmament could be accelerated and the Red Army officer corps strengthened after the bloody purges of 1937-38.

✔ Stalin could now look to create a buffer zone by expanding into the Baltic States.

✔ Stalin presumed that Hitler's planned invasion of Poland (September 1939) would lead to a long drawn-out war between Germany and the western democracies, in which Germany, France and Britain would become exhausted.

Soviet Expansion 1939-40

Within three weeks of Hitler's invasion of Poland on 1st September, 1939, Russian troops invaded eastern Poland. Sandwiched between the Wehrmacht and the Red Army, Polish resistance thereupon collapsed. Germany and the USSR then divided up Poland; western Poland, mainly inhabited by Poles, was placed under German occupation and eastern Poland, mainly consisting of Ukrainians, under Soviet control. In 1940 the NKVD (Soviet secret police) secretly executed about 20,000 Polish prisoners-of-war in the Katyn forest. By late 1940, over 1 million Poles had been deported to Russian labour camps.

In the winter of 1939-40, Estonia, Latvia and Lithuania were forced to sign 'mutual assistance' pacts with the USSR, resulting in their occupation by the Red Army in March 1940. Stalin also seized Bessarabia from Rumania.

The 'Winter War'

Stalin sought to increase Soviet security by pushing back the Russo-Finnish border in the vicinity of Leningrad. Stalin's demand for Finnish territory was rejected and provoked a Russian invasion in November 1939. Although outnumbered by 1 million to 200,000, the Finnish Army embarrassed the Red Army, which was poorly led and equipped. The Red Army's poor performance highlighted the damaging effects of the purges (1937-38) and encouraged Hitler to think that an invasion of the USSR would be easy. Russian aggression against Finland led to the USSR's expulsion from the League of Nations.

The Russo-Japanese Non-Aggression Pact (April 1941)

Stalin's long-term nightmare of a simultaneous attack on the USSR by Germany and Japan was eased by his conclusion of a Non-Aggression Pact with Japan. The Japanese government had abandoned the idea of expanding north at the expense of the USSR and was now preparing for an offensive in South-East Asia aimed at seizing the colonies belonging to the European colonial powers and the USA. This led to the attack on Pearl Harbor in December 1941.

Hitler's invasion of the USSR (June 1941)

Stalin became increasingly anxious about the possibility of war with Germany following Hitler's swift defeat of France, Belgium and Holland in May-June 1940 and the German invasion of Yugoslavia and Greece in the spring of 1941.

However, Stalin strove desperately to postpone war with Germany, observing the terms of the Nazi-Soviet Pact by supplying Germany with oil, rubber and wheat. In the early summer of 1941 Stalin chose to ignore warnings from both his own spies and British intelligence that Hitler was about to invade Russia; Hitler's military preparations were clear evidence of his intentions but Stalin refused to take counter-measures for fear of provoking a German attack. Consequently, when Hitler did launch a three-pronged invasion, codenamed Operation Barbarossa, in June 1941, Soviet forces were caught by surprise and Stalin was paralysed into inaction in the crucial first days of the war.

Within 3 weeks of the invasion, over 750,000 Red Army soldiers had been captured. The poor performance of the Red Army, in spite of rearmament by Stalin which saw its size grow from 940,000 (1936) to 5 million (1941), illustrates the damage inflicted by Stalin's purge of its officer corps (1937-38).

By October 1940, the Wehrmacht was within 100 miles of Moscow. However, the combination of severe winter weather, for which Hitler had not prepared, and a brilliant counter-attack in front of Moscow organised by Marshal Zhukov, meant that Moscow was not captured. Instead, the war on the Eastern Front turned into a terrible war of attrition, with the Red Army eventually driving the Germans out of their country by 1944. Three-quarters of Germany's casualties in the Second World War were incurred on the Eastern Front, where Russia's greater economic resources in the end told against the technologically superior Germans.

Revision and essay writing activities on the Rise and Rule of the Russian Communist Party

Below, you will find two essay questions, which cover most of the issues that I have dealt with in the Russia section of the Revision Guide. By examining these questions, you will be able to test your understanding and recall of that material, as well as gaining insights into how to construct responses to IB essay questions. I have given you some ideas about how they could be tackled and then provided you with space to add examples and further points.

1. **"Left wing single party states achieve power as the result of a revolutionary process against tradition." Does this adequately explain how any one single party state that you have studied acquired power?**

NB. In answering this open question, I have chosen the example of Lenin and the Bolsheviks. Lenin is not a named individual on the Paper 2 syllabus but can be used in open questions such as this one.

Firstly, point out that the Bolsheviks were Marxists and, as such, they sought to overthrow the traditional ruling classes and social system in Russia. This they achieved in 1917-21 by means of the October Revolution and the Civil War. However, it is necessary also to examine the February Revolution, which overthrew the traditional system of government in Russia and which involved a popular revolutionary movement. Arguably the Bolsheviks hijacked this popular revolutionary process for their own ends. Finally, think about the key word 'adequate'. The events of 1917-21 can be viewed to a considerable extent as 'a revolutionary process against tradition' but there were also other factors, which require evaluation.

I have divided my answer in two parts. In the first I have outlined the ways in which the Bolshevik acquisition of power can be explained by reference to a 'revolutionary process against tradition'. In the second half, I have considered the ways in which that does not provide an 'adequate' explanation.

To some extent, "yes".

• Marxism aims at the overthrow of social hierarchy; in Russia this meant the Tsar, nobles and industrialists. In *What is to be done*, Lenin argued that the Bolsheviks must act as a vanguard party to lead a proletarian revolution.

• The fall of the monarchy in the February Revolution of 1917 can be seen as a revolt against tradition. The traditional form of government (Tsarism) had been discredited by its military, political and economic shortcomings in the First World War. However, the February Revolution was not brought about by the Bolsheviks but by the workers and soldiers of Petrograd; the Duma felt obliged to acknowledge the Petrograd Soviet and accept the fall of the monarchy (the Duma would have preferred to exchange Nicholas II for an alternative tsar).

• Lenin's April Theses constituted a manifesto for revolutionary change. Lenin controversially argued for a second revolution. He rejected the notion of bourgeois parliamentary government as insufficiently revolutionary. Government by the traditional ruling classes had to be replaced by a soviet/workers' government; Russia should be immediately withdrawn from the First World War as it was an imperialist war.

• One of the key reasons for the Bolsheviks' growing support in 1917 was that Lenin rejected any idea of compromise with the propertied classes, whereas the other socialist parties, the Mensheviks and Social Revolutionaries, continued to support the Provisional Government.

- Even before October 1917, a popular revolution was underway, characterised by the establishment of soviets, workers' seizure of factories and peasant seizure of land from the nobles. In the view of historians like Orlando Figes, the Bolsheviks hijacked this popular revolution and distorted it for their own ends. This is how the Kronstadt rebels who rose against the Bolsheviks saw it in 1921.

- The October Revolution to some extent depended on the Bolsheviks' harnessing the revolutionary mood of the workers and garrison soldiers. The Petrograd Soviet and Red Guards supported the overthrow of the Provisional Government because they felt it did not represent their interests whereas the Bolsheviks promised the overthrow of the traditional order. Lenin created a new type of government, Sovnarkom, a socialist coalition (the Bolsheviks and Left SRs), to replace the Duma-based government that the Provisional Government essentially was.

- Sovnarkom's first measures to an extent represented a revolution against tradition: it issued decrees allowing peasants to take land from the nobles, church and tsar; it empowered workers to set up factory committees to take control of factories.

- During the Civil War, the Bolsheviks implemented policies which undermined the traditional order and these, to an extent, contributed to their consolidation of power. War Communism (1918-21) involved nationalisation of all factories. The Bolsheviks murdered the royal family in 1918 in order to prevent the Whites ('traditional' forces) from using them as a rallying point. Lenin set up Comintern (1919) to promote worldwide revolution and the overthrow of 'tradition' internationally. The Bolsheviks attacked 'traditional' beliefs in the shape of the Orthodox Church and fought the Whites who represented the landowners and tsarist officers – i.e. the old order.

Your points <u>for</u> the statement:

....

....

....

....

....

....

....

....

....

BUT not an "adequate" explanation because:

• The February Revolution (which made the October Revolution possible) was a limited revolution against tradition – it saw the transfer of political power to the educated classes (Duma) and it was made to a considerable extent by the elites (generals, Duma) deserting the Tsar.

• Some of the Bolsheviks' early measures were not that 'revolutionary', e.g. the Decree on Land (October 1917) was not Marxist because it allowed peasants to enlarge their private holdings of land.

• During the Civil War, the Bolsheviks could be very pragmatic; Trotsky and Lenin used the forces of tradition in their war against the Whites, e.g. the Bolsheviks employed 50,000 ex-tsarist officers and brought back many former managers to run factories. Lenin and Trotsky rejected "revolutionary warfare" and instead raised a conscript army (5 million).

Other factors contributed to the Bolsheviks' acquisition of power:

• Both the February and October Revolutions were the product of intense crisis brought about by Russia's inability to fight successfully against a more modernised Germany in the First World War.

• The workers of Petrograd were primarily protesting about food shortages and inflation, not "tradition" (though they held Nicholas II's government responsible).

• The October Revolution was the **product of other factors** too; e.g. Lenin's flexibility in revising Marx's ideas and persuading the Bolsheviks that a proletarian revolution was possible in relatively backward Russia. The Kornilov Affair undermined the Provisional Government as did its inability to manage the war and the economy.

• The Bolsheviks' victory in the Civil war also **due to other factors:** e.g. the divisions among the Whites; the geopolitical advantages of the Reds (control of the heart of the railway network, more cohesive territory).

• Even after the Civil War, the Bolsheviks realised that in order to stay in power they could not reject 'tradition' entirely, or, at least, not yet. Lenin introduced the New Economic Policy, which represented a retreat from socialism; private profit was permitted in the countryside and small industries could be privately owned.

• The Bolsheviks did not feel strong enough to take on 'tradition' in the countryside in the form of peasant ownership of farmland until 1929 when the "real" revolution occurred with the "revolution from above", in the form of collectivisation. Equally, only in 1928 did the Bolsheviks completely end 'traditional' patterns of private ownership of industry when the First Five Year Plan was launched.

Your points <u>against</u> the statement:

....

....

....

....

....

....

....

....

....

Conclusion

Yes, the Bolshevik acquisition of power is adequately explained by reference to a revolutionary process against tradition because the Bolsheviks were consciously seeking to overthrow the traditional order in Russia. In 1917, under Lenin's leadership, the Bolsheviks aimed at wholesale change that would destroy the power and wealth of Russia's propertied classes. To a considerable extent, the Bolsheviks capitalised on a growing popular movement, particularly in the shape of the soviets, to seize power and retain it. The Bolsheviks then distorted the revolutionary process in Russia by creating a ruthless single party dictatorship, instead of allowing the people to take power themselves. Although an adequate explanation, the statement does not provide a full explanation of why the Bolsheviks achieved power. For that, it is necessary to consider the crisis facing Russia by 1917 and other factors such as the leadership of Lenin and Trotsky and the weaknesses of the Provisional Government and of the Whites.

2.   How far was the single party regime in Russia successful by 1940 in achieving its aims?

In answering this question, first it is necessary to identify what the Bolsheviks' aims were. The question does not specify foreign or domestic policy (the reference to 'in Russia' is to the regime, not to its policies in Russia), so both areas of policy should be considered. Below I have started by identifying their main aims, taking into account that Lenin and Stalin did not have identical aims. Following this, I have created a detailed plan, which evaluates the Bolsheviks' success in certain areas of policy. I have also just indicated certain other aims that would merit assessment in this essay and I have left space for you to provide your own points and examples/evidence you might use in answering this question.

What were the Bolsheviks' aims?

The Bolsheviks were reasonably united in terms of aims; this was the product of a shared commitment to Marxist ideology. However, there were significant differences between the aims of Lenin and Stalin in that the latter sought to develop his own personal power and a personality cult, neither of which can be counted as Lenin's objectives. Furthermore, the Party was badly divided over the USSR's foreign relations. Left Communists sought to promote 'Permanent' or 'World-wide' revolution, whereas Right Communists favoured 'Socialism in One Country'. However, it must be stressed that both Right and Left Communists looked forward to the spread of international socialism; their disagreement was over priorities, feasibility and timings. Certainly, whatever broad consensus on aims there was among the Party leadership, there were huge divisions about methods.

Domestic policy

Political:
- To destroy / suppress opposition and maintain a monopoly of political power for the Communist Party.
- To create a totalitarian state in which all aspects of Russians' lives were controlled and to indoctrinate the population with Marxist ideology.
- Stalin aimed to achieve a personal ascendancy over the Party and to develop a personality cult.

Economic:
- To create a socialist economy.
  To create a modern economy that would allow Russia to match and overtake the West.

Social:
- To establish a classless society and raise living standards for all.
- Social reform, e.g. eliminating illiteracy.

Foreign policy:

- To maintain the security of the USSR.
- To export socialist revolution abroad (however, see above for disagreements about this within the Party).

How successful were these aims?

1.   Political

(a)   Maintaining a monopoly of political power for the Communist Party.
    Very successful
• Lenin had always aimed at a single party dictatorship and had quarrelled in 1917 with other Bolsheviks who favoured a coalition of socialist parties, including the Mensheviks and Socialist Revolutionaries. The closure of the Constituent Assembly (January 1918) underlined that intention. From March 1918, Sovnarkom consisted solely of Bolsheviks. After the Civil War, Lenin banned the Socialist Revolutionaries and Mensheviks and 2000 Mensheviks were arrested (1921). In 1922 several SR leaders were executed. The 1923 and 1936 Constitutions permitted only the Communist Party to exist.
• From 1918, the Party achieved total dominance over state institutions. Real power lay in the Party hierarchy rather than in the soviet structures.
• Lenin created a secret police (Cheka) and prison camp system to suppress opposition. This was continued and expanded massively by Stalin. During Stalin's Purges, the secret police (OGPU and, later, the NKVD) arrested millions of ordinary citizens in the 1930s, creating a climate of terror.
• Dissent within the Communist Party was increasingly suppressed after the Decree on Party Unity (1921), which banned factions. Stalin took this much further.
• Both Lenin and Stalin carried out regular purges of the Party, in order to weed out the uncommitted, dissidents and former members of other parties. Lenin expelled 150,000 Party members in 1921. Stalin's purges were much more savage; 600,000 Party members were executed in the Great Terror (1936-38).
• Collectivisation of agriculture and the creation of the command economy during the Five Year Plans (1928-41), gave the Party much greater control over the people. Prior to collectivisation, Communist control of the countryside had been fragile. After 1929, the peasants were supervised by Party officials attached to each Kolkohz and NKVD units were stationed at each Motor Tractor Station.

(b) To create a totalitarian state in which all aspects of Russians' lives were controlled.

Historians disagree about the extent to which the USSR was a totalitarian society. According to traditional accounts, the Soviet people were very tightly controlled by the Party, with the leadership in Moscow able to enforce its will on the country as a whole. Revisionist historians like J. Arch Getty have challenged this view, arguing that the Party leadership was far from all-powerful. They cite the collectivisation drive of 1929-30 and the Great Terror of 1936-38 as evidence for policies emanating from the centre developing a momentum of their own at local level and indeed in both cases revisionist historians claim that the leadership to some extent lost control over events.
• The media was tightly controlled by the Party and propaganda was used to promote support for the Party. Initially, artists were allowed some freedom but from 1922 restrictions were tightened; dozens of leading Russian scholars and writers were deported in 1922, including the world-renowned philosopher, Nikolai Berdyaev. From 1932 Andrei Zhdanov was charged with ensuring that all art conformed to Socialist Realism.
• Mass organisations/movements were set up to mobilise the people and ensure their loyalty. Young people and students were organised into the Little Octobrists, the Lenin Pioneers and Komsomol.
• Internal passports were reintroduced in 1932 to control people's movements within the USSR.

1. (c) **Stalin aimed to achieve a personal ascendancy over the Party and to develop a personality cult.**

....

....

....

....

....

....

2. Economic: (a) **To create a socialist economy.**

....

....

....

....

....

....

(b) To make Russia into a modern industrial state.

....

....

....

....

....

....

....

....

3.   Social: (a) To establish a classless society.

....

....

....

....

....

(b)   **To implement social reform.**

....

....

....

....

....

....

4. Foreign policy: (a) To maintain the security of the USSR.

....

....

....

....

(b)   **To export socialist revolution abroad.**

....

....

....

....

....

....

....

Your Conclusion:

....

....

....

....

....

....

....

....

THE RISE AND RULE OF THE SINGLE PARTY STATE IN CHINA: 1900-76

A NOTE ON SPELLING

There are two systems of transliterating Chinese characters into English. Most textbooks now use the more modern Pinyin version but some still use the older Wade-Giles system. For example, the older version of Mao's name is Mao Tse-tung whilst the newer version is Mao Zedong; the older version of the Nationalist leader's name is Chiang Kai-shek, the newer version is Jiang Jieshi. Don't worry because it does not matter which you use.

Origins of the Single Party State

In October 1949 Mao Zedong proclaimed the establishment of the People's Republic of China, and, although initially several other political parties were tolerated, 1949 effectively marked the beginning of single party rule by the CCP (Chinese Communist Party). In order to explain the rise of the CCP, it is necessary to examine the failure of both the Qing (or Manchu) dynasty and the Guomindang government of Chiang Kai-Shek to establish stable government. In addition, the CCP's strengths must be analysed, to determine how they successfully exploited conditions, enabling them to seize power in 1949 and achieve effective control over virtually the whole of the former Chinese Empire.

Q. What weaknesses did governments prior to 1949 exhibit?

1. A failure to prevent increasing encroachment by foreign powers.
2. A failure to address widespread peasant poverty.
3. An inability to promote effective control over the provinces.

BACKGROUND

For about three thousand years, China was ruled by a series of imperial dynasties. From the mid-17th century, the Qing dynasty, originally from Manchuria (hence they are often referred to as the Manchu), reigned in China. The 19th century saw the Qing dynasty in decline, struggling to cope with foreign aggression and internal rebellions. In 1911 the Revolution of "The Double Tenth" (10th October), destroyed Qing power and China officially became a Republic in 1912, following the abdication of Pu Yi, the last emperor.

China is forced to open up to the West

Before the mid-19th century, Chinese emperors showed little interest in contact and trade with the West. Their isolationism was fuelled by a belief that the Chinese Empire was the only civilised country in the world. However, starting with the Opium Wars (1839-42) in which the British defeated Chinese forces, the Chinese government was compelled to open up to the West. The Qing were forced by militarily and industrially advanced powers, notably GB, France, Germany, Russia and Japan, to grant commercial bases and rights and to allow Christian missionaries to operate in China. As a result of a whole series of 'unequal treaties', foreign merchants gained control of China's import and export trade. Major ports, e.g. Shanghai, had large foreign-controlled districts. Foreign powers completely took over peripheral areas of China, e.g. Russia claimed Manchuria in 1900, France seized Indo-China in the 1880s-1890s and Japan took Taiwan and Korea in 1895.

Internal rebellion

The 19th century was marked by a series of large-scale rebellions as the Imperial government in Beijing found it increasingly difficult to exercise effective control over the whole of the Empire. The Manchu armies deteriorated in quality during the 19th century and the Manchu court increasingly allowed regional armies to develop which were outside the main Imperial army. The most serious rebellions were the Taiping Rebellion (1850-1864) and the Boxer Rebellion (1898-1900). During the latter, the Boxers murdered missionaries and Christian converts. The foreign powers eventually crushed the Boxers in 1900 and imposed the *Boxer Protocol of 1901* on the Imperial government, a fine of $330 million; this further undermined support for the Qing dynasty among their subjects.

Peasant poverty

One cause of the growing unrest in China was the poverty of its peasant masses. Arable land constituted only 10% of China and much of it periodically suffered from natural disasters, such as flooding. Huge population growth in the 18th century (a rise from an estimated 120 million in 1712 to 440 million by 1900) made for growing land hunger, exacerbated by the custom of dividing land among all the sons of a family. Devastating local famines became increasingly frequent. By 1900 landlords and prosperous peasants, who made up 10% of the rural population, owned 70% of the land, most of which they rented out. Many peasants were constantly in debt and they gave 50–80% of their crop as rent. The urban population was small and there were few modern industrial centres, except on the eastern seaboard and most were foreign-owned.

The Hundred Days (1898): A brief flowering of reform

Many Chinese were angered by China's inability to stand up to foreign encroachment and believed the solution lay in reform and modernisation by the Imperial government. Kang Youwei, in the *Hundred Days of Reform*, persuaded the Emperor Guang Xu to introduce reforms in order to modernise the bureaucracy, the armed forces and the transport system and to develop industry but this reforming phase was brought to an abrupt halt by the powerful Empress Dowager Cixi who hated reform and western ideas. Her conservatism was a powerful barrier to reform from 1861 until her death in 1908.

Sun Yatsen and revolutionary nationalism

Many Chinese nationalists believed that only the overthrow of the Qing and the establishment of a republic could save China. The most prominent republican leader was Sun Yatsen. Sun had been trained as a doctor in Hawaii and Hong Kong. In Hawaii (1894), he created the *Revive China Society* and, in 1905 in Japan, Sun brought about a coalition of several Chinese revolutionary groups known as the *Revolutionary Alliance (Tongmenghui)*. Sun's ideas were influenced by Western ideas, but he was also very impressed by the modernisation of Japan since 1868. In his writings, Sun outlined the *Three People's Principles*: People's Nationalism, People's Democracy and People's Livelihood. Sun sought to end foreign domination of China and to create a strong, unified China under a republican government. His idea of People's Livelihood fell far short of full-blown socialism but rather represented a desire to see greater social justice and a fairer distribution of wealth.

Reform by the Imperial government: too little, too late

Nationalist resentment at foreign aggression against China and at the Imperial government's inability to stand up to it reached new heights after 1894-5 when China and Japan went to war and as a result China lost Korea and Formosa (Taiwan). This encouraged other foreign powers to make further demands on China. Japan inflicted a humiliating defeat on Russia in 1905, leading to increased Japanese influence in Manchuria and in 1910 Japan officially annexed Korea.

The rise of Japan as a major Asian power impressed many educated Chinese who saw Japan as a model that China should copy. Since 1868, Japan had modernised its armed forces and its system of government and had embarked on a programme of industrialisation. The Imperial government in China belatedly came to realise the need to follow suit and it introduced a series of reforms, including the abolition of the ancient examination system (by which educated Chinese gained appointments in the Imperial bureaucracy) and the modernisation of parts of the army. Elected provincial assemblies were set up in 1909 and a national consultative assembly was called in 1910, but they wielded little political power.

The Revolution of the Double Tenth (1911)

Q. What caused the 1911 Revolution?

(a)   Nationalist resentment at the continuing feebleness of the government
(b)   The disappointment of many educated Chinese that the reform programme had not gone far enough.
(c)   Anger at the government's nationalisation of several privately owned railway networks and the poor financial compensation offered. This was compounded by the fact that the government turned to foreign banks for a loan to finance its railway programme.
(d)   Severe flooding and harvest failure in the south
(e)   Revolutionary conspiracy by new army units stationed in Wuhan.

Sun Yatsen was abroad at the time of the Double Tenth but he returned to China in December and was proclaimed President of the new Chinese Republic by the Revolutionary Alliance in Nanjing. However, the Revolutionary Alliance was too weak on its own to topple the Imperial government; what sealed the fate of the Qing dynasty was the decision of the most powerful of the Imperial generals, Yuan Shikai, to broker a deal with the rebels. Yuan promised to support the revolution on condition that he, rather than Sun, took over as President. Lacking substantial military force of his own, Sun agreed and the Republic formally came into being in February 1912, following the abdication of Emperor Pu Yi.

Yuan Shikai (1912-16): the false dawn of parliamentary government

Yuan Shikai called parliamentary elections in 1913. The Revolutionary Alliance, which had reconstituted itself as the Guomindang (National People's Party) in 1912, won the elections. However, Yuan had no intention of sharing power and, in 1913, having had the Guomindang (GMD) leader Song Jiaoren assassinated, he banned the GMD. In 1914 he closed down parliament and proceeded to rule China very much as if he were an emperor (which he clearly aimed to make himself). Yuan proved no more able to stand up to foreign aggression than the Qing. In 1915 he tamely submitted to most of the *Twenty-One Demands* that Japan made; these included the transfer of German privileges in Shandong to Japan and the granting of rights to exploit mineral resources in southern Manchuria.

The Warlord Era (1916-27)
Yuan died in 1916 and thereafter there was no effective central government in China until 1927. There was a government in Beijing, which foreign powers recognised, but its authority did not extend over much of China. Instead a series of powerful regional generals or warlords held sway. Conditions were terrible for ordinary Chinese as warlord armies frequently attacked each other, pillaged and looted the civilian population and extracted heavy taxes from the peasants. The integrity of the former Chinese Empire was further undermined, as control over Tibet, Xinjiang and Outer Mongolia was lost.

During this period, Sun Yatsen tried to set up a GMD government at Guangzhou, planning to mount a northern military expedition with the aim of reunifying China. However, the GMD's position remained precarious and Sun was dependent on support from local warlords. In 1922 Sun was forced to flee to Shanghai.

The *May Fourth Movement*, 1919

This proved to be a highly significant development in the history of modern China. Massive student demonstrations, joined by workers in the major cities, were organised in protest at the western powers' decision at the Versailles Peace Conference to award Germany's former concessions in Shandong to Japan. The May Fourth demonstrators were protesting at yet another example of foreign powers carving up China in their own interests and also at the revelation that the Chinese government had earlier secretly agreed to this concession to Japan. The May Fourth Movement did much to revive the fortunes of the GMD as it provided a powerful stimulus to nationalist feeling.

Q. What led to the founding of the Chinese Communist Party (1921)?

- The May Fourth Movement was a key factor in the emergence of the Chinese Communist Party (CCP), as many of the founding members of the CCP had been involved in the May Fourth demonstrations, particularly at the Beijing National University.
- The success of Lenin's Bolsheviks in seizing power in Russia in 1917.
- The publication of the first Chinese translation of Karl Marx's *Communist Manifesto*.
- The arrival of Comintern agents in China sent by the Soviet government in 1920. Comintern was the Russian Communist Party's agency for spreading worldwide revolution.

Li Dazhao and Chen Duxiu, both professors, were the leading members of the fledgling CCP. Mao Zedong, a university librarian of peasant background, was also one of the founding members but his influence was limited at this stage. The CCP was tiny at first, numbering only 432 members even by 1923.

The First United Front (1923)

Neither the GMD nor the CCP were strong enough to achieve power in China in the early/mid 1920s but in 1923 the USSR helped to broker an alliance, known as the First United Front, between the two Chinese parties, which would facilitate the establishment of a GMD government in 1927. CCP members were allowed to join the GMD as individual members but there was no merger of the two parties.

The USSR had tried unsuccessfully to establish diplomatic relations with the Beijing government, so decided to work instead with the GMD and CCP. The Soviets aimed to increase their own influence in China by the overthrow of the pro-western government in Beijing. Comintern provided the GMD and CCP with political and military advisers and some financial backing. Acting on Comintern advice, the GMD/CCP set up a military training academy at Whampoa.

In 1925 Sun Yatsen died, just as he was planning the Northern Expedition to take on the warlords. Eventually Chiang Kai-shek (Jiang Jieshi), the commandant of the Whampoa Academy, emerged as the new GMD leader. This proved highly significant as Chiang was politically to the right of Sun Yatsen and was deeply suspicious of the CCP. Chiang's main rival for the GMSD leadership, Wang Jingwei, was much more to the left and therefore may have acted to preserve the United Front.

The Northern Expedition (1926-27) and the White Terror (1927)

In 1926-27 Chiang Kai-shek successfully led joint GMD-CCP forces on the Northern Expedition; the aim was to defeat the various warlords and create an effective national government, whose authority extended over all of China. However, it must be emphasised that Chiang did not defeat all the warlords but rather brokered deals with several, whereby they agreed to join forces with him. The CCP only provided a limited number of troops for the Northern Expedition but they made a major contribution in terms of organising peasant uprisings and urban strikes, distributing propaganda among peasants and factory workers.

Chiang Kaishek became increasingly concerned about the growing strength - 50,000 CCP members by 1927 - and influence of the CCP and feared that their fomenting of strikes would frighten off the GMD's middle-class backers. So at Shanghai, in April 1927, just after the capture of the city, Chiang Kaishek ordered a massacre of thousands of CCP members and trade unionists. This White Terror was extended to other cities during the rest of the year.

The atrocities in Shanghai led to a schism within the GMD as Wang Jingwei and the left of the party, based at Guangzhou, condemned Chiang's actions. However, Chiang proceeded to establish a Nationalist government at Nanjing, which became the new capital of China. Chiang had several key assets, including the support of the main GMD military forces, substantial financial backing from Shanghai businessmen and bankers and the support of several powerful warlords, particularly Feng Yuxiang. Foreign governments duly recognised the new GMD government as the official government of China.

The conditions that led to the establishment of the People's Republic of China in 1949

Given the eventual collapse of GMD rule and the seizure of power by the CCP in 1949, it is all too easy to present the GMD government as doomed from the start. However, this would be misleading as the GMD government did make progress in certain directions during the Nanjing Decade (1927-37) before the Japanese invasion of 1937 and the ensuing Sino-Japanese War (1937-45), which certainly undermined GMD rule, perhaps fatally.

Q. What were the positive achievements of the GMD during the Nanjing Decade (1927-37)?

- Chiang Kaishek brought to an end the chaos of the warlord era.
- Industrial output grew at 6% p.a.
- The railway network expanded from 8000 miles of track to 13,000 miles and from 1936 this extended all the way from Beijing to Hong Kong; the amount of road increased from 18,000 miles to 69,000 miles.
- China's financial institutions were reformed, chiefly by Chiang's brother-in-law, Song Ziwen; Song rescheduled China's foreign debts, abolished the lijin, the tax on internal trade and established a central bank. He also recovered from the foreign powers the right to set customs tariffs.
- Educational provision in the towns expanded. Between 1931 and 1937 the number of children attending primaries increased by 86% and the number of university students rose by 94%.
- A national research institute, Academia Sinica, was set up in 1928.

However, even before the Japanese invasion of 1937 the shortcomings of the GMD were very evident.

Q. What GMD weaknesses were apparent during the Nanjing Decade?

- **Once in power, the GMD lost its revolutionary outlook**, becoming part of the bureaucracy, and, corruption became a growing problem. Many time-servers and careerists who had served the warlord and Imperial governments joined the GMD.

- **The GMD lacked popular support.** In 1927 the GMD purged those of its members who were more left-wing and turned its back on mass organisations of peasants, workers, and young people which it had used in the past, e.g. to mobilise support for the Northern Expedition (1926-27).

- The GMD became increasingly dependent on army support. In the cities, the GMD suppressed the trade unions. Nationally, the GMD had an organised party branch in less than 20% of China. In rural areas, the GMD relied on former warlords and officials to keep order and collect taxes, but otherwise showed little interest in the condition of the peasantry. The historian Chan Han-seng, based on research on Guandong, has argued that peasant poverty worsened in the early 1930s because of landlord exploitation.

- The **GMD failed to introduce parliamentary government**. Sun Yatsen, in his *Three Principles of the People*, had written about the need for a temporary dictatorship until the country was ready for democracy. In 1931 a provisional constitution was issued, establishing a 5 branch system of government (executive, legislative, judicial, examination and control bureau [yuan]); however, there was no evidence of the GMD being prepared to abandon their single party monopoly of power. The GMD relied on a large secret police, the *Special Services*, led by Tai Li. The press was heavily censored.

  The GMD was composed of many different elements, so it was unable to function as a party dictatorship; instead it soon became a Chiang Kaishek dictatorship. Chiang started the Blue Shirts, a fascist organisation of several thousand army officers. The Blue Shirts did much to promote the New Life Movement (1934), which was intended to encourage civic virtue and drew heavily on Confucianism. However, this began to run out of steam after a promising start and it seems to have had little effect in terms of improving the conduct of officials.

- **Most of the industrial expansion in the 1930s took place in foreign-owned factories**. The GMD did not encourage the business classes. Businessmen were subject to high taxes and in Shanghai they were intimidated (often by use of the *Green Gang* criminal organisation) into giving the GMD large sums of money.

- 80% of government spending went on the 5 million strong GMD army, imposing a huge strain on state finances.

- **There was little in the way of social reform**; education was expanded in the cities but this was from a very low base and rural illiteracy was not tackled.

- **The GMD failed to unite China and extend GMD control to China's 400 million people**; it at best only controlled areas containing two-thirds of China's population; this fell drastically following the Japanese invasion of Manchuria in 1931 and the outbreak of the Sino-Japanese War in 1937.

- Even before the Japanese invasion of 1937, **only limited progress was made in ending foreign domination;** Chiang did regain control over China's customs service but was unable to retrieve Outer Mongolia or Tibet and foreign powers retained their trading privileges in many of China's ports and territorial concessions such as Hong Kong.

- Chiang lost support by **failing to provide vigorous defence against the Japanese**, firstly when they took over Manchuria (1931-32) and then when Jehol was attacked in 1933; he preferred to concentrate on destroying the CCP. Chiang declared that the Japanese were merely *a disease of the skin*, whereas the Communists were *a disease of the heart*. The Xian (Sian) Incident (December 1936), when Chiang was kidnapped by some of his own generals, illustrated the resentment this caused among even his own supporters.

- The **GMD had not defeated warlordism** but come to terms with it; therefore GMD control of China was rather superficial; again, the part played by the former warlord of Manchuria, Zhang Xueliang, during the Xian Incident in 1936 reflects that.

- Chiang **failed to destroy the CCP**. Although, as a result of the White Terror, CCP membership had dropped by perhaps 80% by 1928, the bulk of the survivors set up the Jiangxi Soviet. Chiang launched four unsuccessful extermination campaigns (1930-34) against the CCP in Jiangxi, until capturing the CCP base area in a fifth campaign in 1934. However, Mao led the remnant of the CCP, on *the Long March*, to Yanan.

Q. How were GMD weaknesses worsened by the Japanese War (1937-45)?

The GMD were to emerge from the Sino-Japanese War (1937-45) divided, demoralised and discredited, their best troops destroyed and the economy in crisis. Many historians see this as the key to explaining the GMD's defeat in the Civil War of 1946-49.

- After the fall of the eastern coastal region (Beijing, Shanghai, Nanjing) to the Japanese in 1937, the GMD were forced to relocate their government to Chongqing in the south-west. This area was poor and the **GMD were now cut off from their traditional power base** in the Lower Yangzi area.

- Although the GMD offered determined resistance to the Japanese in 1937, for the rest of the Sino-Japanese War (1937-45), the **GMD forces were less active in fighting the Japanese than the Communists** were. This lost the GMD support. Chiang preferred to conserve his forces and weapons for a final showdown with the Communists. The US general who acted, for most of the war, as army liaison officer with the GMD, Joseph Stilwell, was very critical of GMD inaction.

- The GMD **totally mismanaged the economy**, fuelling hyper-inflation by printing vast quantities of paper currency; prices increased to more than 6000 times the level of 1937.

- The **GMD lost many of its best troops during the Japanese War**, particularly as a result of the major Japanese offensive, *Operation Ochigo*, in 1944.

- The **GMD alienated the peasantry** by high levels of conscription and requisitioning of horses and equipment.

- GMD **corruption worsened**; a lot of the supplies sent by the USA, were sold by GMD officials on the black market.

- **GMD relations with intellectuals and students worsened**. The GMD were hostile to liberal elements at the National South-West Associated University in Kunming; the GMD used the Three People's Principles Youth Corps to spy on the staff and students.

Q. What were the strengths of the CCP?

As we have already noted, initially the CCP was a very small movement, founded in 1921, composed largely of intellectuals. The CCP decided, on the advice of Comintern, to form a United Front with the GMD in 1923. However, the CCP soon began to develop popular support as it seemed to offer to many ordinary Chinese the best chance of tackling lower class poverty and ending foreign domination of China.

The CCP prior to the Yanan Era (before 1935)

♦ **The CCP won lower class support**: By 1927 there were 58,000 CCP members, many of them recruited from the factory workers of China's eastern cities, like Shanghai. Mao was in charge of the Peasant Institute in Guangdong; by 1927, 2 million peasants had joined the Peasant Associations set up by the CCP in Guangdong and Hunan.

♦ The White Terror of 1927 was a huge blow to the CCP but the survivors established the Jiangxi Soviet and built support through land reform. Until 1931, land reform was moderate, with only the richest or most exploitative landlords having their land confiscated. However, from 1931 a more extreme policy meant that even richer peasants had land confiscated.

♦ **The CCP leadership showed great resilience** in surviving the White Terror, the various GMD extermination campaigns against the Jiangxi Soviet and the Long March (1934-5). The Long March, an epic journey of nearly 7000 miles, provided the CCP with an inspiring legend to draw on (particularly the crossing of the Luding Bridge) and use for propaganda purposes. After 1927, and, again after 1935, the CCP had to rebuild its membership.

♦ By 1935 the CCP had **begun to acquire strong leadership** in the person of Mao Zedong, although his control over the party was far from complete at this stage. Prior to 1935, there had been bitter divisions over strategy and personal rivalries too. Mao had favoured more moderate land reform, in which landlords were permitted to retain some land, an emphasis on building peasant support and a more defensive response to GMD attacks on Jiangxi. Other CCP leaders, notably the 28 Bolsheviks, who had returned from training in the USSR, argued for more extreme land reform, an emphasis on winning urban working class support and a more aggressive strategy to deal with GMD attacks on the Jiangxi Soviet. Wang Ming and Li Lisan were two of Mao's main rivals for the leadership. Mao was ruthless in dealing with rivals, as he demonstrated in the Futian Incident (December 1930-January 1931), when thousands of CCP members were tortured or executed, allegedly because they were GMD agents but probably because they supported Mao's rivals. Mao was eventually chosen as Chairman of the Standing Committee of the Politburo in January 1935 at the Zunyi conference during the Long March.

Q. What strengths did the CCP display during the Yanan Era (1935-46)?

The factors outlined below laid the foundations for CCP success in the Civil War of 1946-49; the CCP were to emerge from the Japanese War more united, with an enlarged army, wider support and control over a much greater area than previously.

♦ **The CCP united under Mao.** It was at Yanan that Mao asserted his dominance over the CCP, by a combination of intellectual brilliance and ruthlessness. The Rectification of Conduct Campaign of 1942 established Mao's ideas as official CCP ideology. 'Rectification' became a regular feature within the CCP; party members had to scrutinise their behaviour and engage in self-criticism and criticism of each other, in order to ensure they remained faithful to the ideals of the party. Mao also used rectification to maintain his own ascendancy over the party. A leadership cult began to develop from 1943; CCP ideology was referred to as 'Mao Zedong Thought'.

♦ Under Mao, the **CCP adapted Marxism to Chinese conditions,** *sinifying* it, e.g. it departed from orthodox Marxism in that the CCP came to see the peasantry as the main revolutionary class. This view had been developed by Mao from the late 1920s and had been opposed by many of the CCP's leaders, particularly the so-called 28 Bolsheviks.

♦ The **CCP broadened its support base** by appealing beyond the peasantry to other classes. At the Wayaobu Conference (December 1935), the Party approved Mao's policy of allowing even bourgeoisie and gentry into the CCP. In 1940 Mao wrote *On New Democracy* (1940), in which he appealed for an alliance of four revolutionary classes (national bourgeoisie, petite bourgeoisie, peasants, industrial workers) to defeat the Japanese and landlordism. During this period the CCP pursued a moderate land policy, insisting on rent reductions but only expropriating landlords who had collaborated with the Japanese.

Year	CCP membership
1937	40,000
1945	1.2 million

♦ **The CCP won peasant support,** through land and educational reforms; also the CCP helped the peasants organise their own associations. Mao advocated the *Mass Line*: CCP officials were to live among the peasants and learn from them. From 1940 the CCP followed the *'three-thirds policy'*, which meant CCP members only occupied a maximum of one third of local posts; in 1941 only 25% of government officials in the Yanan area were CCP members.

♦ The **CCP had the opportunity to expand massively the area under its control** because the Japanese drove the GMD southwards but were too thinly spread out to prevent the CCP controlling much of the countryside in northern China. By the end of the Japanese War, the CCP controlled an area occupied by about 90 million Chinese.

♦ **The Red Army based at Shaanxi, led by Zhu De and Peng Dehuai, was much better disciplined** than the GMD forces. Mao's *Eight Rules of Conduct* laid the basis for good relations with the peasants. As well as combating the Japanese, the Red Army had important non-fighting roles in distributing propaganda and helping to organise Peasant Associations.

Year	Red Army membership
1936	22,000
1945	900,000

♦ The **CCP established stronger nationalist credentials than the GMD**. The CCP's decision in December 1936 to allow Chiang's release (during the Xian Incident) in exchange for the Second United Front was greeted approvingly by many Chinese.

The CCP took a more active part in resisting the Japanese (1937-45) than the GMD. Mao favoured using the Communist Eighth Route Army to fight a guerrilla war, aided by peasants, behind enemy lines. The only time the Communists mounted a major conventional attack against the Japanese was in 1940, known as the Hundred Regiments Offensive. This inflicted heavy casualties on the Japanese but Communist losses were high too and the Japanese conducted terrible reprisals on Chinese civilians.

The Main Events of the Civil War (1946-49)

1946-1947: The Battle for Manchuria Part 1 – the PLA retreat

In March 1946, the truce brokered by Marshall broke down and there was renewed fighting in Manchuria. By June, there was full-scale GMD-CCP warfare in much of northern and central China. In the first year of the Civil War, Mao employed the same strategy as he had used against the GMD in Jiangxi and the Japanese in 1937-45; giving up territory and encouraging the enemy to become overextended, both in Manchuria and elsewhere in northern China. This involved temporarily withdrawing from Yanan and allowing the GMD to capture it in March 1947.

However, the Civil War of 1946-49 was fundamentally different from the fighting experienced by the Communists in the past. Prior to 1946, the Red Army had been engaged in battles to secure the countryside, now the People's Liberation Army was aiming to win control of China's major cities. Mao ordered his commanders to avoid battle unless they were certain of victory against smaller GMD detachments.

Chiang Kaishek made the fatal error of concentrating too many of his troops in the battle for Manchuria, without first gaining control of the areas of northern and central China which lay between GMD-held southern China and Manchuria in the north-east. In Manchuria, the GMD forces held the cities but were thinly spread out, with the PLA controlling the countryside in between the major towns. This allowed the PLA to cut communications between the different GMD garrisons.

1947-1948: The Battle for Manchuria Part 2 – the PLA counter-attack

The summer of 1947 saw the PLA's best commander, Lin Biao, launch a three-pronged offensive in Manchuria, which, over the next 6 months, resulted in the Communists securing control of the main north-south railway line and inflicting 640,000 casualties on the GMD. In addition, about 1 million GMD soldiers surrendered, many of them then being absorbed in to the PLA. By April 1948, the PLA had captured all bar three major towns in Manchuria.

To the south of Manchuria, other PLA forces captured much of northern China between Beijing and the Yangzi River. When the GMD lost control of Manchuria, at the end of 1948, the best of their forces had been destroyed.

1948-49 Three decisive battles

1. **The climax of the Manchurian campaign**. In October-November 1948 Lin Biao successfully attacked the last three Manchurian cities (Jinzhou, Shenyang and Changchun) in GMD hands. Mao was astonished by the speed and completeness of the PLA's triumph in Manchuria. Chiang Kaishek lost 500,000 of his best soldiers in the process.

2. **The battle for Tianjin and Beijing**. Lin Biao took his forces 600 miles south, to link up with the Communist North-Eastern Army. Their objective was the capture of the key cities of Tianjin and Beijing. Mao ordered Lin Biao to encircle the two cities and then in January 1949 the PLA stormed Tianjin, leading to the surrender of Beijing a week later.

3. **The Huaihai campaign**. This was conducted over four northern provinces (Anhui, Henan, Jiangsu and Shandong) and lasted between December 1948 and January 1949. The PLA and GMD both had about half a million troops engaged in this campaign but the PLA had significant help in the shape of peasant militias. By mid-January, almost all 500,000 GMD troops had been killed or captured, most of them at the decisive PLA victory at Xuzhou.

In the four months from October 1948 to January 1949, the GMD lost 1.5 million troops. Chiang Kaishek stepped down as president in January, with Li Zongren taking over.

The Conquest of the South: 1949

Mao certainly had not envisaged such a rapid collapse by the GMD. It was at this point that Stalin urged Mao not to cross the Yangzi River but instead be content with control of just northern China. Stalin was concerned lest a PLA offensive into southern China triggered intervention by the USA and was probably also anxious about the prospect of a potentially powerful, reunited China on the USSR's southern border. Mao ignored Stalin's advice and in April 1949 the PLA crossed the Yanzi River. Nanjing fell to the Communists in April; Shanghai fell in May. Chiang Kaishek resumed the presidency and in December 1949 he crossed over to the island of Taiwan with many of the remaining GMD forces and $300 million in gold and foreign currencies. On October 1, 1949, in Beijing, Mao proclaimed the establishment of the People's Republic of China.

Q. What GMD weaknesses led to their defeat in the Civil War?

♦ **Many Chinese blamed the GMD for the resumption of the civil war** in 1946. Chiang Kaishek, wanting to preserve a monopoly of power for the GMD, refused to accept the suggestion of a coalition government, including the CCP, which the USA urged Chiang to agree to. In December 1946 there were widespread student demonstrations in Beijing and Shanghai against the GMD government.

♦ **The way in which the GMD behaved in reoccupying areas formerly held by the Japanese lost them support.**

  (i) The GMD failed to punish those who had collaborated with the Japanese.
  (ii) GMD officials and officers who took control of Taiwan were corrupt, provoking a rebellion in 1947.
  (iii) The GMD appointed officials and commanders drawn from outside Manchuria to run the region.

♦ **The GMD became increasingly repressive**.
  This led to a number of factions within the party breaking off and going into opposition, e.g. the Revolutionary Alliance. The most infamous victim of political assassination by the GMD was the popular poet Wen Yiduo, who was a professor at South-West Associated University at Kunming. In 1948 the GMD secret police killed many of the GMD's opponents in cold blood on the streets of Shanghai.

♦ **The government's attempts to control inflation failed disastrously**.
  In August 1948 the gold yuan note was introduced to replace the national currency. People were encouraged to convert their gold and foreign currency into gold yuan. In November the gold yuan collapsed and, with it, many people lost their savings.

♦ **Chiang Kaishek had miscalculated about how the war in Asia would end.**
  Chiang had assumed there would be large-scale US intervention in China to drive out the Japanese; he had hoped to persuade the USA, once the Japanese had been defeated, to use its troops against the CCP. Instead the war ended abruptly following the Nagasaki A-bomb (August 1945).

- **The USA only provided limited support to the GMD.**
  The US government had hoped to broker a peace between the GMD and CCP and sent General George Marshall to China for that purpose in 1945-46. The Truman administration was disappointed by the failure of the Marshall Mission. Following the renewal of civil war, the US government severely restricted aid to Chiang as it was concerned by reports of the corruption of his regime. By 1948, when the US government realised that Chiang was in serious danger of losing, it proved too late for increased US aid ($463 million) to have a significant impact.

- **Chiang's key military mistake was to commit most of his troops to the occupation and retention of Manchuria.**
  The GMD forces were overextended and were vulnerable to counter-offensives by the People's Liberation Army (the CCP's army). Chiang interfered disastrously in military decision-making.

- **GMD army morale was low.**
  Although the GMD Army was much bigger than the PLA at the start of the civil war, the morale of many soldiers was low and discipline was brutal. Many GMD soldiers were conscripts and were often roped together to try to stop them deserting. Desertion rates in GMD units regularly ran at 70% a year.

Q. What strengths led the CCP to win the Civil War (1946-49)?

- **At the end of the Japanese War, the People's Liberation Army (PLA) were in a better position to take the surrender of Japanese weapons in Manchuria.**
  Soviet troops, taking the Japanese surrender, did hand over captured weapons to the PLA; otherwise, the USSR provided no help to the CCP during the Civil War. In fact, Stalin tried to dissuade Mao from crossing the Yangzi into southern China in 1949, urging him to be content with CCP control of just the north.

- **The PLA sensibly did not, at first, try to contest GMD control of Manchuria's towns.**
  They retreated encouraging the GMD to overextend themselves. In June 1947 the PLA went onto the offensive and isolated many of the GMD garrisons; by the end of November 1948, the PLA had captured the whole of Manchuria. This was the decisive campaign in the Civil War.

- **The PLA had able generals, particularly Lin Biao.**
  Mao did not interfere with military decision-making.

- **CCP success in Manchuria was partly the result of peasant support.**
  This was won by the CCP's record against the Japanese and by the CCP's land reforms post-1945.

- **Mao was prepared to be flexible in terms of land policy.**
  In 1946-47 the CCP pursued a radical land policy involving the total expropriation of landlords and some rich peasants; Mao moderated this from 1948 when it became clear that many middle peasants were being alienated.

♦   **The GMD's numerical advantage in troops rapidly eroded during the Civil War.**
Although the GMD army (4.8 million) was much bigger than the PLA (1.2 million) at the start of the Civil War, the PLA was assisted by Peasant Militias. These numbered 2 million and, during the course of the Civil War, many GMD soldiers deserted to the PLA or were prepared to change sides when captured. The CCP encouraged this by promising generous treatment of soldiers who defected to them.

	GMD Army	**PLA**
1946	4.8 million	1.2 million
1949	1.5 million	4 million

♦   **The CCP's growing support is reflected by its membership figures**:

  • 1.2 million at the end of Japanese War
  • 3 million by September 1948.

♦   The CCP managed to infiltrate the GMD armies very successfully, so that they knew in advance most of the GMD's moves. Chiang Kaishek's Assistant Chief of Staff, General Liu Fei, was a Communist agent, as was Guo Rugui, head of the GMD's War Planning Board.

♦   By the end of 1948, Mao had managed to secure an agreement with moderate anti-GMD political parties to set up a National Political Consultative Conference. This was established in September 1949 and was in theory a coalition government. However, in practice the CCP dominated it.

Maoist Ideology

For most of the period from 1942 to 1976, the official ideology of the CCP was defined in terms of 'Mao Zedong Thought'. Prior to 1942, there were bitter and sometimes violent ideological struggles within the CCP; Mao's opponents, particularly the 'Twenty-Eight Bolsheviks', wanted to prepare for a revolution of the industrial proletariat and they dominated the Party until the early 1930s. It was during the early 1940s that Mao established ideological leadership of the Party.

In certain respects, Mao was an orthodox Marxist in that he believed in class struggle, collective ownership of the means of production, and the dictatorship of the proletariat (working class). However, Mao was also highly influenced by Chinese history and culture and adapted Marx's ideas to Chinese conditions. Mao "sinified" Marxism; in other words he produced a Chinese version.

Some key components of Mao Zedong Thought

The peasants as a revolutionary class	Marx had written off the peasantry as incapable of revolutionary consciousness and the Russian Communist Party affirmed Marx's emphasis on the industrial proletariat as the principal revolutionary class. In the first half of the 20th century China had undergone only limited industrialisation and Mao, from the late 1920s, began to argue that the peasant masses could be used to overthrow feudalism and capitalism and then go on to create a socialist society.
Belief in a two stage revolution	In 1940 Mao published *On New Democracy* in which he argued that socialism in China would be created as the result of a two-stage revolution; the first revolution would be bourgeois-democratic and the second socialist. In the "New Democratic" phase, the revolution would begin to be led, not by the bourgeoisie alone (as in Marx's writings), but by a "joint revolutionary-democratic dictatorship" of four revolutionary classes: the proletariat, the peasants, the "national" bourgeoisie (those capitalists who had not collaborated with the Japanese, nor been too exploitative of the poor) and the petite bourgeoisie (shopkeepers, intellectuals). During the National Democratic Revolution, private property would be retained. Later a second, socialist revolution would see property and economic resources collectivised or nationalised. In practice, Mao began to implement this second stage during the early-mid 1950s.
The Mass Line	Mao developed the idea that the Party's role vis-à-vis the masses was to identify what the masses' true interests were, interpret them in the light of Marxist principles, and, then communicate them back to the masses in a way they could understand. The idea of the 'Mass Line' involved developing close relations between the Communist Party and the people. During the Yanan period, CCP cadres were expected to live among the peasants so that they could learn about rural life and be in a better position to educate the peasants about Marxism. After 1949, the Mass Line remained a central Maoist idea. This is illustrated by the regular recourse made by the CCP to mass mobilisation campaigns such as the Three and Five Antis (1951-52); Mao sought to involve the masses in campaigns to build socialism rather than simply sending out officials to impose socialist change on the masses. The way in which to a considerable extent the communes of the Great Leap Forward developed out of initiatives by local officials and peasant experimentation in 1958 reflects Mao's views on the interaction between the Party and the masses.
Continuous Revolution & Rectification	Mao believed that the in addition to the revolutions required to put the CCP into power and to establish a socialist economy, revolution should be a permanent or continuous feature of communist rule. He meant that the Party and people would need to have their outlooks and thought remoulded, corrected and inspected regularly in order to create and maintain a selfless, socialist culture. He developed the concept of "rectification" whilst at Yanan; it involved CCP officials engaging in self-criticism and criticism in order to ensure that they served the people selflessly and remained true to Marxist ideology. Mao also used his first "Rectification Campaign" (1942) and later ones in order to assert and maintain his own authority over the CCP as all cadres were required to study Mao's writings. Mao in the 1950s and 1960s remained convinced that "rectification campaigns" were an essential device for ensuring that the CCP, and especially its officials, remained in touch with the masses and did not develop into a self-seeking elite, as had happened in the USSR. Both the Socialist Education Movement (1962) and the Cultural Revolution (1966) were forms of rectification designed to eliminate corruption and ensure the CCP remained faithful to their socialist ideals.
Worldwide Revolution	Up until 1971-72, Mao was committed to Trotsky's idea of worldwide communist revolution. Mao intervened in the Korean War in 1950 and provided aid to communist guerrilla movements in the Philippines, Vietnam, Malaya, Burma and Indonesia. However, in 1971 Mao departed from this principle by pursuing diplomatic relations with the USA.

The Establishment of Single Party Rule

Consolidation and Recovery: 1949-52

Most historians have viewed the CCP's achievements in this first phase of their rule as remarkable. They succeeded in fulfilling the aims of the May Fourth generation who had dreamt of restoring China's unity and independence from foreign interference. Not only that, but the Communist leadership of the People's Republic decided to take on the technological and military might of the USA in the Korean War, within a year of coming to power, and China was successful in fighting the USA to a standstill and, by doing so, saved communist North Korea from collapse. The CCP's initial success is all the more impressive given that China had suffered from nearly 40 years of war and civil war and that disorder and crime had reached epidemic proportions; perhaps 1 million bandits populated rural areas, while drugs and prostitution blighted the cities. Furthermore, although the CCP had had extensive experience of administering rural areas during the 1930s and 1940s, they had none of running towns or an urban economy.

In order to deal with the huge challenges facing them, the CCP leadership in the early 1950s proved very pragmatic. They were prepared, during this period, to tolerate other political parties (but not, of course, the GMD) and in September 1949 a provisional national assembly for China was set up when the People's Consultative Conference met. The People's Consultative Conference drafted a temporary constitution (the Organic Law) which permitted 8 parties to function. This continued Mao's New Democratic policy of working with other parties in creating a new China.

So the new government initially was a coalition; however, right from the start it was dominated by the CCP. Mao described the new system of government as a 'people's democratic dictatorship'; the 'people' consisted of the 'national' and 'petty' bourgeoisie, the peasants and the industrial proletariat. Mao also made it clear that the CCP would be severe in dealing with those classes not defined as part of the 'people'; he wrote in June 1949, that *"The right to vote is given only to the people and not to the reactionaries. These two aspects, namely democracy among the people and dictatorship over the reactionaries, combine to form the people's democratic dictatorship."*

To facilitate their takeover, for the first years of the PRC, the CCP divided the country into six regions, each run by a bureau in which the military had a key role. China officially became a one-party communist state in 1954 when the Organic Law was replaced by a new constitution. A "parliament", the People's National Congress was created but it only met for a few days each year and had no real power. As in the USSR, power was exercised by a hierarchy of Communist Party committees, with the Politburo at the top.

At the outset, the CCP had to draw on non-communists to help them govern China, because there were just 750,000 CCP cadres in 1949. So many of the 2 million officials who had served the GMD government were kept on by the CCP until it had built up the numbers and administrative competence of its own officials. By 1953, CCP membership had increased from 4 million to 6.1 million and that growth allowed the Party to dispense with many non-communist officials. Communist suspicions about the reliability of the latter were greatly heightened by the outbreak of the Korean War (1950).

The restoration of unified control over what had been the Chinese Empire had been a major aim of the CCP leadership. This was not completed in 1949 as much of South-West China was still under GMD control and the PLA's assault on Quemoy (Jinmen), an island close to Taiwan, failed. Chiang Kaishek spent

November and December in Sichuan on the mainland. However, by the end of 1950, the CCP had been almost totally successful in reunifying China. Xinjiang was captured in March 1950, Hainan Island in April and Tibet in October 1950. This only left Hong Kong (British), Macao (Portuguese), Outer Mongolia, Taiwan and a few other small GMD-controlled islands, outside of the PRC; Mao was furious that he was obliged to abort plans for an invasion of Taiwan in 1950 when the Korean War broke out.

National Capitalism: 1949-52

On taking power, the CCP's central economic goal was to achieve recovery after the damage and dislocation caused by the Sino-Japanese War and the Civil War. To that end, the CCP was keen to work with 'national capitalists', or 'national bourgeoisie', that is those businessmen who had not had close connections with the GMD. The CCP needed their management and financial skills and experience.

Under National Capitalism, the state took over ownership of heavy industry and the banking system. This was made easier by the fact that the GMD government had exercised considerable control over industry, for example, 75% of chemical industries had been state-run. Lighter industry and smaller factories were not nationalised at this stage; they remained under private ownership. However, although the national bourgeoisie could continue to make profits, they were subject to increasing state regulation in terms of wages and prices. Even when all factories and businesses were nationalised in 1955, many former owners were kept on as managers and received an annual share of the profits.

Industrial and agricultural production recovered very successfully. In the period 1949-52, the value of industrial output increased by two and a half times. By 1952, grain production was actually 10% higher than it had been in 1936. The Communists also tackled the hyperinflation which had totally destabilised China's economy under the GMD. A new, carefully controlled, currency, the *renminbi*, was introduced: the currency was exchanged at a rate of 10,000 old to 1 new yuan. The budget was balanced, partly as a result of the CCP being much more effective at taxing the population than the GMD had been.

Land Reform (June 1950)

One of the biggest changes introduced by the CCP in the early years of its rule was land reform. In contrast to the relatively moderate land policy that Mao had followed for most of the Jiangxi and Yanan periods, the Land Reform of 1950 saw the destruction of the power and wealth of the landlord class. Before the Land Reform, 4% of landowners had owned 40% of China's arable land.

CCP cadres were sent out to the villages but, in keeping with Mao's emphasis on mobilisation of the masses, the peasants were encouraged to take the lead in attacking their landlords, denouncing them in organised "Speak Bitterness" sessions.

Q. **What were the results of the Land Reform?**

- Historians cite different figures for the number of landlords who were killed, often beaten to death by the peasants, but somewhere in the region of 2 million landlords died.
- A much larger number survived but had much of their land taken away and redistributed to middle and poor peasants.
- Land reform was not complete until 1952.

- One important effect, just as the CCP intended, was to give the peasants a stake in the revolution, as they now had something to lose if the CCP were overthrown.
- At this stage, ownership of land remained private; the CCP only moved gradually towards socialisation of agriculture from the early 1950s.

Mass Movements and Thought Reform

The CCP launched a number of campaigns to reshape the attitudes and habits of the Chinese population, as part of their drive to establish political control over its citizens. They were aiming not just at a socialist economy but also at a socialist culture and mindset. To achieve this, the CCP employed the same methods that they had used before coming to power: mass movements to mobilise and galvanise the population, rectification campaigns involving criticism and self-criticism, struggle sessions.

In order to establish tight control over the Chinese people, particularly in the towns where the CCP had not previously held sway, the CCP created structures to ensure everyone was subject to surveillance. *Danwei,* work or neighbourhood units, were set up to which all citizens had to belong.

A series of mass organisations were created, including the National Women's Association, New Democratic Youth League (for 14-25 year olds), and the Children's Pioneer Corps (ages 9-14). Children were instructed in the Five Loves – for country, people, labour, science and public property.

The Campaign against Counter-Revolutionaries (1950)

In spite of having to make use, for a time, with officials who had served under the GMD, Mao was particularly concerned to identify and eliminate anyone within the PRC who continued to support the GMD. The outbreak of the Korean War (1950), which, by October, saw US troops perilously close to North Korea's border with Manchuria and which, in turn triggered China's military intervention, heightened the CCP's anxiety about potential 'enemies within' and led to a bloody campaign against Counter-Revolutionaries.

- The Party organised mass demonstrations against the USA and other capitalist countries. China's population was mobilised to identify spies and traitors.

- Within six months, over 700,000 people, most of them with former GMD links, were executed.

- In addition, 500,000 were imprisoned in the 'reform through labour' camps.

The Three and Five-Antis Campaigns (1951-52)

Even before the official end to the National Capitalist phase, the CCP began to put greater pressure on former GMD officials and the bourgeoisie who had remained behind when the GMD leadership had fled to Taiwan. In 1951-52 the CCP launched two campaigns with a view to clamping down on corruption:

The Three Anti (*San Fan*) Campaign (1951) targeted corruption, waste and elitism. It was directed against officials, both former GMD officials and members of the CCP. Officials were obliged to undergo self-criticism and criticism, both at the hands of colleagues and the public.

The Five Anti (*Wu Fan*) Campaign (1952) targeted bribery, tax evasion, fraud, theft of government property and of economic secrets. This was directed against the business community.

In the case of both campaigns, offenders, on the whole, were treated mildly compared to the Campaign Against Counter-Revolutionaries. Fines and prison sentences or dismissal from official posts were the most common punishments. About 5-10% of officials were either censured or punished. Businessmen collectively had fines imposed on them totalling somewhere between $1 billion and $2 billion.

Thought Reform Movement (September 1951)

The CCP also sought to eradicate bourgeois and capitalist ideas from intellectuals. In the autumn of 1951, 6500 intellectuals and university professors were obliged to undertake courses in Communist thought run by the Party.

Art and literature had to conform to the CCP's political dictates. Back in 1942, Mao in his *Talks at the Yanan Forum on Literature and Art*, stated that *"There is in fact no such thing as art for art's sake, art that stands above classes, art that is detached from or independent of politics."* Art was required to promote class struggle and loyalty to the Party. "Bourgeois individualism" was condemned. The Party silenced artists and writers who did not conform.

Social Reform

War on crime

The CCP was keen to tackle problems of organised crime and banditry. The CCP approached them in a decisive but measured fashion, punishing, often executing, major criminals but treating prostitutes and drug addicts as victims and providing them with rehabilitation programmes. CCP officials raided and closed down brothels and gambling dens.

Education

On coming to power, the CCP, in keeping with their pre-1949 policies, launched a massive drive to increase literacy and expand educational provision. In 1949, only 24 million children attended primary schools and only 1.27 million were in secondary education. By 1953, 51 million children were in primary education and 3.13 million in secondary. However, even by the mid-1950s, illiteracy rates remained very high, with perhaps as much as 80% of the population unable to read and write. During the 1950s, the CCP received a lot of help from the USSR in the form of Russians teaching in Chinese schools and universities and Chinese being trained in Russian universities.

Marriage Reform

The CCP did try to improve the position of women in society. In 1950, the Marriage Law banned arranged and child marriages and polygamy. Women were also given the right to divorce and the right to own property. This led to a huge increase in divorce, with 1.3 million divorce petitions filed in 1953. However, changing men's attitudes, particularly in rural areas, proved very difficult and women continued to be treated as inferiors by many men, receiving lower pay and continuing to marry outside their native villages, as was the custom.

Socialist Transition

The First Five Year Plan, 1953-57

The First Five Year Plan ended the National Capitalist phase and saw, by February 1956, the nationalisation of all private industries and businesses in China.

Given the backing that the GMD had received from the USA, it is not surprising, that Mao decided that the PRC must 'lean to one side' in international relations and look, despite receiving very little help from Stalin in the past, to the Russian comrades for friendship. Furthermore, it was natural, given their lack of experience in industrial planning, for the CCP to turn to the USSR for advice and help in building a socialist economy. In February 1950 the PRC signed the Sino-Soviet Friendship Treaty. Under its terms, the USSR provided China with $300 million in loans (repayable at low interest) and Russian technicians and economic advisors. 11,000 Soviet experts were working in China in the 1950s and 28,000 Chinese received training in the USSR.

China's First Five Year (1953-57) followed the Soviet model, planning was highly centralised and concentrated on heavy industry. Huge new industrial centres such as the Anshan steel complex, employing 35,000 workers, were built. Factory management changed from a more team-based approach to one-man management, as in Russian industry.

Q. What were the First Five Year Plan's results?

• It completed the process of nationalisation of industry. On the eve of the Five Year Plan, 20% of heavy industry and 60% of light industry had still been under private ownership.

• It boosted urbanisation. China's urban population increased from 57 million (1949) to 100 million (1957).

• There were important infrastructure improvements such as the Yangzi River Rail and Road Bridge linking north and south China.

• Over the course of the Five Year Plan, heavy industrial output nearly trebled and light industrial output rose by 70%. Overall targets were exceeded by 20%.

• The $300 million lent by the USSR represented only 3% of total investment under the Five Year Plan, so the Chinese government had to raise the money to fund the Plan from its own population. Consequently, agriculture was squeezed to pay for heavy industrial expansion; the state set grain prices low, to produce a large profit which could be invested in industry.

• Agricultural investment was low as 90% of state investment was in industry. This is one reason for the relatively slow growth in agricultural output (just 3.8% p.a.)

The Socialisation of Agriculture

Aware of the disasters that had accompanied Stalin's collectivisation of Russian agriculture in the 1930s and drawing on their considerable experience of working with the peasants, the CCP adopted a gradualist approach to introducing socialism into the countryside. The CCP leadership was convinced that collectivisation was essential for increasing agricultural efficiency as well as for fulfilling their ideological aims. However, from the early 1950s onwards, the CCP leadership quarrelled over the pace at which the PRC moved towards full collectivisation.

After the Land Reform of 1950, the CCP encouraged peasants to pool their equipment and animals at certain times of the year, whilst retaining private ownership of land and other resources. This was acceptable to the peasants and, by 1953, 40% of peasant households belonged to mutual-aid teams. Starting properly in 1954, the CCP began to organise peasants in some parts of the country into Agricultural Producers' Co-operatives. In these larger units, land was pooled but private ownership was still retained and the peasants were rewarded in terms of what they contributed to the co-operatives in terms of land, equipment and labour. Rich peasants were not allowed to join these Lower Level APCs.

Between 1953 and 1956 the CCP's policy towards co-operatives oscillated wildly; for example, in 1953 Mao condemned the speed of change (*Rash Advance*) but then criticised the resulting fall-off in the number of co-operatives (*Rash Retreat*). A similar stop-start pattern occurred in 1955. Liu Shaoqi advocated a slower, more cautious approach but Mao won over the Party leadership to his policy of rapid collectivisation. By 1956, 80% of rural households were in co-operatives. Encouraged by this success, Mao ordered the transition to bigger, Higher Level Agricultural Producers' Co-operatives (APCs) in which land was collectively owned. This was a radical step as all peasants now worked for wages, regardless of their input of land or equipment. Within a year nearly 90% of peasants were incorporated into Higher Level APCs.

Q. What were the results of collectivisation?

- The CCP achieved far greater control over the countryside than any previous regime. The historian, John King Fairbank, described this as '*a modern serfdom under party control*'.

- From 1953, the state became the sole buyer and seller of grain and peasants were obliged to sell fixed quotas of grain to the state.

- The gradual introduction of collectivisation in China meant that it was achieved much more peacefully than had been the case in Russia. The differences in wealth between the peasants in the early 1950s was relatively small so that most peasants did not feel they would lose out by pooling their resources.

- Historians disagree about the extent of resistance to collectivisation; Marc Blecher suggests that it was limited to rich peasants who were unhappy about their share of the co-operatives' income, which resulted in them slaughtering their livestock.

However, Philip Short, in his biography of Mao, argues that it was serious peasant rioting in 1954 that led Mao, in January 1955, to call a temporary halt to the process.

- Collectivisation was achieved without major disruption to the rural economy and 1957 saw a 5% increase in agricultural output.

Staged ollectivisation

Date begun	Type of organisation	Number of households	Features
1950	**Mutual-Aid Teams**	5-10	Equipment and animals pooled at harvest time but private ownership retained
1954	**(Lower Level) Agricultural Producers' Co-operatives (APCs)**	30-50	Pooling of land but share of profits partly based on how much land/equipment contributed.
1956	**Higher Level APCs**	200-300	Land collectively owned; small allotments permitted.
1958	**Communes**	5000	Land collectively owned, not even small private plots/ allotments permitted.

The *Hundred Flowers* Campaign, 1957

In 1957 the CCP briefly lifted censorship and encouraged intellectuals to voice criticism of how the Party was working. The *"Hundred Flowers Campaign"* was very much Mao's initiative and he had been trying to launch it since May 1956 when he announced *"Let a hundred flowers bloom. Let a hundred schools of thought contend."* At that stage, intellectuals did not respond, not surprisingly given the controls they had been subjected to by the Party and the treatment dissidents had received in the past. Many of them would have viewed this invitation as a trap, designed to lure them into making known their misgivings about the CCP so that they could be punished. However, Mao continued to make calls urging intellectuals to speak out and, following the publication of a speech by Mao in the *People's Daily* in April 1957, the campaign finally got under way in May.

After a slow start, a torrent of criticism was unleashed in which many claimed that the CCP had become a privileged caste, alienated from the masses. The movement spread to the universities as students called for multi-party elections and a Democracy Wall was created at Beijing University where students and lecturers pinned posters. Within six weeks, the CCP leadership, alarmed at the way its authority was being undermined, decided to bring the campaign to a halt.

A purge of intellectuals and other critics then followed, known as the Anti-Rightist Campaign. In this, over 500,000 people were forced to undergo labour reform or were sent to the countryside to learn from the peasants. Many academics were dismissed from their university posts. Intellectuals would never trust Mao again and Mao remained suspicious of intellectuals for the rest of his life.

Q. **How have historians interpreted Mao's motives for launching the** *Hundred Flowers*?

> • For some, Mao saw the *Hundred Flowers* as a form of rectification. Opening up the CCP to criticism would keep it pure and prevent it from developing into a privileged elite. There is no doubt that Mao believed that the revolutionary disturbances in Communist Poland and Hungary in 1956 were the result of criticism being stifled and grievances building up as the communist parties of Eastern Europe had become increasingly out of touch with the people. So, on one level, it is likely that Mao saw the *Hundred Flowers* as a safety-valve, designed to let off steam so that grievances did not accumulate to exploding-point.

- Philip Short suggests that Mao was trying to combine a *"totalitarian system with democratic checks and balances"*. Certainly, it appears that Mao was not sure what would happen when the *Hundred Flowers* got going but wanted to experiment; however, he massively misjudged the likely scale of the condemnation that would ensue and had not foreseen there would be widespread calls for the end to the CCP's monopoly of power.

- Alternatively, as many intellectuals suspected, the *Hundred Flowers* can be viewed as a trap set by Mao to flush out critics. Finally, the *Hundred Flowers* coincided with the rapid industrialisation of China and the CCP leadership was perhaps seeking to encourage intellectuals as their talents would be invaluable in this process.

The Great Leap Forward, 1958

It is clear that Mao had growing reservations about the Soviet-style First Five Year Plan. As early as December 1953, the arrest of the top Party leader, Gao Gang, was probably, in part, motivated by Mao's misgivings about being too closely tied to the USSR, as Gao, the CCP boss in Manchuria, was a strong advocate of Soviet-style industrialisation. In May 1956 Mao delivered an important speech, which became known as *On the Ten Great Relationships*, in which he outlined a set of economic priorities which were fundamentally at odds with the Five Year Plan and which the Great Leap Forward would be based on when it was launched in 1958.

In October 1957, Mao persuaded the Central Committee to cancel a Second Five Year Plan, due to be implemented in 1958, and instead adopt a radical new plan which set very ambitious targets and which would abandon the Soviet model. This became known as the Great Leap Forward (the slogan was first used in late 1957).

Q. Why did Mao decide to abandon the Soviet model of economic planning and adopt the Great Leap Forward?

i.   Under the Five Year Plan, with its massive emphasis on heavy industry, light industry and agriculture had been neglected. Mao wanted China to *"walk on two legs"*: to develop simultaneously agriculture and industry.

ii.   Since 1956, material incentives in the form of pay differentials for skilled and unskilled workers had reappeared. This clashed with the Marxist idea of rewarding each according to his needs.

iii.   The Five Year Plan focused on capital-intensive projects but the PRC was short of capital to invest in industry, particularly as agricultural productivity was rising only slowly.

iv.   Mao was keen to change the nature of China's economic planning and development because the First Five Year Plan was Russian in inspiration and direction and Mao wanted to assert China's independence and do things his own way.

v.   By 1957, Mao was impatient to accelerate the speed of economic growth. The rapid collectivisation of agriculture in 1956-57 encouraged Mao to believe that willpower and mobilisation of the masses could deliver huge advances in industry and agriculture. In October 1957 Mao spoke of quadrupling steel output (to 20 million tons p.a.) and in November, whilst attending a Communist Conference in Moscow, he predicted that China would overtake Great Britain in industrial production within 15 years.

vi.   Mao was worried that the CCP might be losing its revolutionary spirit and that the CCP and government officials were becoming a self-interested elite. He aimed to reduce the influence of the central planning ministries in Beijing and increase the influence of provincial CCP agencies. As importantly, Mao wanted to revive the "Yanan spirit" and mobilise both the Party and the masses to create a modern, socialist economy. So the GLF had political as well as economic aims (see below).

The launching of the Great Leap Forward

Mao undertook a tour of China in January-April 1958 and returned to Beijing, fired with enthusiasm for a Great Leap Forward. In particular, he had between encouraged by massive irrigation schemes, involving 100 million peasants digging dykes and channels to provide water for almost 20 million acres of farmland. This had been achieved by combining the labour of many co-operatives. Mao decided that this was the way to transform the Chinese economy, by focusing on labour-intensive projects and so, in August 1958, he called for the amalgamation of the co-operatives into much larger units, the communes. The term 'commune' was coined in memory of the revolutionary Paris Commune of 1871. The first had been set up in April 1958 in Henan province by radical, local cadres and Mao seized on this as the answer to his search for a way to accelerate economic and socialist progress.

The 26,000 communes that were set up in 1958 were gigantic units, containing an average of 5000 households. Mao believed that such large-scale organisation would mean a significant surplus of labour available for large projects such as land reclamation, irrigation or industrial production. Canteens and crèches were set up in order to free women for agricultural and industrial work. By 1959, 70% of children were in nurseries.

However, the communes were not just agricultural enterprises, but were also responsible for industry, education and defence. In terms of defence, Mao planned to use the communes to set up a People's Militia; the CCP was concerned about security at this stage because of the international tension over Quemoy and Matsu, Nationalist islands off Taiwan, which the PRC shelled in 1958. The CCP leaders were aiming to develop industry in the countryside as well as in the towns. Under the "backyard furnace" policy, the communes were instructed to set up blast furnaces in the countryside. In 1958 the government set a target for steel production to double to 10.7 million tons a year by 1959 and to rise to 60 million tons by 1960.

There were attempts to set up communes in the towns, so that they encompassed agricultural production as well as industry. However, lack of space and lack of time, in the case of factory workers, meant that few were established. Nonetheless, industry underwent major changes as planning and management became more decentralised. Within individual factories, decision-making power was transferred from a single manager to collective management including worker representatives.

Mao and the more radical elements of the CCP leadership saw the GLF not just as a means to economic progress but also in cultural and political terms. They intended the establishment of communes to break down the distinction between peasant and worker, town and countryside and transform the outlook of the people so that they put aside narrow loyalties to their families and villages and instead think in terms of the good of the Party and the country.

The announcement below, from a CCP declaration of August 1958, makes the leadership's political and cultural agenda very clear:

In the present circumstances, the establishment of people's communes with all-round management of agriculture, forestry, animal husbandry, side occupations, and fishery, where industry (the worker), agriculture (the peasant), exchange (the trader), culture and education (the student), and military affairs (the militiaman) merge into one, is the fundamental policy to guide the peasants, to accelerate socialist construction, complete the building of socialism ahead of time, and carry out the gradual transition to communism.

Q. What were the results of the Great Leap Forward?

Industry

- Overall China's GNI (Gross National Income) increased by 8% in 1958 but fell by 30% in 1960.

- 600,000 backyard furnaces were built in 1958 and steel production more or less reached the target laid down by the government.

- But the steel produced by the backyard furnaces was of such poor quality, that most of it could not be used. The programme was therefore abandoned in 1959. The government had not taken into account factors such as the availability of coal, iron ore and transport.

- In spite of the failure of the backyard furnace scheme, the GLF marked the beginning of rural industrialisation, which became a very important feature of China's economy in the long-term. The communes had considerable success in manufacturing agricultural tools, the production of chemical fertilizers and in uranium mining (which helped accelerate China's atomic programme).

- The Communes also contributed to large-scale irrigation and hydroelectric projects. This model of labour-intensive development was to have considerable appeal to Third World countries.

Agriculture

The impact of the Great Leap was much more disastrous on the countryside:

- The 1958 harvest was good (200 million tons of grain). However, the government published the inflated figure of 260 million tons and set wildly unrealistic targets for 1959.

- The 1959 and 1960 harvests were poor (only 170 million tons and 144 million tons respectively).

- China experienced a catastrophic famine: the death rate rose steeply in 1959 (from 1.08% to 1.46% of the population) and then hugely in 1960 to 2.54% of the population. The rate remained high in 1961 (1.7%). 1959-61 are known as the *'Three Bitter Years'* when possibly in excess of 20 million people died in the famine.

Grain production 1957-60

Year	Grain output (million tons)
1957	196
1958	200
1959	170
1960	144

Year	Deaths (millions)
1957	7
1959	9.6
1960	17
1961	11

Figures for deaths in Chinese population 1957-61

Q. **Why did the Great Leap fail so disastrously?**

» CCP officials were unable to deal with the huge challenges posed by the GLF. In particular, local cadres were totally unprepared for managing the vast size of the communes. The GLF took off in 1958 with very little prior planning.

» Mass mobilisation – the intensive use of labour - could not, contrary to Mao's philosophy, compensate for the lack of capital investment in technologically advanced processes such as steel production, hence the failure of the "backyard furnace" programme.

» In 1960 the Sino-Soviet split occurred and Khrushchev abruptly withdrew thousands of soviet advisers from China who were helping the Chinese on industrial projects. This, in part, explains the slump in industrial production in 1960-61.

» Flawed agricultural reforms, derived from the ideas of the Russian agronomist, Lysenko, were imposed on the peasants. These included close planting, deep ploughing and a campaign against the "Four Pests" (rats, sparrows, flies and mosquitoes). The sparrow population was all but wiped out, which allowed an explosion of caterpillars, which devastated crops.

» Grain production fell partly because peasants were heavily involved in industrial projects and land reclamation. After the initial enthusiasm of 1958 wore off, many became exhausted by the demands being made of them. In the autumn of 1958, about 90 million people temporarily abandoned their normal occupations to get involved in steel production.

» The withdrawal of material incentives contributed to falling levels of agricultural and industrial output. The peasants disliked the huge size of the communes and the regimented lifestyle and resented the loss of their private plots. In industry, the ending of higher wages for skilled workers and greater output, demotivated factory workers.

» China suffered abnormally bad weather in 1959-61, leading to severe drought in the North-East and flooding in the South. 60% of China's arable land was affected.

» Although the harvests were poor in 1959-60, they were not so disastrous that a famine should have ensued. Famine was more the product of the CCP's refusal to admit to failure. Officials at both local and national level claimed a record harvest in 1959 (supposedly 282 million tons) and so the state took 28% of the peasants' grain (as opposed to just 17% in 1957).

» Most of the blame for this failure by officials to report honestly must be laid at Mao's door. He had, by 1958, created a climate of fear in which almost no-one, even within the circle of top CCP leaders, dared criticise his policies.

Early in 1959, Mao had begun to accept that there were serious problems with the GLF and had agreed to reduce some of its most extravagant targets, but he reacted very badly to criticism made in July 1959, at a Central Committee meeting at Lushan, by his old comrade, Marshal Peng Dehuai. Mao even threatened to engage in civil war if the Party did not back him, so the rest of the CCP leadership closed ranks behind Mao and Peng was dismissed as Defence Minister. Disastrously, Mao reaffirmed his faith in the GLF, talking of China producing 1,000 million tons of grain and 650 million tons of steel by the end of the 20th century. So the GLF was continued until late 1960 and the famine therefore intensified.

The Great Leap terminated: 1961

By the end of 1960, China was in a state of crisis, suffering its worst ever famine. In some provinces, such as Sichuan and Anhui, a quarter of the population starved to death. Armed rebellion by desperate peasants broke out in four western provinces and in Tibet; the PLA had to be deployed to restore order. In the face of this, the CCP turned to Liu Shaoqi (PRC Chairman) and Deng Xiaoping (CCP General Secretary) to restore the economy and grain supplies. The Great Leap was quietly abandoned under the direction of Liu and Deng. These 'pragmatists' emphasised the need to pursue economic policies that worked, rather than placing strict adherence to communist principles above all else. In 1962, Deng famously quoted an old Sichuanese saying:

> 'It doesn't matter if the cat is black or white; so long as it catches the mouse, it is a good cat.'

Nonetheless, it took five years for agricultural production to recover fully from the damage inflicted by the Great Leap. Industrial output revived much more quickly and, aided by the discovery of huge oil and gas-fields in Daqing, it doubled by 1965.

Q. How did Liu and Deng bring about economic recovery in the early 1960s?

» The CCP reverted to highly centralised economic planning, returning power to the state planning officials in the central bureaucracy.

» 25 million unemployed urban workers were forced to move back to the countryside.

» Material incentives, including wage differentials for skilled and unskilled workers, were reintroduced.

» Private plots and markets were encouraged in the countryside, although most arable land remained under the control of the communes. By late 1961, CCP local cadres in some provinces were introducing 'household responsibility' schemes whereby individual families contracted to farmland on their own.

» China imported huge amounts of grain from Australia and Canada throughout the 1960s. In 1961, 6 million tons were imported.

» In 1961 the communes were subdivided, reducing them in size by as much as two-thirds. The much smaller unit, the 'production team', became the principal unit of rural organisation and comprised just one village. This marked a major retreat from the radical collectivisation of the late 1950s.

Mao retires to the 'second front'

It appears that, since the early 1950s, Mao had been planning to step back from the day-to-day running of the government and Party and, as he put it, retire to the 'second front', where he would concentrate on strategic thinking and planning, leaving younger colleagues to take over the reins. In accordance with this, Mao gave up his position as PRC Chairman in 1959. This came before the CCP officially declared the Great Leap to have failed. But because of the disasters of the GLF Mao was forced further into the political background than he had anticipated, treated in his words as a "dead ancestor" (respected but not consulted). However, historians disagree about the extent to which Mao's influence was limited in the early 1960s. Philip Short argues that even in 1961-62 Liu and Deng were considerably constrained in what they did by a need to maintain Mao's approval for their policies.

The CCP leadership divides: 1962-65

Q. Why did increasingly bitter faction-fighting develop within the Party?

- From 1962, serious divisions emerged between radical Communists (particularly Mao himself) and the 'pragmatists' or modernisers who supported Liu and Deng's more ideologically flexible economic policies.

- Mao became alarmed about the direction of Deng and Liu's economic reforms. Up until 1962, Mao seems to have continued to regard Liu Shaoqi as his most likely successor. However, in January 1962 Mao began to have serious doubts about Liu after the latter had, at the '7,000-cadre big conference', openly supported the 'household responsibility' system which CCP officials had experimented with in some areas. Mao saw this system as tantamount to abandoning socialism and he was horrified to see it extended so that by the summer of 1962, 20% of arable land was being farmed individually.

- From 1962 onwards, therefore, Mao sought to restore his influence over the CCP. He was desperate to prevent the Party becoming, in his eyes, increasingly 'revisionist' and going further down the 'capitalist road'.

Q. Why did Mao launch the Socialist Education Movement (1962-63)?

» In order to reassert his control, Mao typically turned to mass mobilisation and rectification in the shape of the *Socialist Education Movement*.

» The *Socialist Education Movement* was an attempt to re-educate the masses politically and bring about a fundamental change in the way the Chinese masses saw the world so that they took on new socialist attitudes.

» Mao intended that CCP officials should undergo self-criticism and subject themselves to criticism by the masses.

However, throughout 1962-63, Deng and Liu obstructed Mao's attempt to mobilise the masses. They issued directions which fundamentally altered the Socialist Education Movement; rather than mass mobilisation, the CCP leadership organised work teams to go into schools and factories in order to educate the people and with the objective of identifying and removing corrupt local officials. It would take Mao until 1966 to get a mass campaign off the ground; this became known as the 'Cultural Revolution'.

Q. How did Mao develop his power-base in order to launch the Cultural Revolution?

» Mao was able to rely on the unswerving loyalty of Lin Biao, the Defence Minister from 1959. Lin encouraged a cult of Mao within the People's Liberation Army. In 1963 Lin published Mao's 'Little Red Book', which became daily study for the PLA and the population who as a whole were encouraged to read it as their 'bible'. A fictional work (presented as fact) called the *Diary of Lei Feng* about a lorry driver whose every action was inspired by Mao, was also published in 1963. Both 'The Thoughts of Chairman Mao' ('The Little Red Book') and the *Diary of Lei Feng* became school set texts.

» Mao's wife, Jiang Qing, and a group of radicals known as the Shanghai Forum, promoted the idea of a total transformation of the arts in China, so that all pre-1949 art and literature and all western culture were rejected.

» In 1965-66 the 'Shanghai Forum', led by Jiang Qing and Yao Wenyuan, staged a campaign against Wu Han's play '*The Dismissal of Hai Rai from Office*'. This was not just an argument about culture because they believed that the play was a thinly veiled attack on Mao's dismissal of Marshal Peng in 1959. Hai Rai had been a virtuous medieval official unfairly sacked for criticising a corrupt emperor. The radicals were not just trying to silence one intellectual because Wu Han was also Vice-Mayor of Beijing and his boss and patron, Peng Zhen, Mayor of Beijing, was a close associate of Liu Shaoqi. In June 1966, the Cultural Revolution Committee (a sub-committee of the Politburo), dominated by radical Maoists, purged the so-called Group of Five, including Peng Zhen, who were moderates trying to reconcile the radicals and Pragmatists (Deng and Liu's supporters).

The Cultural Revolution, 1966-76

In 1966, Mao initiated the Cultural Revolution, which caused the greatest disorder in modern Chinese history. Although Mao intended a huge upheaval, it seems clear that events got too far out of the Party's control, even for Mao's liking, and by 1969 the worst of the disruption was halted by action by the CCP and the PLA. However, officially the Cultural Revolution did not end until Mao's death in 1976.

Q. What were Mao's motives in embarking on the Cultural Revolution?

➤ He sought to reassert his authority over the CCP, ending Liu Shaoqi and Deng Xiaoping's influence.

- He was desperate to stop the CCP's movement towards developing an elite of officials and managers.

- He wanted to change cultural values and sought to attack 'bourgeois', western and traditional Chinese values. The historians Roderick MacFarquhar and Michael Schoenhals chose as the title for their major work on the Cultural Revolution, *'Mao's Last Revolution'*; Mao was 73 in 1966 and, conscious of his own mortality, sought to remould the mentality and outlook of the Chinese people.

- Mao intended to restore the CCP's revolutionary zeal. Mao was looking to provide China's young generation with a revolutionary challenge. They were China's future but they had not been through the crucible of the Long March and the Civil War.

Q. How did the Cultural Revolution begin?

- From May 1966 there was growing unrest in the universities, encouraged by visiting members of the Cultural Revolution Group. As the struggle between radical Maoists and the pragmatists intensified, Liu sent work teams into schools and universities to try to prevent the radicals using them to cause disruption. The work teams tried to focus students' criticism on selected targets. However, this time Mao's efforts to launch a radical mass campaign were not to be thwarted. Students and high school pupils in Beijing began to organise themselves in to Red Guard units, dedicated to carrying out Mao's will.

- In July 1966 Mao staged his 'Great Swim' in the Yangzi River in order to demonstrate his virility and that he was 'back'.

- In August 1966 Mao publicly expressed his support for the Red Guard movement in Beijing; this led to Red Guard units being set up all over China. Also in August, Mao, in a wall-poster, called on students to "bombard the [CCP] headquarters" – to seek out and destroy all those who were taking the "capitalist road" within the CCP. The resulting wave of revolutionary enthusiasm was supposedly spontaneous but was orchestrated to a considerable degree from above.

- In August 1966 the first huge Maoist rally of over 1 million Red Guards took place in Tiananmen Square. The PLA took over the railway network on behalf of the radical Maoists and young people were given free transport to Beijing. There, they attended hysterical mass rallies before returning to their homes to seek out those in authority who were taking the capitalist road.

Q. How did the Cultural Revolution develop?

Deng and Liu were dismissed in October 1966. Liu died in prison in 1969. Widespread purges were carried out by the Red Guards. Mao proclaimed 'it is right to rebel' and urged the Red Guards to attack *'the Four Olds'* (old thought, old culture, old practices, old customs). The Red Guards launched violent attacks on 'bad elements' – many CCP officials, teachers, intellectuals and former bourgeoisie were subjected to terrifying psychological and physical assaults. The security Minister, Xie Fuzhi, instructed the police not to intervene to prevent Red Guard violence and Kang Sheng, the head of the secret police, helped Red Guards to identify targets within the Party.

Although the Cultural Revolution originated with organised activism, once started it proved very difficult to control. Schools and universities closed down.

Once the Cultural Revolution started, Mao withdrew to a large degree to central China, leaving Lin Biao and Jiang Qing to direct affairs. Soon clashes developed between rival Red Guard factions and between workers and students. In 1966-67 a democratic workers' movement emerged in Shanghai, which set up the People's Commune. Mao and other party leaders became worried that China was on the verge of civil war. Thousands were killed at Wuzhou in southern China in clashes between rival Red Guard units. In Guangxi province, ceremonial cannibalism of 'Rightists' by Red Guards appears to have occurred.

Zhou Enlai and other moderate Maoists insisted on the restoration of order. In September 1967 Zhou called on the Red Guards to stop their violence and return home. When Red Guard violence did not stop, the PLA sent into restore order. In 1967/68 the PLA was given the key role on new Revolutionary Committees, which were set up in each province. It took a long time to turn off the revolutionary violence, but, by late 1968, the Revolutionary Committees had restored order in most places. In December 1968 Mao called on the Red Guards to leave the cities and go into countryside. 12 million did over the next four years.

Q. Why did Mao retreat from radicalism?

- The purges and violence probably went much further than Mao had intended.

- The emergence of the Shanghai People's Commune threatened the CCP's monopoly of power in China.

- The Cultural Revolution was causing chaos, at a time when the CCP leadership was increasingly worried by the prospect of war with the USSR.

- A number of military commanders, but not Lin Biao, became worried that the purges of the Cultural Revolution might be extended to the PLA.

Q. What were the results of the Cultural Revolution?

a)   The defeat of Liu Shaoqi, Deng Xiaoping and the "revisionists." However, Deng would be rehabilitated in 1973 and helped shape China's economic policies from then on (with the exception of 1976 when he was temporarily disgraced).

b)   The cult of Mao reached its height. In 1969, a new constitution defined 'Marxism-Leninism-Mao-Zedong Thought' as the guiding line of the CCP.

c)   About 500,000 people died (some estimates suggest millions). The main victims were intellectuals and officials, not peasants as in the Great Leap Forward. The prison camp system (*laogai*) expanded.

d)   The period 1968-70 saw the massive transfer of 20 to 30 million urban inhabitants to the countryside.

e)   "May 7th Schools" were set up to re-educate Party officials each year in Maoist thought and by working in the fields.

f)   Education, particularly higher education, was disastrously disrupted. During the Cultural Revolution admission to university was based on 'political consciousness' rather than academic qualifications.

g)   Chinese art and literature became very sterile as Jiang Qing imposed strict controls on what could be displayed, performed and published. The Red Guards destroyed a lot of ancient Chinese art, including Buddhist temples.

h)   The People's Republic became increasingly isolated internationally. Westerners were attacked in China and in August 1967 the British embassy was sacked by a mob.

i)   The economy was not severely damaged by the Cultural Revolution. There was some disruption to industry but by 1970 industrial output had risen to record levels. However, much of the state's investment in 1964-1971 was in the "Third Front", military-industrial development in North-West and South-West China and this was a waste of resources.

Assessing the Cultural Revolution

Mao saw the Cultural Revolution as over by 1970, having defeated his revisionist opponents. However, the period of Maoist indoctrination and domination, which the Cultural Revolution represents, did not end until 1976 (Mao's death).

The Cultural Revolution can be viewed as the escalation of certain features present in the People's Republic since 1949 - namely, public denunciation, struggle sessions and mass mobilisation. It had essentially been an urban phenomenon and the countryside had suffered much less disruption than the towns.

Mao's last years: 1971-76

The Rise and Fall of Lin Biao

Initially Lin Biao seemed to have emerged from the Cultural Revolution in a very strong position. In 1969 he was officially confirmed as Mao's successor and in the same year 10 of the 16 Politburo members were members of the armed forces. However, only 3 of these 10 were supporters of Lin, and, Mao was already having doubts about Lin. In September 1971 Lin mysteriously disappeared; the CCP claimed that he had been planning a coup and an assassination attempt on Mao, and had fled by plane to Russia but had died in a crash over Mongolia.

Lin seems to have been purged by Mao because he was opposed to closer links with the USA. Zhou En-lai pushed for a rapprochement with the USA because of the very strained relations between China and the USSR - in 1969 there had been military clashes along the Sino-Soviet border and the CCP leadership had been alarmed at the Soviet invasion of Czechoslovakia in 1968. Also China needed Western investment to boost its economy. In 1971 Henry Kissinger (the US Secretary of State) secretly visited China and in 1972 the world was stunned by President Nixon's visit to China. The USA withdrew its opposition to the People's Republic entering the United Nations. However, full diplomatic relations were not officially restored until 1979.

Faction struggle continues (1971-76): the Radicals and Pragmatists battle for control of the Party

From 1971 Zhou Enlai and Mao were effectively running the Party but both were ageing and in 1972 Zhou was diagnosed with cancer. Deng Xiaoping was allowed back to Beijing in 1973 and appointed a Vice-Premier. It was not clear whether the radicals or pragmatists would secure control of the Party on Mao's death. There was an on-going debate in the 1970s about the direction of economic policy; the radicals argued for maintaining centralised controls and emphasised the importance of mass mobilisation and production focused on quantity and speed. The modernisers, led by Deng and, up to 1976, Zhou Enlai, stressed gradualism, quality production and the expansion of incentives and wage differentials. In 1975-6 this debate centred around Deng and Zhou's proposed "Four Modernisations."

» The radicals were still a force in the Party, particularly Jiang Qing, Zhang Chunquiao, Yao Wenyuan and Wang Hongwen. In 1973 three of them were appointed to the Politburo; Wang Hongwen, a radical Shanghai trade union leader, was presented as Mao's successor.

» In order to balance the radicals, Mao decided that Deng Xiaoping should be rehabilitated and restored to the Central Committee in 1973.

» In 1973 the radicals launched a propaganda attack on Zhou and his revisionist policies in the so-called *"Criticise Confucius and Lin Biao"* campaign.

» In January 1976 Zhou Enlai died and Mao backed the relatively obscure Hua Guofeng as the new Premier. He was essentially a compromise candidate, a moderate Maoist (between the radicals and pragmatists). In April 1976 Deng was sacked as Vice-Premier, following demonstrations in Tiananmen Square in Zhou Enlai's memory. At this point, Hua Guofeng sided with the radicals against Deng Xiaoping.

» In September 1976 Mao died and, within weeks, Hua Guofeng ordered the arrest of the radicals who were dubbed "the Gang of Four". They were accused of planning a coup and were eventually put on trial in 1980. Jiang was sentenced to death but this was commuted to life imprisonment; she died in 1991.

In 1977 Deng was appointed as number three in the Party hierarchy (CCP Secretary) and he increasingly shaped China's economic policies. From the late 1970s, through to his death in 1997, Deng was the dominant figure in the CCP. He was a moderniser, seeking greater trade with the USA and Japan and introducing reforms such as increased incentives and decentralisation.

Postscript: Deng takes China down the 'capitalist road'

After Mao's death, Deng Xiaoping began to increasingly take China down what Mao would have viewed as the 'capitalist road'.

Agriculture

In the late 1970s Deng introduced two reforms which would lead to a marked increase in agricultural productivity:-

1) From 1979, the peasants were encouraged to maximise the use of their private plots. By 1982 the income from these private plots made up nearly 40% of peasant families' total income.

2) Begun in 1978, but extended throughout China in 1981, the "household responsibility system" was introduced (this amounted to 15% of all cultivated land). Each peasant household could farm its own land (though still technically part of the collective farms) and take responsibility for producing an agreed amount of grain, which the state was obliged to buy. The peasants were allowed to sell any surplus above this quota on the open market.

So, by the late 1970s, the CCP had recognised that collectivisation was not going to allow the development of a modern, efficient agricultural system. Therefore, incentives and greater autonomy for the peasants had to be provided. However, these reforms did not resolve the basic shortage of arable land in China.

Industry

Again, up until the 1980s, there was no fundamental movement away from centralised planning and control of industry. In 1976 a Ten Year Plan was started which concentrated largely on heavy industry and set unrealistically high production targets. However, from the late 1970s major reforms were initiated:

1) In 1978 China abandoned its policy of national economic self-sufficiency and joined the International Monetary Fund and the World Bank. In 1979 four Special Economic Zones were created to attract foreign capital (the PRC provided an improved infrastructure and tax concessions). These measures massively increased foreign investment in China and China's foreign trade (already increased in the 1970s following China's search for better relations with the West). China signed trade agreements with both the USA and Japan in 1978.

2) Greater emphasis was placed on the production of consumer goods in order to provide incentives for workers and peasants.

3) In 1984 state control over industry was reduced, e.g. the fixing of prices by the state was partially ended (it was retained for some goods but market forces were allowed to determine the price of shortage goods). This did lead to significant inflation but also very substantial industrial growth; between 1981 and 1986 China's industrial output nearly doubled.

By 1994 China was the world's fourth largest aggregate economy. However, this progress was achieved at a cost as a number of social problems intensified as a result of this economic growth, including increasing social inequality, rising unemployment and an upsurge in the number of strikes.

The CCP liberalise the economy but maintain political controls: The Democracy Movement and the Tiananmen Square Massacre, 1989

As economic reforms got underway, the 1980s saw demands for greater political freedom, partly stimulated by the Chinese government's policy (from 1978) of sending thousands of students abroad to foreign universities. There were major student demonstrations in 1986.

Students and workers in China were encouraged by Mikhail Gorbachev's reforms in the USSR and by his visit to Beijing in May 1989. The demonstrators, who occupied Tiananmen Square in Beijing, were protesting against a slump in the economy in the late 1980s, which had led to rising unemployment. There was a stand off for some time as the CCP leadership was divided about how to respond. Zhao Ziyang favoured concessions and some liberalisation but Premier Li Ping and, Deng Xiaoping himself, advocated repression. Zhao was sacked and troops were sent in to clear the demonstrators; perhaps a thousand were killed, maybe many more. So the CCP has continued to cling on to single party rule, in spite of the radical departure from Marxism in economic matters. How far this dichotomy (contradiction) can continue remains to be seen.

Chinese Foreign Policy 1949-76

The People's Republic was founded just as the Cold War was developing; this inevitably had profound consequences for the PRC's international relations. For much of the period 1949-76, Mao looked to formulate foreign policy in line with Marxist-Leninist ideas about worldwide revolution – for example, the PRC provided aid to the Huk guerrillas who unsuccessfully tried to establish communist rule in Malaya. However, the desire to export revolution abroad was balanced by considerations of national security. Mao, Zhou Enlai and other CCP leaders were part of the May Fourth generation and consequently they sought to restore Chinese sovereignty and make China in to a great power, as it had been in imperial times before the decline of the Qing dynasty.

The Establishment of the People's Republic of China (1949)

When, in 1945, civil war in China between the CCP and the GMD broke out again, President Truman of the USA sent General George Marshall to China to try unsuccessfully to broker a peace. The Marshall Mission ended in January 1947. In 1945 the USA had helped the GMD by carrying out a massive airlift of GMD troops to Manchuria and in 1948 Congress passed the China Aid Act, but this support was limited as the USA realised how corrupt the GMD government was.

Diplomatic relations severed by the USA

Mao's victory over Chiang Kai-shek in October 1949 came as a shock to the US public. At first it seemed as if the USA might recognise the People's Republic but there was a huge outcry in the USA against Dean Acheson, the US Secretary of State's, statement in August 1950 that China could not have been saved by US intervention. The Republicans accused the Democratic administration of doing too little, too late. Many in the USA feared the spread of Communism all over South-East Asia, especially after the USSR signed a Friendship Treaty with China in February 1950. This coincided with the beginning in America of the Red Scare and McCarthyism. The USA refused to recognise the People's Republic of China until 1979 (though it allowed its admission to the UN in 1971).

The Sino-Soviet Treaty (1950)

Mao's relations with Stalin had never been close. Mao had opposed the pro-Soviet CCP leaders prior to the Civil War and, during the Civil War, Mao received no direct aid from the USSR, except that the Russians handed over captured Japanese weapons in Manchuria to the PLA. As late as spring 1949, Stalin had urged Mao to be content with control of just northern China. Mao was also keen that the Russians withdraw their troops from Lushun (Port Arthur). However, once it became clear that the USA was likely to be hostile to the PRC and, given the PRC's need for economic aid, Mao decided to *'lean to one side'* in the developing Cold War and to do so in the direction of the USSR.

Mao visited Moscow and signed a friendship treaty with the USSR. Stalin agreed to withdraw from Lushun by 1952 but Mao was shocked by the hard bargain that Stalin struck. The treaty provided China with $300 million in loans but in return the USSR was given economic concessions in Xinjiang and Manchuria. This part of the treaty remained secret as Mao was embarrassed that the PRC was making such concessions, a situation reminiscent of the foreign exploitation that prevailed before the Civil War.

The Korean War (1950-53)

Background

Between 1910 and 1945, Japan had ruled Korea. In September 1945 the Korean People's Republic was set up by a coalition of nationalists and communists who supported land reform. In the same month a right-wing group called the Korean Democratic Party was founded. In August 1945 Soviet troops occupied the north of Korea, while US troops occupied the south in September. The dividing line of the occupying forces was arbitrarily set at the 38th parallel.

During 1946 the USA and USSR helped set up rival governments: Syngman Rhee led the Republic of Korea in the South, Kim Il-Sung led the Democratic People's Republic of Korea in the North. In 1949 Soviet troops left the north, confident the South would collapse of its own. Later that same year US troops withdrew from South Korea.

The North invades the South (June 1950)

In January 1950 Dean Acheson, the US Secretary of State, delivered his "perimeter speech" in which he outlined which areas of Asia the USA was committed to defending; in it, he did not refer to Korea or Taiwan. Acheson was probably anxious to restrain Rhee from attacking the north. However, it seems to have encouraged Kim Il-Sung to believe that the USA would not intervene if North Korea invaded South Korea.

Kim visited Moscow in 1949 and was refused permission to invade South Korea; however, on a second visit in 1950, Stalin agreed but he told Kim to consult Mao before going ahead. There is no evidence that Mao was keen on the scheme but he was grateful to the Korean Communists who had provided 100,000 troops during the battle for Manchuria in 1946-47.

In June 1950 North Korea invaded the South. The USA decided that the invasion was a test of containment and got the UN, in the absence of the USSR, to agree to send troops to Korea. The USSR was temporarily boycotting the UN in protest at the PRC's exclusion from the UN.

Initially the North Koreans swept easily through the South, so by September 1950 South Korean and UN forces were confined to the 'Pusan Pocket' at the southern tip of South Korea. However, in September 1950, General MacArthur audaciously turned the tide of the war by launching an amphibious landing at Inchon, deep inside North Korean held territory. Soon the North Koreans were fleeing back over the 38th Parallel and US policy changed from simply driving the North Koreans out of the South to liberating the whole of Korea from communism. The UN advance towards the China's border led to the intervention of 200,000 Chinese troops.

Many within the Chinese Politburo, including Lin Biao, had argued against intervening in the Korean War, particularly as Stalin would not agree to providing Soviet support. However, Mao, backed by Peng Dehuai, managed to persuade the Politburo to send in Chinese troops in late October 1950. This proved brilliantly successful and the Chinese 'People's Volunteers' as they were called, forced the UN forces back over the 38th Parallel and captured Seoul, the South's capital. Mao now got over ambitious and sought to unify Korea under communist rule; Chinese troops suffered huge losses and the UN recaptured Seoul. Mao now supported ceasefire negotiations which began in July 1951. However, it took until July 1953 for an armistice to be arranged, which left Korea divided at the 38th Parallel.

Q. What were the Korean War's results?

- In many ways the Korean War was a triumph for Mao as the PRC had saved North Korea and stood up to the world's greatest military power.

- However, this was earned at great cost; the Chinese suffered between 400,000 and 800,000 casualties.

- Furthermore, the Korean War led the USA to commit itself to the defence of Taiwan and to supporting the French in their struggle against the Vietminh (in Vietnam).

- The USA also sought to contain communism in SE Asia by the creation of SEATO (1954), which was an alliance of South East Asian states; its members were the USA, GB, France, Australia, New Zealand, the Philippines, Pakistan and Thailand.

Taiwan

In 1949, Chiang Kai-shek's Nationalist government had withdrawn to the island of Taiwan. The USA continued to recognise it as the rightful government of China and blocked the PRC's admission to the UN until 1971. In 1954, the USA signed a Defence Treaty with Taiwan when the PRC threatened the islands of Quemoy and Matsu (held by the Nationalists). In 1958, the PRC again threatened the two islands, and the USA sent the 7th Fleet to patrol off Taiwan. On both occasions the PRC backed down, partly because the USSR was unwilling to support the PRC in this dispute.

The Sino-Soviet Split

As the CCP became increasingly self-confident, its leadership became less willing to accept a subordinate role in the Communist bloc. The CCP leaders were angry about Khrushchev's Destalinisation speech (1956) because the CCP had praised Stalin in public. Mao strongly disagreed with Khrushchev's policy of peaceful co-existence. He saw conditions as very different in SE Asia where violent conflict could and did work, e.g. in Vietnam. The Soviet leadership saw Mao as dangerously reckless and Khrushchev soon regretted promising to help the PRC build an A-bomb. The Russians were alarmed by Mao's comments that the world could survive a nuclear war and that it would be the capitalists who would perish.

Sino-Soviet relations really deteriorated from 1958 when Mao felt that Khrushchev had not given the PRC sufficient support in the second crisis over the GMD islands of Quemoy and Matsu. 1959 saw Khrushchev renege on his promise to help develop a Chinese atom bomb and Mao was angered by Khrushchev's public criticism of the Great Leap Forward. He suspected Marshall Peng Dehuai had been conspiring with Khrushchev against Mao when Peng had visited Moscow in March 1959. In 1960 Khrushchev abruptly withdrew all Soviet engineers and technicians from China. In 1960 the split became public when the Chinese and Russian communist parties clashed at a congress of in Bucharest.

In 1962 Khrushchev publicly criticised the PRC's behaviour in the Sino-Indian border war; this hurt the CCP leadership as it seems clear now that the Indians were the aggressors. In the same year the CCP angered Khrushchev by their criticism of his conduct during the Cuban Missile Crisis, arguing that he had capitulated to Kennedy. The CCP denounced the Test Ban Treaty of 1963; it was seen as Soviet-Imperialist collaboration to deny the PRC the atom bomb. In 1963 Deng Xiaoping led a delegation to Moscow for a final attempt to heal the rift but these talks failed and this marked the end of formal contact between the two countries for 26 years. The low-point in Sino-Soviet relations came in 1969 with military clashes along their border at Damansky Island in the Ussuri River.

Rapprochement with the USA (1971-72)

In 1971-72, Mao, after years of denouncing the Russians' policy of peaceful co-existence, shocked the world by resuming diplomatic relations with the USA. This reflects Mao's concerns about the risks of war with the USSR. This about-turn in Mao's foreign policy did much to facilitate the general improvement in East-West relations in the early 1970s known as 'Détente'. It also laid the foundations for the huge growth in China's foreign trade, which, along with Deng Xiaoping's reforms from the 1980s, led to China becoming a global economic force and, consequently, a global political player.

China and the 'Third World'

China developed strong links with a number of Asian and African countries, in part as an attempt to promote worldwide revolution but also to extend China's influence. Mao's brand of Marxism, with its emphasis on peasant revolution, had potentially greater appeal to "Third World" countries. The CCP supplied weapons to the Vietminh in their struggle with the French and later with the Americans; they also provided aid for communist guerrillas in Malaysia, the Philippines and Burma but none of these movements proved successful.

At the Bandung Conference (Indonesia) in 1955, Zhou Enlai raised the PRC's international profile by taking a lead in creating the 'non-aligned' movement of African and Asian states, which sought to avoid domination by the more advanced western countries. The PRC provided economic aid to several African countries, for example, helping build the Tan-Zam Railway.

Chronology of Key Events

1911	Revolution of the Double Tenth against the Qing Dynasty
1912	Emperor Pu Yi abdicates; Yuan Shikai became President
1916	Yuan Shikai's death; start of the Warlord Era
1919	May Fourth Movement; protest at Versailles Treaty
1921	Creation of the Chinese Communist Party
1923	First United Front between GMD and CCP
1925	Death of Sun Yatsen; succeeded as GMD leader by Chiang Kai-shek
1926	Northern Expedition
1927	White Terror in Shanghai GMD government established at Nanjing Mao Zedong sets up Jiangxi Soviet
1931	Japanese invasion of Manchuria
1934	Beginning of the Long March
1935	Mao chosen as Chairman at Zunyi Conference End of Long March; CCP set up base at Yanan
1936	Xian Incident (Chiang kidnapped)
1937	Second United Front Marco Polo Bridge Incident; start of Sino-Japanese War
1938	GMD government moves to Chongqing
1940	Mao publishes 'On New Democracy'
1942	Mao's Rectification Campaign
1944	Operation Ochigo (major Japanese offensive against GMD)
1945	World War Two ended with the Japanese surrender
1946	US Marshall Mission failed to prevent renewal of civil war
1948	The PLA won the Battle for Manchuria and the Battle of Huai-Hai
1949	Chiang fled to Taiwan; People's Republic of China established.
1950	The PLA invaded Tibet Mao visited Moscow; Sino-Soviet Friendship Treaty Land Reform; perhaps 2 million landlords were killed Outbreak of Korean War; China intervened on North Korea's side Campaign against Counter-Revolutionaries
1951	Three Antis campaign; aimed at corrupt officials
1952	Five Antis campaign; aimed at corrupt businessmen
1953	First Five Year Plan started End of the Korean War

1954   Constitution introduced; China officially a one-party state

1957   The Hundred Flowers campaign; followed by Anti-Rightist campaign

1958   Beginning of the Great Leap Forward
CCP shelled Jinmen (Quemoy) and Matsu

1959   Beginning of severe famine which lasted into 1961
Marshal Peng Dehuai sacked after criticising Mao at the Lushan
Conference; Mao stepped down as Head of State (Chairman)

1960   Soviet experts withdrawn from China; the Great Leap abandoned; Liu
Shaoqi and Deng Xiaoping entrusted with economic recovery.

1962   Border clashes between China and India
Socialist Education Movement announced by Mao

1963   Publication of *"Quotations from Chairman Mao Zedong"*

1964   China exploded first atom bomb

1966   Start of the Cultural Revolution

1968   Clamp down on the Red Guards

1971   Mysterious death of Lin Biao
Henry Kissinger's secret visit to China
People's Republic admitted to the United Nations

1972   President Nixon visits Beijing

1973   Deng Xiaoping rehabilitated

1976   Death of Zhou Enlai
Death of Mao Zedong
Hua Guofeng orders arrest of the 'Gang of Four'

Revision and essay writing activities on the Rise and Rule of the Chinese Communist Party

Below, you will find two essay questions, which cover most of the issues that I have dealt with in the China section of the Revision Guide. By examining these questions, you will be able to test your understanding and recall of that material, as well as gaining insights into how to construct responses to IB essay questions. I have given you some ideas about how they could be tackled and then provided you with space to add examples and further points.

1. How successful was Mao Zedong as ruler of China between 1949 and 1976?

In answering this question, first it is necessary to point out that though Mao dominated the CCP, there were times when his influence on CCP policy was less complete, for example in the aftermath of the Great leap Forward when Liu Shaoqi and Deng Xiaoping led China's economic recovery. Next it is necessary to identify what Mao's aims were. The question does not specify foreign or domestic policy, so both areas of policy should be considered. Below I have started by examining briefly some of the differing historical interpretations surrounding his aims and then listed what his main aims were. Following this, I have created a detailed plan, which evaluates Mao's success in certain areas of policy. I have also indicated other aims that would merit assessment in this essay and I have left space for you to provide your own points and examples/evidence you might use in answering this question.

What were Mao's aims?

Mao's recent biographers, Jung Chang and Jon Halliday have argued that the paramount consideration for Mao was securing and maintaining his own control over the Party; that a lust for power and indeed violence was what drove Mao as ruler of China. However, other, rather more balanced biographies, such as Philip Short's, whilst accepting that Mao sought to dominate the Party at all times, portray Mao as a politician whose aims were shaped by his Marxist ideology (though a 'sinified' version) and by China's weakness and exploitation by foreigners since the 19th Century.

- In the short-term Mao was intent on consolidating Communist political control and promoting economic recovery after the Japanese War and the Civil War; so full-blooded socialist policies were postponed.
- To create a classless society and build a socialist economy
- To raise living standards and and promote social reform for China's masses
- As well as seeking to maintain the CCP's monopoly of power, Mao was intent on retaining his own ascendancy over the Party.
- To create a communist culture among China's population and prevent the sort of "back-sliding" that had occurred in the USSR: need for *continuous revolution*.
- To make China into a modern power, freeing it from foreign domination.
- To help spread communist revolution in Asia.

How successful was Mao?

1. In terms of consolidation of power and maintaining political control?
A single party state was created and maintained up to and beyond Mao's death.

• The PLA quickly established control over most of what had been the Chinese Empire (e.g. invasion of Tibet, 1950). This was in great contrast to GMD failure. China was run by 6 military commissions until 1954.
• Use of mass organisations (e.g. Women's Federation) to reach the public and of mass campaigns.
• Expansion of CCP membership; 2.7million in 1947, 6.1 million by 1953.
• Creation of a single party state by 1954; CCP continued to pursue *New Democracy* until 1954; People's Consultative Conference (1949) established temporary constitution; other parties tolerated to a degree (less so after 1950) until formal constitution of 1954. At first, CCP prepared to keep most of the 2 million+ GMD officials in their posts; only 750,000 CCP cadres available.
• Terror against opponents - Campaign against Counter-Revolutionaries (1950); purges of dissidents, e.g. the Anti-Rightist campaign (1957).
• Use of secret police, e.g. Kang Sheng, Head of Security Forces, organised purges during the Cultural Revolution, and establishment of prison camps (laogai).

2. Economic recovery after the Japanese War and the Civil War?
This was completed by 1953.

• National Capitalism until 1953; many factory owners allowed to retain ownership until the Five Year Plan (1953-7) and the CCP employed the vast majority of GMD officials who had worked for the National Resources Commission. This reflects CCP's lack of urban experience.
• Inflation brought under control (down to 15% p.a. in 1951); infrastructure repaired and communications expanded (railways increased by 33% to 24,000km by 1953); the economy did recover by 1953 (grain production was 10% higher than 1936).

3. To make China into a modern economic power?
Though progress was made in 1953-57 and 1961-65, China was not a major world economic power by Mao's death, partly because of his disastrous policies in 1958-60 and from 1966.

• The First Five Year Plan had led to impressive growth in heavy industry (grew at 9% p.a. compared to India in 1950s whose industrial growth was less than 2%) but Mao was disappointed at agricultural growth (just 3.7% p.a. and the population increased by 2.4% p.a.) and wanted rapidly to catch up with the West; hence the radical Great Leap Forward (1958-60). Its results were disastrous; China's economic development was put back. Gross National Income fell by 30% between 1958 & 1960; the harvest in 1960 was 26% less than in 1957.
• Recovery under Liu and Deng 1961-65: heavy industrial output had doubled by 1965, aided by the discovery of the Daqing oilfield; by 1965, grain output had recovered to 1957 level but population had risen by 80 million. The economy was further disrupted by the Cultural Revolution (1966-76), though not that badly. However, much of the state's investment in 1964-1971 was in the "Third Front", military-industrial development in North-West and South-West China and this was a waste of resources.

Limited progress in agriculture (average p.a. increase in grain production 1957-78 was just 2%, China's population roughly doubled in the period 1949-1990); foreign trade hardly increased at all between 1959 and 1970 (by less than 0.5%).

China took off as a modern industrial power only in the 1980s and 1990s as a result of Deng Xiaoping's reforms; Deng introduced elements of capitalism and the free market and encouraged trade/investment from the West. China's economy grew at 9% p.a. 1977-2000.

4. How far had Mao created a classless society and socialist economy?
By the mid-1950s the old ruling elites had been eliminated and private enterprise ended.

....

....

....

....

....

....

....

....

5. How far was Mao successful in creating 'socialist man'?
Mao failed to inculcate communist values among the population at large and despite frequent rectification campaigns, was unable to prevent CCP officials emerging as a new ruling elite.

....

....

....

....

....

....

....

....

....

6. How far did Mao raise living standards and promote social reform?

There was some progress in terms of social reform, notably in provision of health care and primary education, but living standards did not rise significantly until after Mao's death.

....

....

....

....

....

....

....

....

7. How far did Mao make China into a world power, promoting communist revolution?

The PRC ended foreign domination of China and built powerful armed forces, becoming a nuclear power, but attempts to promote communist revolution largely failed and in the 1970s Mao abandoned permanent revolution.

....

....

....

....

....

....

Conclusion:

....

....

....

....

....

....

2. Identify the main principles of Communism and assess how far these principles were put into practice by Mao Zedong.

In answering this question, it will be necessary first to explain what the main principles of Communism are, as derived originally from Karl Marx. Having done this, each of the following paragraphs should focus on a particular principle and assess how far Mao adhered (or indeed intended to adhere) to it. It is imperative that you evaluate the extent to which Mao followed communist principles, rather than just the ways in which he did. Therefore, Mao's deviation from communist principles must also be examined. Below I have written an introduction, the first two paragraphs and a conclusion. In addition, I have provided you with the first sentence of several other paragraphs and then left you space to expand and illustrate that first, key sentence and to include an alternative conclusion or other points.

Karl Marx, in his '*Communist Manifesto*', argued that human history was shaped by class struggle and that all societies would pass through two stages of revolution; a bourgeois revolution and a proletarian revolution. The proletarian revolution would be the result of the growing exploitation of the working class by the capitalist bourgeoisie in a fully industrialised society. Following the revolution, the dictatorship of the proletariat would be established in which the enemies of the proletariat would be eliminated and private ownership would give way to collective ownership and a classless society operating on the principle of "from each according to his ability and to each according to his needs". Mao Zedong, the leader of the Chinese Communist Party, incorporated the main principles of communism into his policies, seeking not only to create a socialist economy but also a socialist culture in China. However, responding to China's particular circumstances, Mao did alter some of Marx's ideas, particularly in relation to the peasants, and formed his own Chinese version of communism, which became known as Mao Zedong Thought.

The most important deviation that Mao made from orthodox Marxist principle was to focus on the peasants, rejected by Marx as incapable of revolutionary consciousness, rather than the proletariat, as the primary revolutionary class. The fundamental reason for this alteration was pragmatic: China, still highly agricultural and way behind the USSR and other countries in industrialisation, had a tiny proletarian class in the first half of the 20th century, while there were hundreds of millions of peasants. Implementation of land reform and rent reduction in the areas under CCP control during the Yanan era and the expropriation of the landlord class in 1950 earned the party widespread peasant support.

Mao also revised Marx in the policy he adopted towards the bourgeoisie during the 1940s. In an article entitled 'On New Democracy', he suggested that there should be two stages of revolutions; the bourgeois–democratic stage in which capitalism would still play a role, and which would be fought by a 'joint revolutionary-democratic dictatorship' of four classes: the peasants, the proletariat, the 'national bourgeoisie' and the petite bourgeoisie, and the proletarian or socialist revolution which would follow later. Mao's purpose was to broaden the CCP's appeal beyond the peasants, so he had to pragmatically revise communist ideology, thus casting the CCP as a nationalist party representing the vast majority of the Chinese people in their fight against Japanese occupation and GMD corruption.

Mao was genuinely committed to the Marxist principle of collective rather than private ownership of property and resources, although for the first phase of CCP rule, known as National Capitalism, Mao did not attempt to implement socialist restructuring of the economy and society.

....

....

....

....

....

....

....

....

....

Although, Mao was a firm believer in Marxist principles, he developed further Leon Trotsky's idea of permanent or continuous revolution, itself a revision of Marxism. Mao believed in the need for a succession of revolutions, including regular rectification campaigns, in order to foster a socialist outlook among both the Party and the people.

....

....

....

....

....

....

....

....

....

....

Mao not only aimed at the development of communism in China but also in other parts of the world, in the spirit of 'worldwide revolution'; again another Leninist/Trotskyite revision of Marxism.

....

....

....

....

....

....

My conclusion

Although Mao often acted pragmatically, chiefly in the years before 1954, and, like Lenin in Russia, revised certain aspects of Marxism to suit his purposes and Chinese conditions, he did attempt to instigate the main principles of communism and they played a major role in most of his key decisions. However, when Mao tried too hastily to build a communist utopia, notably in the Great Leap Forward and the Cultural Revolution, the result was disaster on an unprecedented scale. The People's Republic made much greater progress, in the years 1949-57, 1961-65 and most dramatically from 1977 onwards, towards driving up the living standards of the working classes, one of Marxism's ultimate goals, when pragmatists such as Deng Xiaoping, guided by the view that it does not matter what colour the cat if it catches the mouse, were shaping CCP policy.

Your conclusion/other points you might wish to include:

....

....

....

....

....

....

....

....

....

....

THE RISE AND RULE OF THE SINGLE PARTY STATE IN ITALY

NB   Mussolini is not a named individual on the Paper 2 syllabus but can be used in open questions which are set on single party and authoritarian states.

The Origins of the Single Party State

Overview

Italy was only formed as a unified country in 1861. Prior to that it had been made up of a series of independent states and a bloc of territory, Lombardy and Venetia, belonging to the Austrian Empire. The 1859 War between Austria, on the one hand, and Piedmont and France, on the other, launched the unification process, which, by 1861, incorporated most, but not all, of the Italian peninsula. In 1866 Italy fought alongside Prussia against Austria and was rewarded with Venetia. The new Italian state was a constitutional monarchy under the House of Savoy. Initially the capital was Turin, the capital of Piedmont, which had led the process of unification. However, in 1870 the French troops garrisoning Rome were removed and Rome became the new capital of Italy. The Pope withdrew to the Vatican and, from then until 1929, relations between the Italian state and the Papacy were hostile.

The period between 1861 and 1922 is normally referred to as 'Liberal Italy'. During the First World War, Italy at first remained neutral but, after bitter arguments during the 'Intervention Crisis', Prime Minister Antonio Salandra led Italy into the war on the side of Britain and France in 1915. The post-war years were marked by economic and political crises and saw the emergence of the Fascist movement.

In 1922 King Victor Emmanuel III appointed Benito Mussolini, the leader and founder of Fascism, Prime Minister in a coalition government. Three years later Mussolini established a Fascist dictatorship, which was to last until 1943. Mussolini allied Italy to Hitler's Germany and the Second World War led to Mussolini's downfall after Italy's disastrous performance in the war. In 1943, Mussolini was dismissed by King Victor Emmanuel III and arrested, but he was then rescued by German troops and installed as the puppet ruler of the Salo Republic in northern Italy. In 1945 Mussolini was captured and shot by Italian communist partisans.

Q. What conditions led to the establishment of a single party state in Italy?

'Liberal Italy' suffered from a number of chronic weaknesses, which formed part of the context out of which Fascism emerged in 1919. However, these weaknesses did not make the rise of Fascism inevitable. Other factors need to be considered in order to explain why parliamentary rule failed and why, when it failed, it was replaced by a Fascist dictatorship, rather than by a socialist republic or a more authoritarian monarchy.

1. Long-term causes/weaknesses 1861-1914

(a) The process of unification had been largely artificial and only a minority of Italians had a developed sense of national consciousness. As D'Azeglio commented, shortly after unification, *"We have made Italy, now we have to make Italians."*

To a large extent Piedmont had absorbed the rest of the Italian states and then imposed its laws, political system and administration on the rest of the peninsula. Consequently regional loyalties remained strong, particularly in the South, and the government based in Rome commanded little in the way of popular support. The 'question of the South' remained a huge issue throughout the period, as the peasants of the South continued to live in poverty and illiteracy while the North forged ahead economically and socially.

(b) The mass of Italians had no involvement in, and, little interest in, the political system that operated in Italy prior to 1912.

Historians agree that in this period there was a fundamental division between 'legal' Italy - the upper and middle classes who dominated the political system and 'real' Italy – the peasant masses and the small but growing industrial proletariat. Until 1881 only half a million Italians out of a total population of 32 million had the vote; the electorate was then expanded but still only comprised about 2 million voters until the 1912 the electoral law enfranchised all men aged over 30.

(c) There was a damaging rift between the Italian state and the Catholic Church, which undermined support for the former among the mass of devout churchgoing Italians.

This stand-off was the result of both the absorption of the Papal States and Rome by the Italian kingdom during the process of unification and the anti-clerical (anti-Church) policies pursued by the liberals. Until 1904 the Vatican instructed Catholics not to vote in parliamentary elections.

(d) Government during the period of 'Liberal Italy' had a reputation for corruption and pursuing narrow class interests.

Although there were frequent changes of government, these rarely constituted a different political direction as most politicians, as the historian John Pollard put it, were "merely of different shadings of a broadly liberal-conservative hue." The system by which the different liberal leaders constructed their governments, using patronage networks, bribery and vote-rigging, is known as *'trasformismo'*. The liberal politicians represented the interests of the upper and middle classes and did little for the masses, for example, responding to industrial unrest in the 1890s with brutal repression.

(e) There was growing working-class and peasant unrest from the 1890s, culminating in the General Strike of 1914.

In the late 19th century Italy, particularly the South, was backward economically, both in terms of its agriculture and industry. However, from the 1890s major economic changes began to occur. Agriculture in parts of the North, particularly the fertile Po Valley, started to modernise with the introduction of chemical fertilisers and machinery. This put immense strain on small peasant farmers who struggled to compete with the bigger landowners who were turning to capitalist farming methods. Industry also took off from 1896 onwards, particularly in the North-West, with the rapid growth of heavy industries such as steel, shipbuilding and hydro-electric power. This led to the development of a growing industrial proletariat.

These socio-economic changes led to the development of working-class movements; trade unions and peasant leagues proliferated. In 1892 the Italian Socialist Party (PSI) was founded. A down-turn in the world economy in the 1890s, combined with bad harvests, sparked off strikes and land seizures, which the liberal government met with force, closing down many trade unions and even banning the PSI for a time.

(f)   The failure of liberal governments to reconcile the masses.

The only liberal politician who recognised the need to reconcile the mass of the Italian people to the government was Giovanni Giolitti who dominated Italian politics in the first decade and a half of the 20th century (he was Prime Minister three times in the period 1903-14). Unlike other liberal politicians, Giolitti tried to create a working relationship with the moderate wing of the PSI and win popular support by means of welfare and electoral reform. Giolitti also sought to improve relations with the Papacy by permitting religious education in schools where the local authorities approved.

Unfortunately, after some initial success, Giolitti's strategy failed partly because the economic growth of the early 1900s gave way to a serious recession (1909 onwards) and partly because Giolitti's decision to pursue colonies led him to seize Libya from Turkey, which infuriated the PSI. In 1912 the PSI, which was split between a revolutionary 'Maximalist' wing and a more moderate 'Reformist' wing, swung towards the extreme left and rejected the idea of working with the liberal parties.

(g)   Giolitti's decision to broaden political participation backfired.

Giolitti decided to extend the vote to the majority of adult males in 1912 in the hope that this would give the mass of Italians a stake in the political system. However, the liberal parties proved incapable of adapting to democratic politics and it was the PSI who benefited most by the enlargement of the electorate. This trend was increased after the First World War when the PSI and PPI (a Catholic party founded in 1919) became the largest parties, leaving the liberals struggling to maintain their domination of the Italian Chamber (the lower house of Parliament).

(h)   Many Italians blamed the liberal governments before the First World War for failing to make Italy either a great or an imperial power. Furthermore, Italian nationalists regarded unification as incomplete because many Italian-speakers still lived in 'unredeemed' parts of the Austrian Empire.

After unification many Italians expected Italy to become one of the great European powers. However, its economic backwardness and relatively small population meant that Italy did not achieve that status. The late 19th century saw the European powers engaged in the 'scramble for Africa'; however, Italy made only meagre gains in the shape of Eritrea (1885) and part of Somaliland (1889). The attempt to conquer Abyssinia ended in disaster and humiliation at the Battle of Adowa in 1896. Giolitti did succeed in wresting Libya off Turkey in 1911 in a very expensive campaign.

The failure of the liberal governments to make Italy into a Great Power, led to the rise of Nationalism as an aggressive and restless force in Italian politics, critical of the weakness of the government. The Italian Nationalist Association was established in 1910, with Enrico Corradini its leading figure. At the same time, the poet, Filippo Marinetti, founded an influential artistic movement, known as Futurism. The Futurists glorified mechanisation and war and criticised 'Liberal Italy' for its feebleness.

2. Medium and Short-Term Causes: 1914-22

(a) The Impact of the Intervention Crisis (1914-15)

Italian politicians were bitterly divided by the 'Intervention Crisis'. When the First World War broke out in August 1914, Italy remained neutral. Since 1882, it had been part of the Triple Alliance with Germany and Austria-Hungary. However, over the course of autumn 1914 through to spring 1915, a political debate raged over whether Italy should join the war.

Those who favoured intervention included:

- Right-wing liberals, notably the Prime Minister, Antonio Salandra and the Foreign Minister, Sidney Sonnino. They hoped that intervention on the side of the Triple Entente (Britain, France and Russia) would result in Italy gaining Italian-speaking areas of the Austrian Empire, such as Trieste and the South Tyrol. They also expected the war to strengthen the Liberal state by rallying Italians around the government's war effort. Salandra was the driving force behind the Treaty of London (April 1915), which Italy signed with Britain and France. Salandra persuaded King Victor Emmanuel to approve the treaty but the Italian Chamber was not consulted in the negotiations.

- The Nationalists and Futurists who believed war would galvanise and unite the Italian people and lead to the 'redemption' of the Italian-speaking areas still under Austrian rule.

- Left-wing interventionists included revolutionary syndicalists who had either broken away from the PSI in the years before the war or did so in 1914-15. In the latter category, the most important figure was the editor of the Socialist newspaper, *Avanti*, Benito Mussolini who had originally opposed the war but from October 1914 argued in favour of intervention. He was promptly expelled by the PSI. Revolutionary syndicalists argued that the war would transform society, possibly lead to revolution and, in the process, destroy 'Liberal Italy'.

  Mussolini founded the newspaper '*Popolo d'Italia*' to press for intervention. Left-wing interventionists formed *fasci di azione rivoluzionaria* (revolutionary action groups) to campaign and demonstrate in favour of intervention; these groups can be seen as the forerunners to the later Fascist movement.

Those who opposed intervention included:

- Giolitti and his supporters among the liberals. Most of the Chamber opposed the decision to sign the Treaty of London. Giolittians saw no advantage to be gained from entering the war.

- The PSI attacked the war as an imperialist war and campaigned against intervention.

- On the whole, the Catholic Church was not in favour of Italy joining the war, particularly as Catholic Austria would be Italy's main enemy in the war.

(b)   The Impact of the First World War on Italy (1915-18)

The Italian army fought on a front in Northern Italy against the Austrians and Germans. Three years of largely static, trench-warfare cost Italy 600,000 dead. In October 1917 Italy suffered a major defeat at Caporetto, which saw the Austrians and Germans advance over 100 kilometres. Right at the end of the war in October 1918 Italy scored a victory over the Austrians at Vittorio Veneto.

o   The war widened the political and social divisions within Italy, rather than uniting Italians as many of the interventionists had hoped. The intervention crisis split the liberals irrevocably.

o   5 million Italians served in the armed forces and many of them, particularly the junior officers and NCOs who were drawn largely from the lower middle class, were politicised by the experience. They blamed the liberal politicians for mismanaging the war and hated the Socialists for failing to support the war.

o   The Italian economy was mobilised to support 'total war'. Industrial output expanded rapidly, for example, Fiat's production of vehicles went up by 500% during the war, whilst its workforce grew from 4000 to 40,000. Inevitably this would lead to huge economic dislocation when the war ended and the economy reverted to a peace-time footing.

o   Inflation and food shortages became serious issues, with prices quadrupling between 1914 and 1918. To finance the war, the Italian government borrowed greatly. The government spent 148,000 million lire on the war; that was twice the total government expenditure in the entire period 1861-1914.

o   There was growing unrest among the industrial working class as they suffered from price inflation, shortages and military-style discipline in factories producing war-related goods. In August 1917, the police and army killed 50 protestors in Turin after working-class demonstrations against prices and shortages. The increased militancy of the industrial workers was reflected in the expansion of trade union membership and the growth of the PSI.

(c)   The Post-War Crisis (1918-22)

Italy faced serious economic, social and political crises after the First World War. These crises provided Mussolini with the opportunity to create, and, then rapidly expand, his new Fascist movement. There was nothing inevitable about Mussolini's rise to power but what is certain is that the liberal politicians who had controlled Italy for the past 50 years proved incapable of coping with the difficult post-war conditions.

Although, at first sight, post-war Italian politics saw 'business as usual' with 4 of the 5 governments of the period 1918-22 led by liberal politicians - Orlando, Nitti, Giolitti and Facta (Bonomi, a moderate socialist was the odd man out) - this impression is highly misleading.

The Liberals' grip on power was very fragile as their traditional political control was undermined by the following:

1. The advent of democracy and mass politics; an end to 'trasformismo'

During the war, the Liberals had promised the extension of the vote to all adult males and duly introduced universal male suffrage (December 1918) and proportional representation (August 1919). However, the Liberals did not adapt to the new era of mass politics. As the historian Martin Kitchen has observed, it was *'no longer possible to control parliament by the traditional liberal methods of political horse trading and influence peddling known as trasformismo".* In the 1919 elections, the Liberals gained less than half the seats in the Chamber while the PSI and the newly formed Catholic party, the PPI, or Popolari, emerged as the biggest parties. The Popolari won 100 seats whilst the PSI gained 156 and its membership expanded from 50,000 to 200,000 in 1918-20.

The governments of 1918-22 were all highly unstable because the three major groups or groupings (the Liberals were not a united party as such) proved incapable of working together to form strong coalition governments. The PSI and the Popolari were unwilling and unable to work together because the Socialists (PSI) were hostile to the influence of the Catholic Church. Furthermore, the Liberals could not create an effective working partnership with either the Popolari – because the Liberals were anti-clerical – or the Socialists because of the Socialists' commitment to extensive (indeed radical in the case of the PSI's left-wing) social and economic reform. The PPI did join some of the Liberal coalitions of the period but the PPI-Liberal partnership was always fraught with difficulties and so none of these coalitions endured long.

Italian politics became increasingly fragmented in the post-war period, with the Liberals struggling to construct majorities in the Chamber to support the government. The result was a series of short-lived coalition governments, which undermined many Italians' confidence in the democratic parliamentary system. In 1921, the rise of the Fascists as an electoral force and the breakaway by revolutionary socialists to found the Italian Communist Party (PCI) increased the political polarisation and instability. The 1921 elections saw the PNF (Fascists) win 35 seats in the Chamber, the PSI (Socialists) and PCI (Communists) win 138 and the PPI 108. In all, there were 13 different groupings in the Chamber in 1921.

2. The 'mutilated victory'

Italian Nationalists were furious at the terms of the peace treaties signed in Paris in 1919 and they were able to create the impression that the Italian army's victories had been betrayed by Italy's Allies who failed to give Italy greater gains and by the Italian government of Vittorio Orlando for not standing up sufficiently for Italy's interests. Italy was granted South Tyrol, Trieste and Trentino but did not receive Fiume or Dalmatia.

The nationalist poet, Gabriele D'Annunzio, coined the phrase 'the mutilated victory', to characterise the disappointment Italian patriots felt at having won the war but 'lost the peace'. D'Annunzio led a force of 2000 ex-soldiers, Nationalists and Futurists, and occupied Fiume in September 1919 in protest at the Italian government's decision to hand it over to Yugoslavia as the Treaty of St Germain dictated. The government of Francesco Nitti felt unable to drive D'Annunzio out, so the occupation continued until Giolitti returned as Prime Minister and ejected D'Annunzio and his paramilitaries in December 1920.

3. Economic crisis and social unrest

The transition from wartime to peacetime economy proved very painful for Italy. Inflation continued to rise rapidly - prices increased by 50% in 1918-20, hitting those on fixed incomes and those with savings particularly hard. Unemployment rose steeply as 2.5 million Italian soldiers were demobilised and many found no jobs to return home to. Unemployment peaked at 2 million in late 1919. In 1921 the US government placed strict restrictions on immigration into the USA; this worsened the plight of the poor in southern Italy, many of who had in the past sought escape in the form of emigration to the USA.

The Biennio Rosso (1919-20)

The years 1919-20 were marked by huge social unrest and became known as the Biennio Rosso (the 'two red years'). Radical socialists hoped to emulate Russia and stage a Bolshevik-style revolution, whilst many middle and upper class Italians feared for their property in the event of an Italian 'October' (Revolution).

Q. What were the key features of the Biennio Rosso?

• Once the war ended, many southern peasants, led by socialist land leagues seized uncultivated land left fallow by large landowners. The government inadvertently encouraged this because, after the disaster at Caporetto (October 1917), it had sought to maintain the troops' morale by promising land reform. The governments of 1919-20 sanctioned these seizures in the Visochi and Falconi Decrees; this failure to protect property rights shocked many of the landed classes. In the North, peasant unions forced landlords to cut rents and increase wages.

• The trade unions grew enormously; the socialist CGL's membership increased from 250,000 in 1918 to over 2 million by 1920 and the Catholic unions' membership rose from 160,000 to 1,600,000 in the same period.

• With this increase in size, came an increase in militancy. In 1919 and again in 1920 more than 1 million workers went on strike, culminating in a four-week 'occupation of the factories' in August-September when, in many cities, industrial workers staged sit-ins and took over the factories, setting up factory committees. The occupation eventually was called off, partly because Giolitti, the Prime Minister, offered some concessions to the workers; this was bitterly resented by many of the middle and upper classes who saw this as bowing to illegal pressure. The occupation's ultimate failure demoralised many of the factory workers and their militancy lessened somewhat in 1921-22. However, labour disputes still remained very disruptive and in August 1922 the Socialists called a general strike.

• Social unrest spawned growing political violence between the Socialists and the Fascists but the violence was also a consequence of the First World War in that many young men's experience of fighting meant that after the war they sought to resolve political and social issues by confrontation and physical force. Fascist 'squads' – recruited mainly from ex-servicemen - broke up strikes and closed down socialist and trade union offices throughout much of northern and central Italy from 1920 onwards. The Fascist squads were also very successful in combating the socialists and unions in the countryside; from autumn 1920 through to the summer of 1921, they wrested control of large areas of rural and provincial northern and central Italy away from the socialists, trade unions and peasant leagues. In the period 1920-22, Fascists killed over 3,000 socialists.

Italian Election Results, 1919 and 1921

Party	No. seats 1919	No. seats 1921
Fascists	-	35
Nationalists	-	10
Conservative Liberals	41	43
Giolittian Liberals (loose grouping)	168	60
Popolari (PPI)	100	108
Socialists (PSI)	156	123
Communists (PCI)	-	15
Total	508*	535*

*Note that I have not included data for every party in the table, so the sum of the columns does not match the overall total of seats shown for the Chamber. Data taken from: *Compendio di Statistica Elettorale, II*, 1939, cited in *The Fascist Experience in Italy* by John Pollard.

Q. Why did the Socialists not take power during the Biennio Rosso?

Given the huge growth of the PSI and the socialist trade unions in the post-war period and the increased radicalism of the PSI, which in 1918 formally committed itself to establishing the dictatorship of the proletariat, it might seem surprising that the Socialists did not stage a revolution. Certainly this is what many of the middle and upper classes feared, particularly given the example of Bolshevik Russia.

Alternatively, given the fact that the PSI was the largest party in the Chamber and triumphed in local government elections in much of northern and central Italy in 1920, it might appear puzzling that the PSI did not come to power legally.

Factors explaining the Socialists' failure:

- The Socialists had always been badly divided. Many of the most extreme socialists – the revolutionary syndicalists – had, like Mussolini, broken with the PSI over intervention in the First World War. After the war, the PSI was broadly split between a Reformist wing (more moderate) and a Maximalist wing committed to revolution. In 1921, some of the Maximalists broke off to form the Italian Communist Party (PCI). This further undermined the confidence of the PSI.

- Contrary to their revolutionary rhetoric, PSI leaders such as Giacinto Serrati were cautious about the feasibility of revolution. They were unsure that the Italian working class was ready for revolution. The PSI leaders were very passive, reacting to events rather than trying to shape them; this passivity is well reflected by a headline in *Avanti!* From November 1919, *'All we have to do is wait'*.

- Socialist strength had peaked by late 1920. After that, partly because of the failure of the occupation of the factories, but also because of attacks by the Fascist squads, working class militancy lessened.

- The PSI was insufficiently strong to gain power legally because the Party would not work with either the PPI or the Liberals, although Giolitti had offered cabinet posts to the PSI before 1914.

The Rise of Mussolini and Italian Fascism

Mussolini's political career up to 1918

Mussolini joined the Socialist Party in 1910 and achieved prominence as editor of the Socialist newspaper *Avanti!* Mussolini was then expelled from the PSI in 1914 for advocating that Italy should intervene in the war; he argued that the war would lead to revolution in Italy.

Mussolini founded and edited *Il Popolo D"Italia* in November 1914, with financial backing from Milanese businessmen and the French government. He used *Il Popolo* to campaign for intervention. When Italy joined the war in 1915, Mussolini joined the Italian army but was wounded and left the army in 1917.

1919: Mussolini founded a left-wing Fascist movement

When the war ended, Mussolini decided to create a new left-wing political movement, to which he hoped to recruit ex-servicemen, dissident socialists and syndicalists. However, right from its inception, the Fascist movement contained very diverse elements, which included:

» Revolutionary syndicalists who had broken away from the PSI. Radicals like Edmondo Rossoni, the head of the Fascist Union Confederation, wanted to sweep away Liberal Italy and create a new state in which employers and employees came together to control the economy by means of 'corporations'.

» Militants like Roberto Farinacci and Italo Balbo who wanted a Fascist revolution, which would involve the Party taking over the state and fundamentally altering Italy.

» Ex-Nationalists who advocated a more authoritarian system of government and prioritised making Italy into a great power.

Clerico-Fascists who were hostile to the Socialists and sought to heal the longstanding rift between church and state by means of the Fascist Party.

In March 1919 Mussolini set up the *Fasci di Combattimento* in Milan. The word 'fascio' means 'group' or 'bundle' and derives from the bundle of rods carried as a symbol of office by magistrates in ancient Rome. At this stage, Mussolini deliberately avoided calling the fascists a 'party' as he wanted to suggest that the Fascists were rejecting the traditional party structure, which, by 1919, was so discredited in the eyes of many Italians.

Initially Mussolini proved unable to attract more than several hundred followers and he suffered total humiliation in the November 1919 elections, when the Fascists did not win a single seat.

Mussolini's 1919 programme was anti-capitalist, anti-clerical and republican:

» Abolition of the Senate (the upper house of parliament, which the King nominated)

» The election of a National Assembly to draw up a new constitution

» Universal suffrage (male and female)

» A guaranteed minimum wage

» Worker involvement in running factories

» Confiscation of war profits

» Confiscation of church property

Following the disaster in the November 1919 elections, Mussolini's support began to dwindle and it looked as if the movement would collapse.

1920-21: Mussolini moved Fascism to the Right

However, Mussolini immediately began to move the movement's programme to the right, a process that continued through to 1922. Crucially for the Fascists, late 1920 onwards saw the movement make rapid progress in winning support in rural areas of northern and central Italy as the Fascists organised 'squads' to attack the socialists, Catholic unions and peasant leagues. The Fascists were, therefore, able to appeal to the landed classes as champions of property rights. Simultaneously, but with not quite such success, the Fascists challenged the socialists and trade unions in the cities and major towns of the industrial north. Fascist support and influence in the South was much more limited.

Mussolini increasingly posed as a respectable politician and courted support from the elites and liberal politicians. In April 1921, Giolitti offered Mussolini the opportunity to join the government's 'national bloc' in the forthcoming elections. The PNF now began to develop as a parliamentary party as they won 35 seats in the May 1921 elections. Giolitti's new coalition was highly unstable and in July 1921 it collapsed when the Popolari withdrew. Giolitti was replaced as Prime Minister by a moderate socialist, Ivanoe Bonomi, but Bonomi's coalition proved no more durable than Giolitti's.

In June 1921, in his maiden parliamentary speech, Mussolini publicly renounced the Fascists' earlier anti-clericalism, declaring that, *'Fascism neither practises nor preaches anti-clericalism...I believe...that the Latin and Imperial traditions of Rome are today represented by Catholicism'.*

As part of Mussolini's search for political respectability, he concluded the Pact of Pacification with the Socialists in August 1921. However, this led to a rift with the Ras who regarded Mussolini's negotiations with the liberals and elites as a betrayal of their commitment to a more extreme transformation of Italy. Mussolini briefly resigned as Fascist leader (but not as leader of the Fascist group within the Chamber), probably calculating that the Ras would eventually recognise that the Fascism could not survive without him; that he was the 'cement' that bound the disparate elements of Fascism together into a national movement. In November, at the third Fascist Congress, Mussolini publicly rejected the Pact of Pacification and was reinstated as Fascist leader or *'Duce'*.

In October 1921, Mussolini relaunched the Fascist movement as a predominantly right-wing party, the *Partito Nazionale Fascista* (the PNF), which emphasised a fervent nationalism and a hatred of socialism.

The 1921 Fascist programme advocated:

» The privatisation of all sectors of industry currently under state control (e.g. the railways)

» The right to private property to be guaranteed

» Resolving industrial and agrarian disputes by creating corporations representing all classes

» The incorporation of any Italian-speaking areas still not part of Italy; Italy to play a dominant role in the Mediterranean

1922: Mussolini appointed Prime Minister

Bonomi's coalition government fell apart in February 1922 and was succeeded by a very weak liberal-conservative coalition led by Luigi Facta. Fascist violence increased in 1922 and Facta's government was unable to restore order. The Socialists and Communists called a general strike for August 1922 as a protest against the Fascists but this backfired disastrously because the Fascist squads then broke up the general strike and many of the propertied classes were now strengthened in their conviction that only a government containing Mussolini could maintain law and order. In September 1922, in a speech in Udine, Mussolini made clear his commitment to supporting the monarchy.

By late 1922, Mussolini was walking a political tightrope, under intense pressure from the Ras, the regional Fascist bosses, to seize power by force and then create a dictatorship. However, at the same time, Mussolini was negotiating with liberal and conservative politicians to win support for his appointment as prime minister; in October 1922, Mussolini demanded 5 cabinet posts.

The March on Rome (October 1922) was a successful bluff on Mussolini's part. The Fascists mobilised 30,000 poorly armed squadristi for the March on Rome. They would have been no match for the regular army. On October 27, Facta asked King Victor Emmanuel to declare martial law in preparation for suppressing the Fascist march. Crucially, after initially agreeing to Facta's request, King Victor Emmanuel lost his nerve and cancelled the order. Facta immediately resigned. Victor Emmanuel probably feared that civil war might break out if the Army was ordered to confront the Fascist squads and he seems to have been concerned lest the Army prove unreliable (although all the evidence suggests the Army would have obeyed orders to suppress the squads).

Liberals and conservatives close to the King, such as Luigi Federzoni, then advised him to appoint Mussolini as Prime Minister; they believed that Mussolini could be 'tamed' and that, in power, as part of a coalition with the Liberals and Nationalists, the Fascists could be induced to moderate their behaviour and programme. In a word, the liberal-conservative politicians were resorting to their traditional 'trasformismo' tactics. Mussolini was duly appointed Prime Minister on 29 October. The Fascist squads were then invited to march through Rome on 30 October as a victory parade.

Q. Why did the Fascist movement grow so rapidly between 1919 and 1922, propelling Mussolini to the premiership by October 1922?

The rise of Fascism is a remarkable phenomenon; from just a few hundred members in 1919, the movement grew to over 300,000 by October 1922.

➢ Mussolini was a brilliant journalist and orator. He had the ability to whip up emotions and the 'common touch', in stark contrast to the liberal politicians. Mussolini offered charismatic, authoritarian leadership, promising to restore national greatness and revive the glory of ancient Rome.

Mussolini's posturing and his dynamism helped create an exaggerated impression of how powerful the Fascists were. Serrati, the Socialist leader, described Mussolini as, *'a rabbit - a phenomenal rabbit; he roars. Observers who do not know him mistake him for a lion'.*

➢ Mussolini was pragmatic and flexible – he once declared that, *'Only maniacs never change'.* His transformation of the Fascists' programme, from predominantly left-wing wing in 1919 to predominantly right-wing by late 1921, illustrates that and explains the growing appeal of Fascism to the middle classes. Mussolini made clear his lack of attachment to any particular ideological position in a speech to the chamber in December 1921 in which he stated that, *'the Fascist programme is not a theory of dogmas…our programme is a process of continual elaboration and transformation'.*

➢ Mussolini and the Fascists exploited bourgeois and upper class fears of socialist revolution, which appeared to many during the Biennio Rosso to be imminent. For many property-owners, the squadristi seemed to offer the best defence against a left-wing revolution.

➢ Many of the Fascists were recruited from the middle class and, even more so from the lower middle classes – small farmers, skilled craftsmen, shopkeepers, teachers and civil servants. This social group had dominated the ranks of the junior officers and NCOs during the war and the war politicised them. After the war, they resented the privileged position and power of the ruling classes but were also hostile to the trade unions and socialists, fearing that they would be levelled down to the status of the labouring classes.

➢ Mussolini was the 'glue' that held the various and competing strands of Fascism together. Although, his authority over the movement was often challenged by the independently-minded Ras, ultimately no-one else emerged as a credible alternative leader. It was Mussolini who had the political skills required to negotiate with the established politicians and it was Mussolini who made Fascism into a national movement, rather than a jumble of regional groups.

The leading British historian Denis Mack Smith characterised the disparate nature of Fascism in the following terms:

'Fascism had elements of both [Left and Right]…It was revolutionary, but could also sometimes claim to be conservative. It was monarchist but also republican, at different times. It was Catholic, but also anti-clerical; it claimed to be Socialist, but could also be strongly capitalist whenever it suited the Duce to be so…'

> Mussolini was able to appeal to and balance elite support (e.g. that of the industrialist Alberto Pirelli) and that of the squadristi. This was an extremely difficult juggling act for Mussolini. If he leaned too much towards the violent authoritarianism of the Ras or the radicalism of the ex-revolutionary syndicalists, he risked alienating his supporters among the elites. Conversely, if he appeared too much the moderate and the defender of the ruling classes, he might lose the backing of the Ras.

> The violence of the squads was both an asset and a liability for Mussolini. The squads' destruction of the unions and socialist organisations met with the approval of many big landowners, industrialists and leading figures within the armed forces, police and the Vatican. However, too much violence threatened a descent into anarchy and alarmed the propertied classes. This explains the Pact of Pacification that Mussolini signed with the reformist wing of the PSI in the summer of 1921. However, the Pact was denounced by the *Ras*, the powerful regional Fascist bosses like Italo Balbo of Ferrara, who continued their attacks on the socialists. Mussolini, therefore, abandoned the Pact.

Sometimes Mussolini was forced to go further and faster than he wanted by the Ras, e.g. Mussolini was pushed into the March on Rome (October 1922). Italo Balbo told Mussolini, *'We are going, either with you or without you.'*

> Increasingly Mussolini was able to win the backing of powerful elements within the ruling elites who did not become Fascists but saw in Mussolini a valuable ally in the fight against socialism. In 1922, there was a new pope, Pius XI, who was sympathetic to Mussolini and sensed in him an opportunity of improving church-state relations.

> The police and Army were favourably inclined towards the squadristi and helped them in their battles with the Socialists, either by turning a blind eye to squad violence or by supplying the squads with weapons.

> The Liberals miscalculated, they thought they could use Mussolini; therefore, the 1921 elections saw the PNF invited to join the government list by Giolitti. Similarly, Salandra, in October 1922, advised Victor Emmanuel to appoint Mussolini Prime Minister, wanting to prevent his longstanding rival, Giolitti, from coming to power and believing that the Fascists could be tamed.

The Establishment of Single-Party Rule

From Prime Minister to Duce (1922-26)

When Mussolini was appointed Prime Minister in October 1922, his government was a coalition in which there were just three Fascists; the rest of the cabinet comprised Nationalists, Popolari, Liberals and two generals. Mussolini's position was therefore far from unassailable as he depended on the continuing support of the King and, within the Chamber, the Fascists only held 7% of the seats.

Yet by the end of 1926 Mussolini had instituted a single party state in Italy. During the first three years of Mussolini's tenure as Prime Minister, it remained unclear whether Mussolini would pursue constitutional methods or whether he would look to achieve a complete Fascist takeover of the state and society. This ambiguity about the nature of Fascist rule – moderate or revolutionary – was only resolved in 1925-26.

The Matteotti Crisis (1924)

The 'Matteotti Crisis', above all else in the period 1922-26, highlighted the tensions and ambiguities within the Fascist movement and revealed how fragile Mussolini's hold on power was. In June 1924 a political crisis erupted over the murder of the moderate socialist leader, Giacomo Matteotti. Matteotti had delivered a major speech in the Chamber at the end of May, in which he launched a scathing attack on the illegal methods employed by the Fascists in the recent elections; just under two weeks later he was abducted in broad daylight in Rome and his body was eventually discovered in a ditch in August. It was clear that his murderers were Fascists, what was less so was the extent to which Mussolini was involved. The outrage caused by the murder threatened to overwhelm Mussolini and for a time it looked as if Mussolini would not survive as Prime Minister.

Moderate Fascists such as De Stefani and Federzoni put pressure on Mussolini to expel the extremists who were damaging the reputation of Fascism. Mussolini responded by appointing Federzoni Minister of the Interior and Alfredo Rocco Minister of Justice (both men were former Nationalists and had great influence within Italy's ruling classes). He also dismissed Cesare Rossi, head of the Fascist press office, who was directly linked to Matteotti's murder and Emilio de Bono, the Fascist Director of Public Security. The Ras and more militant elements in the Fascist movement were furious at these measures.

Mussolini managed to ride out the crisis because the opposition was weak and divided and made the mistake of walking out of the Chamber, which did nothing to undermine Mussolini's position. Equally important to Mussolini's survival was the continuing support of the King and of the Vatican. Victor Emmanuel preferred to retain Mussolini as Prime Minister rather than risk seeing a revival of the fortunes of the Left or a revolt by Fascist extremists.

Q. **How was Mussolini able to consolidate his power and create a single party state?**

1. **Mussolini, posing as a respectable politician, successfully wooed the upper and middle classes by:**

a. Merging the Nationalist Party with the PNF (1923); this gave Fascism greater respectability as Nationalists like Alfredo Rocco and Luigi Federzoni (see above) had influential connections among big landowners and industrialists, the armed forces, civil service and the royal court.

b. In 1924-5 Mussolini's Finance Minister, De Stefani, reassured the business class by pursuing orthodox financial policies, cutting government spending and balancing the budget. In this, De Stefani was helped by an upturn in the world economy.

c. Cancelling the Falconi and Visocchi Decrees, which had legalised peasant land seizures. This reassured the big landowners.

d. Banning strikes and ending independent trade unions (only Fascist unions were permitted) in a law of April 1926, which followed on from the Palazzo Vidoni Pact of October 1925 between the Italian Confederation of Industry and the Fascist trade unions.

e. Pursuing an assertive foreign policy during the Corfu Incident (1923), when Mussolini bullied Greece into paying compensation for the murder of Italian officers by Greek bandits. Mussolini also pleased nationalists by successfully negotiating with Yugoslavia for the transfer of Fiume to Italy (1924).

f. Making concessions to the Catholic Church. The 1923 Education Act made religious education compulsory in primary schools and allowed secondary schools to offer it. Schools were also permitted to place crucifixes in classrooms. In January 1923, Mussolini had talks with the Vatican Secretary of State, Cardinal Pietro Gasparri, in which he declared his desire to resolve the long-running dispute between the Italian state and the Vatican.

2. Mussolini successfully extended his control within and over the Chamber by:

o   Arresting the leaders of the Communist Party in December 1922; in moving against the Communists, Mussolini used emergency powers granted to him for one year by the Chamber.

o   Breaking the PPI as a political force in 1923. The PPI was very divided between right-wing members, who favoured close ties with Mussolini because they feared the Socialists and wanted to end the rift between Church and state, and more reformist, or left-wing members, who hated the Fascists who attacked the Catholic unions.

Mussolini sacked the PPI members of his coalition government in April 1923. Pope Pius XI, desperate to avoid confrontation with the Fascists, forced the leader of the PPI, Dom Luigi Sturzo, to resign. The PPI split over the Acerbo Law (see below); some right-wing deputies voting for it and most deciding to abstain.

o   Getting the Chamber to pass the Acerbo Law (November 1923). This gave the Party with the most votes in an election two-thirds of the seats in the Chamber. Mussolini was anxious to get this measure passed because elections were due in 1924 and he wanted to ensure that the Fascists dominated the Chamber, rather than having to rely on a coalition with other parties.

o   Winning the parliamentary elections in April 1924. Mussolini presented a government list of candidates, including Liberals and some Popolari, to the electorate. Government candidates won 66% of the seats (375 out of 575), with PNF members securing over 50%.

The Fascists used unprecedented violence and intimidation against opponents in the 1924 elections. Vote-rigging and bribery by the Fascists were widespread, particularly in the South where these methods had traditionally been effective. The Fascists won over 80% of the votes in the South but only 54% in the North, where the working classes still largely voted for the Socialists.

3. Mussolini was <u>partially</u> successful in increasing his control over the Fascist Party by:

o   Establishing the Fascist Militia (Voluntary Militia for National Security or MSVN for short) in 1923. The MSVN absorbed all of the local squads into a national militia. Mussolini hoped that this would lead to greater discipline and centralised control over the squadristi, thereby undermining the independent power of the Ras. This only proved a step towards increasing Mussolini's control over the rank and file of the Fascist movement; his control remained incomplete at this stage.

o   Creating the Fascist Grand Council in December 1922. This was presented as a way of improving communication between the Fascist Party and the government but again Mussolini saw this as a vehicle for asserting his personal control over the PNF and particularly over the Ras.

4.   Liberal and conservative politicians continued to underestimate Mussolini and were outmanoeuvred by him:

o   They supported the Acerbo Law (1923). The Liberals voted for the Acerbo Law because they believed that proportional representation had, since 1919, favoured the Socialists and produced weak coalition governments.

o   The opposition parties blundered in their response to the political crisis sparked off by the murder of the moderate socialist leader, Giacomo Matteotti in June 1924. This was a serious crisis for Mussolini and initially it looked as if Mussolini would not survive as Prime Minister.

When Mussolini was implicated in the murder, most of the opposition deputies (but not the Popolari) walked out of the Chamber. However, the so-called Aventine Secession simply strengthened the Fascist grip on the Chamber and achieved nothing. When they tried to return to the Chamber in 1925, they were refused admission.

Constitutional Rule or Dictatorship? The Question Resolved (January 1925)

The Matteotti Crisis brought to a head the tensions within the Fascist movement. A delegation of 30 consuls (as the Ras were now known) delivered Mussolini an ultimatum on New Year's Eve: either Mussolini took steps towards establishing a dictatorship or they would depose him as leader. Three days later Mussolini made a speech in the Chamber in which he announced his intention to establish authoritarian government. In the speech Mussolini declared his responsibility for Fascist violence without admitting to any involvement in Matteotti's murder:

'If all the violence has been the result of a particular historical, political and moral climate, then responsibility for this is mine, because I have created this climate with a propaganda that has lasted from the Intervention Crisis until today.'

Q.   What steps did Mussolini take towards establishing a single party state?

o   The Socialist Party (PSI) was banned in October 1925.
o   Censorship was increased by the Press Law of December 1925. All journalists now had to be registered by the Fascist authorities. Prefects were empowered to dismiss editors or close down newspapers.
o   In 1926 Mussolini acquired the power to issue decrees; he issued over 100,000 in the next 17 years.
o   Locally elected mayors were replaced by podestas appointed by the prefects (1926).
o   Free trade unions were banned (1926); consequently, the Catholic and Socialist trade union confederations dissolved themselves. This just left the Fascist trade unions.
o   All opposition parties were banned in November 1926; this followed on a series of four separate assassination attempts on Mussolini. The PNF was now the sole legal party.
o   Public Safety Law (1926); increased powers of arrest. Suspected subversives could be sentenced to 5 years internal exile. Approximately 10,000 people were held in '*confino*', usually on off-shore islands like Lipari.
o   The creation of a secret police (OVRA) in 1926; OVRA arrested or detained hundreds of people every week.
o   A Special Tribunal was established in 1926 for trying political offences; trial by jury was thereby removed in political cases. The Tribunal convicted over 5000 people over the period 1927-43 but only 49 were sentenced to death.
o   The democratic electoral system was abolished and replaced by a plebiscitary system in the 1928 Electoral Law. The Fascist Grand Council was to draw up a list of 400 candidates, after nominations by unions and employers, and then the 'electorate' had to approve or reject the whole list.

In the 1929 'elections', 95% of the 'electorate' approved the Grand Council's list of candidates. In 1939 the Chamber was abolished and replaced by the 'Chamber of Fasces and Corporations'.

However, to a considerable extent Mussolini subordinated the Fascist Party to the power of the state:

o   In January 1927 a decree obliged Fascist officials to accept the superior authority of the Prefects (chief state official in each province).

o   The *Statuto* remained Italy's constitution and the King retained his positions as Head of State and Commander-in-Chief. Mussolini was designated Head of Government and Duce of the Fascist Party.

o   The civil service, including the prefects, and police were still dominated by career-officials, rather than by Fascists; for example, Arturo Bocchini, a non-Fascist, was Chief of Police (1926-40).

o   The PNF's membership expanded massively (from 783,000 in 1923 to 1,851,000 by 1934) and most of those joining were careerists and public officials. Consequently, the PNF became increasingly an organisation of bureaucrats and professionals, rather than militant activists.

Mussolini now created a personal dictatorship, extending his control over the Fascist Party by:

o   Appointing Roberto Farinacci, one of the Ras, in 1925 as PNF Secretary with instructions to impose greater discipline on the unruly elements within the Party.

o   Sacking Farinacci as PNF Secretary (April 1926) when Farinacci proved too independent-minded.

o   Appointing the compliant Augusto Turati as PNF Secretary to replace Farinacci. Turati then set about, over the next three years, purging 60,000 members of the PNF. Most of those expelled were radicals or militant squad members. During the 1930s another Mussolini loyalist, Achille Starace, occupied the post of PNF Secretary.

o   A Party statute of 1926 laid down that all party posts were to be appointed from above (PNF headquarters in Rome), rather than elected from below or appointed by local Fascist bosses.

Mussolini now dominated the Fascist Party. Furthermore Mussolini was not entirely dependent on the PNF's support because he had close relations with non-Fascist centres of power such as the Church, the King, the armed forces and big business. From 1925 a personality cult of the 'Duce' developed and this further elevated Mussolini's position above that of any other individual, whether a government or Party member.

So by 1929 the Fascist Party had been subordinated to the state and centralised under the personal control of Mussolini. Its role now had effectively been limited to organising propaganda and rallies, overseeing mass organisations like Dopolavoro (in charge of recreation and sport) and supervising the youth organisations.

FASCIST RULE

The Corporate State

Fascist propaganda suggested that what distinguished Mussolini's regime from the rest of the world was Corporatism. Indeed, there is no doubt that, internationally, the 'Corporate State' established in Italy had many admirers. In theory, Corporatism was a third way between Communism and Capitalism and would bring about harmonious labour relations. Corporatism was an influential idea in pre-war Italy, particularly associated with Filippo Corrodoni, an anarcho-syndicalist. Some leading Fascists had for a long time been passionate advocates of Corporatism, including Michele Bianchi and Edmondo Rossoni, Secretary of the Confederation of Fascist Syndical Corporations (the Fascist trade unions).

Syndicalists wanted to transform society by reorganising it on the basis of different economic spheres of activity. In each sphere, syndicates would represent both workers and employers and these joint-representatives would resolve issues concerning both working conditions and economic management. Syndicalists envisaged the corporations having a major say in directing the economy and, ultimately, Corporations replacing the traditional parliamentary system; instead representatives from different corporations would wield political power.

In the early to mid-1920s, opinion within the Fascist movement was strongly divided about how far a Corporate state should be established. This reflected the wider debate about the nature of Fascism and the pressures being placed on Mussolini by the various factions among his supporters. Mussolini needed the support of industrialists and landowners but sections of the PNF demanded a fascist revolution. In 1925, Rossoni organised a strike by 100,000 workers in Lombardy, which alarmed employers and Mussolini.

In contrast to the syndicalists, many other Fascists were decidedly hostile to Corporatism as it raised the prospect of much greater power for the working classes. Conservatives like Alfredo Rocco sought to use Corporatism simply as a way of keeping the workers in order and supporting the interests of the big employers. Ultimately, although the structures of a corporate state were erected, Mussolini came down decisively in favour of a neutered version of corporatism that chimed in with Rocco's views.

The establishment of the 'Corporate state' was a rather haphazard process and it took until 1939 before the corporate edifice was complete. However, beneath the structures, the Corporate state was essentially a sham: the tribunals set up by the Syndical Law (1926) favoured the industrialists and the Charter of Labour (1927) was mere window dressing in terms of safeguarding workers' rights.

	The Creation of the 'Corporate State'
1925	**Vidoni Palace Pact** • The Fascist Labour Confederation (Fascist trade unions) and *Confindustria* (Confederation of Industry), agreed to recognise only each other as representatives of workers and employers in negotiations. Fascist unions were delighted that this excluded the free trade unions (Catholic, Socialist and Communist) from labour relations. Employers were pleased that elected factory councils were abolished. However, they were unhappy at the prospect of binding arbitration in labour disputes.

1926	**Alfredo Rocco's Labour and Anti-Strike Law**
	• Confirmed that only syndicates could engage in labour negotiations.
	• Divided the economy into 7 branches of activity (agriculture, transport etc) and created separate syndicates to represent the workers and the employers. Radical Fascists had wanted mixed or 'integrated' syndicates to include employers and workers.
	• Set up special tribunals to provide compulsory arbitration in industrial disputes. But, in practice, the tribunals favoured the employers and dealt with very few cases.
	• Banned strikes and lockouts (employers locking out workers).
	This advantaged the employers as they were not subject to state or PNF supervision. In disputes, officials represented the workers, whereas employers represented themselves. A Ministry of Corporations was established, with Mussolini as Minister. However, only 1 corporation really functioned at this stage, the corporation for artists and intellectuals.
1927	**Charter of Labour**
	• Affirmed private enterprise.
	• Reaffirmed that strikes and factory councils were illegal.
	• Set out guarantees of workers' rights, but these were not honoured.
1928	Rossoni was sacked as Secretary of the Confederation of Fascist Syndicates. The Confederation was broken up into 6 confederations of syndicates, thereby weakening their bargaining power. Radicals within the PNF were disappointed.
1930	**The National Council of Corporations set up**
	• In theory it established representatives of workers, the PNF and employers to regulate the economy. The National Council appeared to have the power to fix wages, settle disputes and advise on the economy. However, in practice the Council did very little.
1934	**The 'Corporate State' was finally established (on paper)**
	• 22 'mixed' corporations were set up - each consisting of employers and employees. However, the system continued to favour the employers.
	• The corporations lacked any real power. State institutions and big business interests made all the major decisions concerning the economy.
1939	The Chamber of Fasces and Corporations replaced the Chamber, the lower house of parliament. It had no real power and was purely a propaganda exercise on Mussolini's part.

The Economy under the Fascists

Q. What were Mussolini's aims?

Mussolini had little understanding or knowledge of economics when he came to power. Although the original Fascist programme had an anti-capitalist character, by the time Mussolini was appointed Prime Minister, this had been dropped and Fascism from then on was committed to the capitalist system. In theory, the Fascists pursued 'Corporativism' as a third way between capitalism and socialism but in practice this was mere window-dressing. Fascism was supported by, and in turn, protected big business and the *agrari* (large landowners).

Under Fascism, economic policy was inconsistent and erratic; broadly speaking, it was laissez-faire (minimum of state intervention) during the period 1922-25 and then was increasingly marked by state intervention thereafter. The pursuit of 'autarky' (economic self-sufficiency) characterized the mid to late 1930s as Mussolini's foreign policy became more aggressive. Mussolini sought to build up Italy's industry to support foreign wars of conquest. However, in that respect he failed miserably as economically Italy was far from ready to go to war at the end of the 1930s.

Much of Fascist 'policy' was posturing, with little substance. Mussolini asserted that what mattered in economics, as in all spheres of life, were 'will-power' and 'struggle', so he launched a series of economic 'battles' – e.g. the Battle for Grain and the Battle for the Lira. These grandiose campaigns were largely misconceived and tended to damage the economy.

1922-25: Laissez-faire

The period leading up to the establishment of the Fascist dictatorship saw Italy recover from the post-war depression. This was largely the result of an upturn in the world economy from 1923. Mussolini's Finance Minister, De Stefani, followed the same economic policies as previous liberal governments: balancing the budget, cutting taxes and government spending and reducing tariffs on trade. He also privatised several nationalised industries such as the telephone company.

Protectionism and increasing state intervention

In 1925, the Italian economy was suffering a balance of payments crisis as imports, particularly of grain, increased. This, combined, with the falling value of the lira led Mussolini to:

1. Replace De Stefani with Giuseppe Volpi, who had strong links with Italy's financiers and big industrialists.
2. Increase tariffs on foreign imports in order to protect Italian industries. Tariffs were increased in 1925, 1928 and 1929.
3. Launch the Battle for Grain (1925).
4. Revalue the lira (1926).

The Battle for Grain (1925)

Mussolini's goal was to make Italy self-sufficient in wheat production. Tariffs on imported grain were raised and the government provided financial incentives to farmers to switch production from other crops to grain.

Q. What were the results of the Battle for Grain?

• Grain production nearly doubled (1923-38) from 4.5 million metric tons p.a. to 8.2 million metric tons p.a.

• Grain imports fell by 75% in the same period.

• Although successful in increasing grain output, this was achieved at the expense of other crops, and so damaged Italian agriculture. Exports of citrus fruit, olive oil, and wine all fell heavily.

• The policy was particularly damaging in the South where the soil was not conducive to wheat-production but was better suited to fruit and wine growing.
• Livestock levels fell sharply too as farmers switched land-usage from pasture to arable; e.g. the number of cattle in the South dropped by 20%.

• Furthermore, Italian consumers suffered from higher food prices.

As the historian Martin Clark puts it so well,

'Mussolini's wheat policy made little economic sense. But then it was not an economic policy. It was politics and propaganda, like everything else he did: not bread, but circuses.'

The Battle for the Lira (1926)

Mussolini's one major intervention in economic policy prior to the Great Depression (1929), was his decision to revalue the lira. Rising prices and increasing import levels accompanied a sharp fall in the lira's value. For Mussolini, this was a question of prestige; he announced that '*I shall defend the Italia lira to my last breath*'. This proved disastrous as it was fixed at an artificially high rate of 90 lire to the pound (had been 154 to the pound) and so was known as the *quota noventa*.

The revaluation hit Italian exports which became much more expensive as a consequence. Exports were further hit by the tit-for-tat tariff war with other countries that Mussolini's protectionist policy provoked. Consequently, the value of Italian exports was halved in the period 1925-38; from 44 million lire to 22 million lire.

Italian consumers should have benefited from cheaper imports resulting from the revaluation but this was not the case because the Fascist government raised tariffs. Moreover, in 1927, the government introduced a 10% wage cut. Further wage cuts occurred in 1930.

Agriculture (see above also the Battle for Grain)

Overall, with the exception of the Battle for Grain, Fascist economic policy did little to try to address the backward agricultural methods which characterised much of Italy's farming or widespread peasant poverty. Fascist propaganda presented rural life as the ideal but the reality was that the government spent little time or money on agricultural issues (except for the Battle for Grain).

o   Mussolini virtually ignored the South where these problems were most acute.

o   Living standards deteriorated for peasants and agricultural labourers.

o   Nor could poor southerners so easily seek an escape route by emigrating to the USA as immigration controls were tightened considerably by the American authorities.

o With growing underemployment and unemployment in rural areas, increasingly poor farmers migrated to the cities in spite of Fascist attempts to restrict this 'flight from the land'; about 500,000 agricultural labourers or peasant farmers did so during Mussolini's rule.

o The Fascists did nothing to challenge the interests of the traditional big landowners. In the 1930s, 20,000 families owned half of Italy's arable land.

Land Reclamation

In 1928 the 'Mussolini Law' was announced; this declared that the Fascist government intended to invest in land reclamation. Initially it looked as if a radical reform might be instituted, based on proposals drawn up by an agricultural expert, Serpieri. He advocated an 'integral' scheme that would oblige landowners to contribute financially to land reclamation and irrigation projects or have their land confiscated. However, the compulsory element was abandoned after opposition from large landowners.

Little was achieved in terms of land reclamation but there was real success in the draining of the Pontine Marshes, south of Rome. This had been a malaria-infested area but the much publicised reclamation scheme transformed it in to farmland suitable for cultivation. New smallholdings and villages were established there. It also provided much-needed jobs during the Depression. However, this scheme was really the exception as little was achieved elsewhere.

In 1934 the government announced that 4.75 million hectares of land had been or were in the process of being reclaimed. Martin Clark estimates that the real figure was only about 250,000 hectares. The cost of the reclamation schemes amounted to almost 8 billion lire.

The Great Depression: the Italian Economy in the 1930s

The Wall Street Crash in America (1929) hit Italy, like the rest of Europe, hard. Unemployment rose to over 2 million by 1933. The statistics suggest that the Fascist regime coped marginally better than most other Western European governments in tackling the effects of the Depression.

	Italy	Western European average
% Drop in GNP	5.4	7.1
% Drop in industrial output	22.7	23.2

Source: P Ciocca and G Toniolo, *L'Economia Italiana durante il Fascismo*, Bologna, 1976

Several major banks were threatened with collapse in 1931 in Italy during a worldwide banking crisis stemming from the Wall Street Crash. The Bank of Italy itself was at risk. The Fascist government effectively responded by creating the Istituto Mobiliare Italiano (1931); IMI provided financial help to shore up ailing banks and industries.

Even more importantly, the regime set up the Istituto per la Ricostruzione Industriale (IRI) in 1933 in order to rescue banks and firms and take over their shares. By the late 1930s, the government controlled 20% of the capital of Italy's industrial firms, especially in steel, shipping and electricity. Only the USSR had a larger public sector. The IRI had been initially intended as a temporary holding company, with the task of sorting out firms and then returning them to the private sector. However, by 1937, the IRI had become a permanent agency led by the non-fascist, Alberto Beneduce. It became a training ground for a new progressive generation of managers who later contributed significantly to Italy's 'economic miracle' of the 1950s and 1960s.

Fascist economic successes:

✔ There was significant infrastructure investment, e.g. the autostrada (motorway) network was built. However, minor roads were neglected.

✔ IRI did much to mitigate the worst effects of the Depression by rescuing banks and companies threatened with financial collapse.

✔ Hydro-electric power was successfully developed; by 1937, 14.8 billion kilowatt-hours were being produced.

✔ 5000 km of railways were electrified.

✔ Gross Domestic Product (GDP) grew by an average of 1.2% pa between 1922 and 1940, in spite of the Great Depression.

✔ Substantial growth in the chemical, electrical and machine sectors. Italy became the largest exporter of artificial fibre (rayon). Industry overtook agriculture in the 1930s, making up the largest share of GNP (Gross National Product).

✔ Mussolini at last recognised the need to devalue the lira in 1936.

Serious economic failings in the 1930s:

✘ Huge budget deficits mounted up – 12,750 million lire (1938-39) - because of the cost of the Abyssinian War (1935-36) and Italy's intervention in the Spanish Civil War (1936-39).

✘ The Abyssinian invasion led to damaging League of Nations' sanctions, which caused severe raw material shortages. In 1936-38, Italy's imports were only a one third of the 1913 level. Also Italian exports were affected, with a major reorientation of Italy's trade relations; after 1936, 25% of Italy's exports went to Africa and another 25% went to Germany.

✘ The regime failed in its increased drive for autarky (economic self-sufficiency), although there was some success in aluminium and oil. Mussolini had to inform Hitler in 1939 that Italy was not ready to go to war.

✘ Small businesses lost out to a number of huge companies (e.g. Fiat) that virtually monopolised particular economic sectors, e.g. SNIA Viscosa and Montecatini controlled almost the whole chemicals industry.

✘ Mussolini failed to make Italy into a great industrial power. In 1939, Italy produced just 2.4 million tons of steel; Britain, by contrast, produced 13.4 million tons and Germany 22.5 million.

✘ Increased state interference and a growing Fascist bureaucracy were not only very costly but hampered business by the introduction of a lot of 'red tape', regulations and paperwork.

✘ Living standards for most ordinary Italians fell. The government obliged industrial workers to accept wage cuts in 1927, 1930 and 1934. Agricultural wages dropped by between 20 to 40% during the 1930s.

Overall, the social groups who benefited most from Fascist economic policies were the big industrialists and large landowners. Their interests were protected, for example by the imposition of greater discipline on the workforce and the removal of free trade unions. The middle-class gained from an expansion of jobs in the expanded bureaucracy.

As pointed out above, living standards fell for most of the industrial and agricultural labourers. The Fascists did bring in welfare measures in the 1930s, largely as a response to the Depression. In 1934 family allowances were introduced and, later, schemes for insurance against accidents and sickness were added. These initiatives proved very expensive to the state, but Mussolini, as ever, was more concerned with public image.

Fascism and Italian Society

The Fascist takeover was only partial, Italy became much less of a totalitarian state than Nazi Germany; existing institutions (the monarchy, the Senate) and elites (generals, big landowners, industrialists) remained, e.g. the prefects retained a key role in local government and most were not Fascists. Fascist influence over education, particularly the universities, was limited. Just as under the liberal governments, the South was badly neglected by the Fascists, e.g. land reclamation schemes and Dopolavoro were ineffective in the South. The illiteracy rate in Calabria was still nearly 50% in the 1930s.

The Church-State rift healed (1929)

One of the greatest weaknesses of 'Liberal Italy' had been the long-term rift between the Italian state and the Vatican. Initially, Mussolini would have seemed an unlikely candidate for resolving the 'Roman Question' as, prior to 1922, he had shown himself to be strongly anti-clerical and had written a pamphlet entitled, *'God Does Not Exist'*. However, Mussolini recognised the potential gains he could make by means of an agreement with the Vatican. Showing his characteristic pragmatism, he remarried his wife Rachele in a church wedding in 1925 and had his children baptised.

Healing the Church-state rift was arguably Mussolini's most important triumph. By reaching a series of agreements with the Pope in 1929, Mussolini won the approval of millions of Italian Catholics and reassured many conservative Italians, particularly members of the establishment, that the regime had turned its back on the radical origins of the Fascist movement. The resolution of the 'Roman Question' also won the regime prestige abroad. The Pope famously referred to Mussolini as, *'the man sent by providence'*.

The signing of the Lateran Treaty (1929), however, angered many radical Fascists who were deeply anti-clerical and the continuing independence of the Catholic Church severely undermined the Fascists' claim to exercise totalitarian rule. The Catholic Church remained a rival source of authority and values to Fascism.

Pope Pius XI was keen to reach an accommodation with Mussolini. The Pope was fiercely anti-Socialist and Communist and welcomed the Fascists' destruction of the left in Italy. The Pope had been encouraged by early concessions to the Church made by Mussolini in the early to mid-1920s, e.g. exempting the clergy from paying taxes. In return, Pius XI had forced the resignation of Dom Sturzo, the leader of the Popolari, who had been a powerful opponent of Fascism.

The **Lateran Pacts** contained three agreements signed in **1929**:

1.	The Lateran Treaty involved the recognition of the pope's sovereign rule over the Vatican City.
2.	The Concordat recognised Catholicism as the sole state religion. Church marriages were made legal and religious education in secondary schools became compulsory (Mussolini had already made it compulsory in primary schools). Catholic Action could continue to operate as long as it carried out its *'activities independently of all political parties and immediately subordinate to the Church hierarchy, for the diffusion and realization of Catholic principles.'*
3.	The Vatican received compensation for the loss of the Papal States (1860) and Rome (1870) to the tune of 750 million lire in cash and 1000 million lire in government bonds

In spite of these agreements, there was significant friction between the Fascist government and the Catholic Church in the 1930s. In particular, the Fascists were worried by the activities of Catholic Action, the Catholic lay organisation which had over 1 million members. A major row erupted in 1931 over Catholic Action's involvement in sport, which the Fascist Youth organisation, the *Balilla*, claimed a monopoly over. On this occasion, the Vatican climbed down but Catholic youth movements (under the umbrella of Catholic Action) continued to rival the Fascist youth and student organisations.

The Catholic student organisation, FUCI, was very influential and many of its members, for example Aldo Moro, in the 1930s became leading figures in the Christian Democratic Party in Italy after 1945.

In the late 1930s, the Pope was critical of the anti-semitic laws introduced by Mussolini. Nevertheless, Mussolini's relations with the Church remained reasonably cordial as both sides had much to gain from the Concordat. The Pope applauded the Fascist invasion of Abyssinia (1935-36) as a 'crusade' and praised Mussolini's intervention in the Spanish Civil War (1936-39) against the 'godless' forces of the Left.

Propaganda, Control of the Media and the Arts

Unsurprisingly given his experience and skill as a journalist, Mussolini saw control of the media as vital. Prefects were given the power to censor newspapers in 1923 and the opposition press was suppressed in 1926. However, the Fascist government did not seek to take over the press and only owned 10% of newspapers. Mussolini was, however, determined to control what the newspapers wrote and reported. Journalists and editors who stepped out of line could be fined or banned from journalism, but in practice most editors conformed to the guidelines laid down by the government. The Fascist Press Office instructed newspapers about how events should be reported and insisted on the need to avoid reporting bad news such as crime stories.

Initially Mussolini did not place a great emphasis on the importance of radio, partly because only 40,000 Italians owned a radio in the mid-1920s. However, this changed in the 1930s, as government broadcasts increased and ownership of radios went up to 1 million by the late 1930s. Similarly, at first, the Fascist government did not see film as a particularly important medium. In 1924 a government film agency, *Istituto Luce*, was created to produce newsreels and documentaries. In 1937 the government funded an Italian film studio, called *Cinecitta*. Yet, even then, there was not too great an emphasis on propaganda until the late 1930s.

Mussolini was constantly on the look out for propaganda opportunities to sell himself and the Fascist movement to the Italian people. Fascism concentrated on conveying an image of action and energy. Fascism's aim was to create a new type of Italian – more virile, heroic and selfless - and propaganda was one means the regime sought to use to promote that purpose. From 1925, the cult of the *Duce* was launched. This was aided by the publication of the best-selling biography of Mussolini by his mistress Margherita Sarfatti, entitled *Dux* (1926). As the historian Denis Mack Smith has put it, Mussolini was a 'stupendous poseur' and many Italians appeared to like this! Mussolini was presented as a superman who excelled at all sports, worked relentlessly and was loved by the people. The Fascists regularly organised mass parades and developed elaborate rituals, often using classical Roman imagery. Mussolini sought to revive the Roman spirit.

Mussolini's use of propaganda was never as systematic as in Germany. The Ministry of Popular Culture (popularly known as *Minculpop*) was not set up until 1937. Historians now largely agree that, particularly in the years 1929-36, the Fascist regime did enjoy widespread support. This 'consensus' was partly the result of successful policies such as the Concordat with the Pope but also because of propaganda. However, the limitations of Fascist propaganda can be seen in the regime's failure to win popular support for the German alliance being promoted by Mussolini from the mid-1930s or the anti-semitic policy launched in 1938. During this more radical phase of Fascism, support for Mussolini began to ebb away and this process accelerated once Italy joined the Second World War in 1940.

The Arts

Compared to Nazi Germany or Soviet Russia, Fascist control of the arts was relatively limited and no major artist felt obliged to leave Italy. Fascists were divided over what style of art to encourage. This reflected the radical and conservative factions within the Fascist movement. Neo-classicists preferred art and architecture that drew its inspiration from ancient Rome, whereas modernists encouraged abstract and experimental art. In 1939 these rival tendencies led to the creation of two major artistic prizes – the Cremona Prize and the Bergamo Prize. The Cremona Prize favoured traditional art and art as propaganda and was established by Roberto Farinacci. In 1940 the themes included 'Listening to a speech by the Duce on the radio'. The Bergamo Prize was set up by Bottai to promote experimentation.

The Fascist government organised an average of 50 art exhibitions a year, to try to broaden popular access to art.

Sport

The Fascist regime sought to use sport as a way of keeping the masses happy (see the section on Dopolavoro) and also for propaganda purposes. Mussolini was helped in this respect by the fact that Italy won the football world cup in 1934 and 1938.

The Battle for Births (1927)

In common with many other dictators, Mussolini equated a large population with power. Mussolini, in his desire to make Italy into a great power, sought to increase Italy's population. In 1927 he launched the so-called Battle for Births, with a target of increasing Italy's population from 37 million to 60 million.

To encourage marriage and larger families, the government imposed higher taxes on bachelors and awarded medals to mothers who bore the most children. Italians with 10 or more children were exempted from income tax. Loans were given to married couples, which were partially cancelled each time a child was born. Family allowances were also introduced in 1934. The Criminal Code of 1932 banned contraception, abortion and sterilisation.

The Fascist regime had a very traditional view of women; seeing their role purely in terms of rearing large families and looking after the home. One Fascist slogan described them as 'angels of the hearth'. However, the Fascists were unable to reverse the trend of growing numbers of women attending university and getting public sector jobs.

The Battle for Births was a failure. The birth-rate continued to fall in Italy; in 1911 there had been 147.5 births for every 1000 women of child-bearing age but by 1936 this had fallen to 102.7 births. The overall population rose to just 44 million (1940). This compares with 48 million in Britain and 68 million in Germany.

The slight rise in Italy's population was the result of the falling death rate and the huge drop in emigration; on average 233,000 Italians emigrated to the USA each year in the period 1901-10 but, in the 1920s, this fell to 42,000 and, in the 1930s, to just 11,500. The regime's attempt to promote earlier marriage also failed, with the average age at which Italians married rising in the 1930s.

Anti-Semitic laws (1938)

Q. Why did Mussolini introduce anti-semitic laws?

Historians are divided about why Mussolini introduced anti-semitic legislation in 1938. Fascists had shown racist attitudes towards Africans in Libya and Abyssinia but there had been no evidence of anti-semitism in Mussolini's earlier career or indeed within Fascism as a movement (with the exception of individuals like Farinacci). There were only 56,000 Jews in Italy (0.1% of the population) and Mussolini's mistress (up until 1935), Margherita Sarfatti, was Jewish.

- One theory put forward is that as Mussolini, in the late 1930s, was contemplating war, he wanted to weaken the Jewish community because he was not sure they could be trusted to be loyal.

- By 1938, Mussolini was leaning closer and closer to Nazi Germany and, while there is no sign of Mussolini coming under pressure from Hitler to adopt anti-semitism, Mussolini's introduction of these laws probably stemmed from a desire to establish closer links with Hitler. It is quite likely that their timing (November 1938), coinciding with Kristallnacht (attacks on Jewish shops and synagogues) in Germany, is explained by a desire on Mussolini's part to be in step with the Führer. The introduction of the *passo Romano* (goose step) into the Italian army can be seen as part of this trend.

An article written by Mussolini, published in February 1938, first heralded the campaign against the Jews. In it, Mussolini wrote about the need to reduce the *'disproportionate number of Jews in public life.'* The anti-semitic laws banned marriage between Jews and non-Jews and barred Jews from jobs in the civil service and teaching (with the exception of Jewish war veterans). Jews were also barred from PNF membership. Jewish children were excluded from state schools. Up to 10,000 non-Italian Jews were deported from Italy.

Historians are unanimous in judging the anti-semitic laws a disastrous mistake by Mussolini. The laws were deeply unpopular, even within the Fascist Party, where one third of Italian Jews were members. The Roman Catholic Church criticised the anti-semitic laws. 6,000 Italian Jews left Italy by 1941, many of them successful businessmen, professionals and academics. Many Italians saw, rightly or wrongly, the anti-Jewish campaign as the result of Mussolini 'kowtowing' to Hitler.

Youth policies

The Fascists encouraged a cult of youth; the party song was 'Giovinezza' – 'Youth'. All totalitarian regimes have a particular concern to indoctrinate the young in order to capture the minds of the next generation; Italian Fascism was no different in this respect from Hitler's Germany or Stalin's Russia. In 1926, the Fascists established the Opera Nazionale Balilla, bringing together existing Fascist youth organisations and providing state funding. The Balilla was placed under the control of the Ministry of Education in 1929. Rival youth organisations were closed down, although Catholic youth groups did survive. Membership of the Balilla became obligatory in 1932. However, it is estimated that 40% of Italian children never joined. Membership was low in rural areas, particularly in the South.

There were different sections for boys and girls and for different ages:

Age	Boys	Girls
6-8	'The Sons of the She-Wolf'	'The Daughters of the She-Wolf'
8-13	The *Balilla*	*Piccole Italiano*
14-18	The *Avanguardisti*	*Giovani Italiane*

In 1937 the ONB joined with the Young Fascists (Fasci Giovanili) to create a single youth organisation, GIL (Gioventu Italiana del Littorio), for 6-21 year olds.

The Balilla was highly militarised and political indoctrination was a major characteristic of the movement. However, there were also extensive sporting and recreational activities organised by the Balilla and these did appeal to many children.

Education

At first Italian schools retained considerable freedom over what they taught. Mussolini appointed the philosopher Giovanni Gentile as his first Minister for Education. Gentile drafted the 1923 Education Act, which reformed the education system but more in the spirit of humanism than Fascism. Gentile's reforms increased the elitist nature of the school system, promoting grammar schools (*ginnasio*), and encouraging philosophy and classical studies. He gave less emphasis to technical and vocational education.

In order to ensure that the schools did not propagate anti-Fascist ideas, anti-Fascist teachers were removed in the 1920s and all teachers had to take an oath of loyalty to Mussolini. In 1929 the Ministry of Public Instruction was redesignated the Ministry of National Education; this was a significant change because in Italian '*educazione*' means 'upbringing' and so is a more comprehensive term.

Mussolini's interference in schools was relatively limited until the mid 1930s; only in 1936 were schools obliged to use Fascist textbooks. In 1936 a single history textbook became compulsory, replacing the several hundred then in usage. The Fascists sought to promote a particular version of Italian history that would inspire devotion to the Duce and to the PNF. Physical education was given greater priority, so that children could become fitter and so better conditioned for either war (boys) or motherhood (girls!)

In 1939 the Education Minister, Giuseppe Bottai, launched a Schools Charter, which introduced far-reaching changes, including a greater emphasis on science and technology and the introduction of manual work into the curriculum. However, this reform had too little time to have much impact as Italy joined in the Second World War (1940) and then Fascism collapsed in 1943.

135

Fascist indoctrination was certainly more successful in primary schools than in secondary schools; in the latter, teachers prioritised academic results and subjects like philosophy encouraged independent thinking. It was only after the mid-1930s that the Fascists attempted fundamental changes to the education system. Martin Clark has concluded that, *'Pupils were not hostile to Fascist ideas, indeed they accepted them as normal; but they were not committed enthusiasts either.'*

Italian universities enjoyed considerable intellectual freedom under Mussolini as long as they outwardly conformed and the vast majority of academics were prepared to do so; only 11/1200 university professors refused to take an oath of loyalty in 1931. Lectures and journals were largely unsupervised.

Opera Nazionale Dopolavoro (1925)

Dopolavoro ('after work') was definitely the most popular of all the Fascist organisations and institutions set up by Mussolini. It was an umbrella organisation for recreation and was highly successful in expanding recreational opportunities, particularly for the working classes. Martin Clark points out that its popularity was also the result of the emphasis being on *'fun, not propaganda'*.

Dopolavoro's membership reached 4 million in the 1930s. Dopolavoro owned theatres, libraries, football pitches and billiard halls. It organised free summer holidays for children from poor families and excursions and holidays for workers. Dopolavoro clubhouses were set up in virtually every village and town in North and Central Italy but, in line with most other Fascist agencies, Dopolavoro was very much less effective and active in the South.

Mussolini's Foreign Policy

Mussolini dominated Italian foreign policy, whether personally holding the position of Foreign Minister, as he did for most of the 1920s, or during the tenure of the foreign ministry by Dino Grandi (1928-32) or Galeazzo Ciano (1936-43).

Q. **How have historians interpreted Mussolini's Foreign Policy?**

There is no doubt that Mussolini meant *'To make Italy great, respected and feared.'* However, historians are divided over the extent to which Mussolini's foreign policy marked a break with that of the liberal era and how far there was continuity.

Furthermore, there is considerable historical debate about whether Mussolini's eventual alliance with Nazi Germany was the result of ideology or pragmatism. 'Anti-Fascist' historians such as De Felice and Gentile argue that Fascist Italy could have avoided the 'German embrace' and entry into the Second World War.

By contrast, historians such as Martin Blinkhorn and MacGregor Knox argue that the German alliance and Italy's aggression of the late 1930s and early 1940s were the logical outcome of the Fascist belief in struggle and violence. Blinkorn suggests that Mussolini needed war to keep Fascism alive, that Mussolini was anxious by the early 1930s that *'his movement and regime were growing too comfortable, too paunchy and middle-aged and needed new challenges.'*

Macgregor Knox has put forward an interpretation that stresses the interdependence of Fascist foreign and domestic policy, *'internal consolidation was a prerequisite of foreign conquest and foreign conquest was the decisive prerequisite for a revolution at home'*. Knox, therefore, sees violent struggle, whether at home or abroad, at the heart of Fascism.

136

During the 1920s, Mussolini's foreign policy had much in common with that of the liberal governments before and after the First World War, as he aimed to expand Italy's influence in the Balkans, Near East and East Africa. However, Mussolini's methods were certainly different from those of his liberal predecessors. He was hasty and reckless, prone to make grandiose gestures and, above all, keen to increase Italian prestige and his own.

Mussolini saw an aggressive foreign policy as essential in order to transform the Italian people – to make them into a dynamic, aggressive and united nation. This aim certainly seems increasingly evident in the mid to late 1930s when the Fascist regime, both at home and abroad, became more radical.

By and large, in the 1920s Mussolini appeared prepared to play by the rules of western diplomacy and Italy had an important role in the League of Nations. Mussolini was for the most part content to co-operate with Britain and France, the strongest European powers in the 1920s who dominated the areas Mussolini was keen to expand in, namely the Mediterranean and North Africa.

Examples of Italy co-operating with the rest of the international community:

☑ Mussolini signed the Locarno Pacts (1925), which involved Germany accepting its western frontiers and being admitted to the League of Nations.

☑ Mussolini acquired Fiume from Yugoslavia by diplomacy in 1924 and, in the same year, received small bits of French and British territory in East Africa.

☑ Mussolini signed the Kellogg-Briand Pact (1928) along with over sixty other countries, whereby they pledged to renounce war. Mussolini did not take this agreement seriously.

The explanation for the relatively peaceful and restrained policy conducted by Mussolini during the 1920s lies in the fact that much of his attention was focused on extending and then consolidating his political position within Italy. Furthermore, much of the Italian army was tied up in suppressing rebellion in Libya.

However, even in the 1920s, Mussolini demonstrated a preference for confrontation and aggression:

☒ **The Corfu Crisis (1923).** Italian troops occupied Corfu after the murder of an Italian general by Greek bandits. Mussolini sought to bully Greece into paying compensation to Italy. It is possible that Mussolini had planned to take Corfu permanently but he withdrew after the League of Nations ordered Greece to pay Italy compensation.

☒ **Relations with France and Yugoslavia.** Superficially Mussolini appeared to want good Franco-Italian relations, but he demonstrated a hostile attitude to France in several ways in the 1920s:

   o He encouraged opposition movements in France's Moroccan and Tunisian colonies.

   o He was hostile to Yugoslavia, an ally of France, because it had gained territory Italy had wanted at the end of the First World War. Mussolini funded Croat separatists who sought independence from Yugoslavia.

   o He also helped King Zog seize power in Albania (1926) and turned Albania into a satellite state, to extend Italy's influence to the south of Yugoslavia.

Opportunities for Expansion in the 1930s

'Intentionalist' historians, for example, MacGregor Knox, who believe that Mussolini had long-term aims in foreign policy, argue that in the 1930s Mussolini was at last able to discard the cautious approach of the 1920s in order to realise those aims. 'Structuralist' historians, like De Felice, on the contrary, contend that Mussolini was merely an opportunist, with no fixed plans, and that ideology played no role in his foreign policy. Structuralists view Mussolini's more expansive foreign policy in the 1930s simply in terms of a response to changing international circumstances.

What cannot be doubted is that the international situation in the 1930s was much more favourable to Italian expansion:

- The League of Nations was undermined by the Japanese invasion of Manchuria (1931) and Germany's withdrawal from League membership (1933).

- Hitler came to power in Germany (1933), intent on revising the Versailles Treaty.

- The Wall Street Crash (1929) and the Great Depression undermined international relations as tariffs were increased and countries became more inward-looking.

Initial suspicion of Hitler

At first Mussolini was decidedly cool towards Hitler when he came to power in 1933. Mussolini's first meeting with Hitler – in Venice in June 1934 – was a tense affair. Mussolini wanted Austria as a satellite state of Italy and feared that Hitler would seek to take it over and that he would then demand German-speaking South Tyrol, which Italy had acquired from Austria-Hungary (1919). In July 1934 Austrian Nazis murdered the Austrian chancellor, Dollfuss, who had close links with Mussolini, but the Austrian Nazis failed to seize power. Mussolini moved Italian troops to the Brenner Pass (the Italian-Austrian border) in order to warn Hitler off intervening in Austria (it is not clear whether Hitler had been planning an invasion).

Mussolini courts the Western democracies: The Stresa Front (1935)

When Hitler broke the Versailles Treaty in March 1935, by announcing the reintroduction of conscription and his intention to build up an army of 550,000, Mussolini signed the Stresa Front (April) with Britain and France. The three powers agreed to take collective action in the event of any further German breach of Versailles.

However, this pact collapsed very quickly because:

- Britain did not consult either Italy or France before signing the Anglo-German Naval Agreement with Hitler in June 1935, which permitted Germany to expand its navy beyond the level laid down at Versailles.
- Mussolini invaded Abyssinia in October 1935. Britain and France condemned this aggression.

Mussolini's Invasion of Abyssinia (1935-36)

The Abyssinian War of 1935-36 was much bigger and more brutal than any of the imperialist adventures of the liberal Italian governments. This was a key turning point in Mussolini's foreign policy; as a result of the invasion, his relations with Britain and France deteriorated and he drew closer and closer to Hitler's Germany.

Historians disagree about what led Mussolini to invade Abyssinia. 'Structuralists' (see above) argue that Mussolini did so in an attempt to divert the Italian people's attention away from domestic economic problems. 'Intentionalists' (see above) see it in terms of 'an outgrowth of Fascism itself, its need to fight and win battles' (Martin Blinkhorn).

What were Mussolini's aims in invading Abyssinia?

→ To link up Italy's existing colonies in North-East Africa (Eritrea and Italian Somaliland).

→ To gain revenge for the Italian defeat at Adowa (1896).

→ To satisfy the many Italian nationalists who had been angry at Italy's failure to acquire any colonies as a result of the 1919-20 Peace Settlement.

→ To be able to claim to be recreating the glories of the ancient Roman Empire in North Africa.

Mussolini was certainly considering an attack on Abyssinia from 1932 onwards, if not before. He picked a quarrel with Abyssinia after a small military clash at Wal-Wal in December 1934. Mussolini believed that France and Britain would not take any action against Italy if it invaded Abyssinia as Pierre Laval, the French Foreign Minister, had, in January 1935, agreed that there were no major French interests at stake in Abyssinia. Furthermore, in June 1935, Anthony Eden, the British Foreign secretary, had visited Rome and proposed a deal between Abyssinia and Italy which would have given Italy the Ogaden region and compensated Abyssinia with a piece of British Somaliland, allowing Abyssinia access to the sea.

Contrary to Mussolini's expectations, the League of Nations imposed economic sanctions on Italy following its invasion of Abyssinia in October 1935. This was largely because the British government felt under pressure from public opinion – which was very pro-League – to take a stand against Italy. The imposition of sanctions (even though they did not include oil or steel), and, Britain and France's attempts to prevent Mussolini from gaining all of Abyssinia (e.g. by planning to offer him two-thirds of it in the Hoare-Laval Pact of December 1935) angered Mussolini. By contrast Germany ignored the League sanctions and continue to trade with Italy. Mussolini completed the conquest of Abyssinia in May 1936.

Q. What were the results of the Abyssinian War?

→ Mussolini now turned his back on good relations with Britain and France, which he possibly could have rebuilt.

→ Mussolini drew closer to Hitler, whose own aggression was encouraged by Mussolini's flouting of the League.

→ Mussolini undermined the League of Nations and withdrew Italy from membership.

→ The successful conquest of Abyssinia also made Mussolini more open to take risks and use force but it had paid off in this instance.

→ It was very popular in Italy.

→ Abyssinia did not prove of significant commercial value to Italy; in 1939 only 2% of Italy's trade was with Abyssinia.

→ Sanctions hurt the Italian economy.

→ The war was very expensive, costing 40 million lire, and Italian troops were engaged in fighting Abyssinian guerrillas until 1939.

Intervention in the Spanish Civil War

Both Mussolini and Hitler intervened in the Spanish Civil War, which broke out in July 1936, in support of General Franco's Nationalists against the Republican government. Mussolini sent 70,000 troops to Spain but they performed poorly, suffering a humiliating defeat at Guadalajara in March 1937, where Italian anti-Fascists formed part of the opposing force.

Q. Why did Mussolini intervene in Spain?

→ Mussolini wanted to weaken France (which had a left-wing Popular Front government similar to the Spanish government) by installing a right-wing regime in Spain, which he hoped would become a satellite state of Italy.
→ To acquire naval bases in the Balearic Islands, which would help promote Italian power in the Mediterranean.

However, Mussolini gained very little from intervention in Spain, which proved very costly (approximately 14 million lire).

Closer relations with Nazi Germany

In October 1936 Italy and Germany signed the Rome-Berlin Axis, a commercial and friendship treaty. In September 1937 Mussolini visited Germany and was received very warmly by Hitler. This was followed in November 1937 by Italy signing the Anti-Comintern Pact (originally signed by Germany and Japan in 1936). In December 1937 Italy walked out of the League of Nations, as Germany had done back in 1933.

Probably in an attempt to cement his friendship with Hitler, Mussolini introduced a series of anti-semitic laws in Italy in 1938. There is no doubt that many radical Fascists saw the German alliance as a way of radicalising the Fascist regime in Italy. Mussolini himself certainly came to fall under Hitler's spell.

The Anschluss (March 1938)

As Mussolini drew closer to Hitler, he changed his policy towards Austria and decided to allow Hitler to increase German influence over Austria. In fact in January 1936 Mussolini told Hitler he was happy for Austria to become a client state of Germany. In March 1938 Hitler felt compelled to organise an immediate takeover of Austria after the Austrian chancellor, Schuschnigg, announced he would call a referendum on Austria's independence. When Hitler invaded Austria - having been invited to send troops in by the newly appointed Austrian chancellor, Seyss-Inquart (an Austrian Nazi) - Mussolini did not object.

The Sudeten Crisis and the Munich Conference (1938)

In 1938 a crisis broke out over Hitler's demand that the Czech government allow the German-speaking area of Czechoslovakia – the Sudetenland – to unite with Germany. By September 1938, it looked likely that Germany would invade Czechoslovakia and that Britain and France might then intervene on the Czechs' side.

War was averted when Mussolini helped set up the Munich Conference in September 1938, attended by Germany, Italy, France and Britain. He was keen to avoid war breaking out and was able to pose as a mediator between Hitler and the British and French (the Czech government was not invited to attend). However, again it was Hitler who was dictating the pace and direction of international affairs, not Mussolini. Hitler did not even inform Mussolini before he occupied the rest of Czechoslovakia in March 1939.

Mussolini was encouraged by Britain and France's appeasement of Hitler over the Sudetenland (and the Anschluss), to believe that neither country would stand up to aggression and this in part explains Mussolini's increasingly belligerent foreign policy from the late 1930s onwards.

1939-43: Growing Italian aggression

Mussolini was very much aware of the fact that Italy was the junior partner in the Italian-German relationship – this became increasingly the case in the period 1939-43. That was one reason for his determination to increase Italy's influence and possessions by force. In February 1939, Mussolini announced to the Fascist Grand Council his intention that Italy should break out of the 'prison' of the Mediterranean. He said that the 'bars' of the prison were '*Corsica, Tunisia, Malta and Cyprus; its sentinels Gibraltar and Suez*'.

The Invasion of Albania (April 1939)

This was a publicity stunt by Mussolini as Albania was already virtually under Italian control. Mussolini wanted to show that he had made some gains following on Germany's expansion in 1938-39.

The Pact of Steel (May 1939)

Mussolini now fatally tied Italy to Nazi Germany by signing a military alliance, which obliged both countries to support each other in the event of a war. This worked to Germany's advantage because it was much more likely that Germany would go to war. Mussolini probably hoped to acquire German support for Italian expansion in the Balkans, Mediterranean and North Africa. However, Mussolini had no intention of going to war in 1939 as he knew how unprepared Italy's armed forces were.

The Outbreak of World War Two (September 1939)

Mussolini was very alarmed when he heard in August of Hitler's plans to invade Poland. When Hitler invaded Poland in September and Britain and France declared war, Mussolini announced that Italy was a 'non-belligerent power'. Mussolini told Hitler that he could only enter the war if he received 17,000 trains full of munitions from Germany.

The State of Italy's Armed Forces in 1940

Mussolini's dependence on his German ally in the Second World War was largely the result of Italy's continuing economic weakness and lack of raw materials. During the Second World War this was worsened by Italian imports being disrupted (partly by British attacks).

Between 1935 and 1938 Italy spent 11.8% of its national income on rearmament compared to 6.9% in France and 5.5% in Britain – but there was not much to show for this investment as much of the spending went on inferior weapons.

Q. **What evidence is there of Italy's military weakness in 1940?**

- Italy was particularly short of oil, coal and iron ore. This resulted in a 20% reduction in steel output in 1940-42.

- Mussolini boasted of an army of 8 million but in 1939 only 0.8 million troops were available; by 1940 this had risen to 3 million.

- The Italian Navy had no aircraft carriers and only 8 battleships.

- Italy did have a large submarine fleet but a third of its submarines were destroyed by the British in the first 3 weeks of the war.

- The Army had only 1,500 tanks (and most of them were light).

- The Italian airforce lacked long-range bombers and its fighters were slow. In 1939 Italy had 1500 aircraft compared to Germany's 4200.

- The leadership of Italy's armed forces was old and there was intense rivalry between the army, navy and airforce.

Italy's entry into World War Two (June 1940)

Mussolini kept out of the war for the first 10 months, torn between a desire to share in any spoils won by Germany and a realisation that Italy wasn't ready for war. Mussolini was not comfortable with his position of 'non-belligerency' (as he put it) as it was reminiscent of Italy's stance at the start of the First World War.

After Hitler's swift conquest of Poland, Norway, Denmark, Holland and Belgium in September 1939-June 1940 and, with France on the point of collapse, Mussolini decided to declare war. Mussolini was keen not to lose out on any possible territorial gains. Italy declared war on France just two weeks before it surrendered. Ciano (his son-in-law and foreign minister), King Victor Emmanuel and most of the Italian people were against Mussolini's decision.

Italy gained very little French territory after France surrendered because Hitler wanted to preserve good relations with the new Vichy French government.

Italian campaigns in the Balkans and North Africa (1940-43)

Mussolini wanted to conduct his own campaigns, separate from Hitler's, so he invaded Greece in October 1940. This proved disastrous and Hitler had to send in German troops to help Mussolini out in April 1941. In September 1940 Italian forces in Libya invaded Egypt but were driven out by British forces. Again, in 1941, the Germans had to send troops in and take control of the campaign.

In November 1940, the Royal Air Force destroyed half of the Italian fleet at Taranto and in March 1941 British forces expelled Italian troops from East Africa.

In June 1941 Mussolini weakened his forces in the Balkans and North Africa by sending 200,000 troops to the Eastern Front to help Hitler's attack on the USSR.

In November 1942 British-American armies finally defeated the German-Italian forces in North Africa at El Alamein.

The Fall of Mussolini (July 1943)

In 1943 the Allies invaded Sicily. The war had never been popular in Italy and became increasingly unpopular as defeats mounted up and economic conditions worsened. Real wages fell by 30% in 1940-43; food prices rose by 72% in 1940-42 and rationing was introduced. In March 1943 strikes involving 130,000 workers broke out in several northern cities.

Victor Emmanuel III, some of the generals and the majority of the Fascist Grand Council in the Fascist Party combined to depose and arrest Mussolini in July 1943. Mussolini was replaced by Marshal Badoglio, who surrendered to the Allies in September 1943.

Mussolini was rescued by German troops and spent the rest of the war in northern Italy as puppet ruler of the Salo Republic, which was effectively under German control. In April 1945 he was captured and executed by communist partisans.

Mussolini's Italy

1914	Mussolini expelled from the Socialist Party
1915	Treaty of London - Italy joins the First World War
1918	Universal male suffrage introduced
1919	Proportional representation introduced
	Fasci di Combattimento set up
	Treaty of St Germain
	General election -PSI win 156 seats
1919-20	The "Red Biennium"
1921	Fascist Party founded
	General Election: PNF win 35 seats
1922	March on Rome
	Mussolini appointed PM in a coalition government
1923	Fascist Militia set up
	Education Act
	Nationalist Party merged with the PNF
	Acerbo law
	Corfu Incident
1924	General Election; coalition of PNF and Liberals win 66% seats
	Fiume gained
	Matteotti murdered
	The Aventine Secession
1925	Mussolini announces authoritarian government
	Dopolavoro
	Battle for Grain launched
1926	Mussolini gained power to issue decrees PNF sole legal party
	Public Safety Law

	Purge of squadristi
	Syndical law
	Battle of the Lira
1927	Battle for Births
	Charter of Labour
1928	Electoral law - Fascist Grand Council nominates candidates
1929	Lateran Treaties
1930	National Council of Corporations set up
1933	Institute for Industrial Reconstruction set up
1935-36	Invasion and conquest of Abyssinia Rome-Berlin Axis Mussolini intervenes in Spanish Civil War
1938	Anti-semitic Laws
1939	Pact of Steel Italian invasion of Albania
1940	Italy entered the Second World War
1943	Mussolini overthrown
	Mussolini rescued by the Nazis and set up as leader of the Salo republic
1945	Mussolini captured and executed by partisans

Revision and essay writing activities on the Rise and Rule of the Italian Fascist Party

Below, you will find two essay questions, which cover most of the issues dealt with in the Italy section of the Revision Guide. By examining these questions, you will be able to test your understanding and recall of that material, as well as gaining insights into how to respond to essay questions. I have given you some ideas about how they could be tackled and then provided you with space to add examples and further points.

1. **How far did any one authoritarian ruler you have studied change the country he ruled socially and economically?**

NB.   In answering this open question, I have chosen the example of Mussolini. Mussolini is not a named individual on the Paper 2 syllabus but can be used in open questions such as this one.

In answering this question, first it is necessary to identify what Mussolini's aims were. It is open to question how far Mussolini wanted to bring about change, although it is equally clear that there were many Fascists who were committed to revolutionary change. In terms of the question's parameters, you must focus on Mussolini in power, rather than his rise to power (apart for possibly determining his aims) and you must concentrate on social and economic change and not wander off into political change. After outlining Mussolini's aims for the economy and society, I have created a plan, evaluating the degree of change achieved in the economy. I have also indicated some areas of society that would merit consideration and left space for your own points and for examples/evidence you might use in answering this question.

What were Mussolini's aims for society and the economy?

This is difficult to define precisely because of the incoherent nature of Fascism. Mussolini had originally founded the Fasci di Combattimento as a left-wing movement; within the original programme, there was a commitment to radical transformation of the economy and society. It contained socialist elements which challenged the interests of capitalists, the Church and the monarchy. Mussolini subsequently relaunched his movement as the PNF in 1921 with a broadly rightwing programme. Therefore, as Denis Mack Smith suggests, Mussolini can be seen essentially as an opportunist whose main aim, once in power, was to maintain it. However, other historians argue that ideology did matter to Mussolini and that in the late 1930s the Fascist regime embarked on a more radical stage where Mussolini aimed at more totalitarian control.

Given the fact that the Fascists' takeover of the Italian state had only been partial, the basis for a genuine Fascist revolution was largely missing. In coming to power, Mussolini had compromised with the existing elites in society (big industrialists, large landowners, the Church hierarchy, the Court) and arguably continued to do so right through to 1943. Whatever Mussolini's personal preferences were, there certainly remained a more radical Fascist wing, particularly among the syndicalists and Fascist trade unions, who sought to transform Italy into a genuinely 'Corporate state'.

Mussolini's economic priorities were to create a modern economy capable of supporting an aggressive foreign policy and to achieve self-sufficiency, rather than transforming Italy's economic structures. Furthermore, Mussolini sought to use both economic policy and social policy (education, culture, youth movements, relations with the Church) to generate support for his regime.

1. How far did the establishment of the Corporate state transform the economy and society?

Whilst for many Fascists, 'Corporatism' was seen as a third way between capitalism and communism, and a way of transforming both society and the economy, it appears that Mussolini viewed it largely as a propaganda exercise. Corporate structures were gradually but erratically created over the course of the 1920s and 1930s, culminating in the establishment of 22 'mixed' corporations and the National Council of Corporations. However, neither the National Council nor the later Chamber of Fasces and Corporations had real influence in shaping economic decisions. The corporate state was a façade; in theory, it was supposed to harmonise labour relations by bringing together employers' and workers' representatives, but in practice, the system advantaged big business. Free trade unions and strikes were banned and within the corporate structure workers were unable to choose their own representatives whilst the employers could. Rossoni's dismissal in 1928 as secretary of the confederation of Fascist unions signalled the radical syndicalists' defeat.

2. (a) How far did Mussolini transform Italy's economy into a modern one, capable of supporting his great power aspirations?

Mussolini had little knowledge of economics and Fascist economic policy proved to be far from coherent. Initially, Mussolini's economic policy was directed towards recovery after the post-war economic crisis. Up to 1925, De Stefani successfully followed conventional liberal economic policies and there was minimal government intervention. Thereafter, Mussolini became much more interventionist, launching a series of economic 'battles'. However, none of these campaigns fundamentally altered Italy's economic structures. The power of big business and the great landowners was not challenged. Nor was Italy transformed into a modern industrial power. There were important infrastructure developments, such as the construction of the autostrada and electrification of 5000 Km of railway, but Italian industry continued to lag far behind countries like Germany and Britain. In 1939, Italy produced just 2.4 million tons of steel; Britain, by contrast, produced 13.4 million tons and Germany 22.5 million.

The 'Battles' were fundamentally misconceived, another product of Mussolini's desire to pose rather deliver real change. The Battle for Grain (1925) did end Italy's reliance on wheat imports but it damaged agriculture by encouraging wheat to be grown at the expense of more appropriate crops such as citrus fruit. The Battle for the Lira (1926) resulted in making Italian exports too uncompetitive. During the Great Depression, the Fascist government did take measures to mitigate against its worst effects, notably the creation of the IMI and the IRI, and these did represent significant change because by the late 1930s the government owned 20% of the capital of industries. Only in the USSR was there a bigger public sector.

Public work schemes, notably in the Pontine Marshes, were successful in reclaiming and irrigating land for cultivation. However, more radical plans for 'integral land reclamation', drawn up by Serpieri, were ditched. Furthermore, Mussolini did nothing to address the 'Southern Question' as little land reclamation was carried out in the South whose agriculture remained very unproductive. Fascist attempts to prevent the continuing 'flight from the land' by poor labourers and peasant farmers failed.

---

2. (b) How far did Mussolini achieve 'autarky'?

From the mid-1930s onwards, Mussolini's regime increasingly sought to achieve 'autarky' (economic self-sufficiency). Mussolini wanted to build up Italy's industry and its raw material resources to support foreign wars of conquest. Although there was some success in aluminium and oil, the drive for autarky failed miserably as economically Italy was far from ready to go to war at the end of the 1930s, which Mussolini had to inform Hitler in 1939. The Abyssinian invasion (1935-36) led to damaging League of Nations' sanctions, which actually worsened Italy's raw material shortages. Also Italian exports were affected, with a major reorientation of Italy's trade relations; after 1936, 25% of Italy's exports went to Africa and another 25% went to Germany.

---

3. How far did Mussolini's policies change Italian society?

Changing society, as opposed to using social policy to generate support for his regime, does not appear to have been a major priority for Mussolini. In many ways Mussolini was content to work with and protect the interests of the existing ruling elites in Italy. This certainly frustrated the more radical Fascists like Rossoni and Farinacci. Mussolini's major initiative and success in social policy was restoring relations between the Italian state and the Catholic Church. This limited the change Fascism could bring about as the Lateran Treaties recognised the Church as a rival centre of values and authority. However, from the mid 1930s onwards, there is a case for arguing that Mussolini began to attempt more fundamental social change as government intervention in education increased and anti-semitic laws were introduced.

(a) Relations with the Catholic Church

....

....

....

....

....

....

....

(b)   Education and Youth movements

....

....

....

....

....

....

....

(c)   The Battle for Births

....

....

....

....

....

(d)   The Media and Arts

....

....

....

....

....

....

....

(e)   Racial policies (Anti-semitic laws)

....

....

....

....

....

....

(f)   Other areas/points of your own

....

....

....

....

....

....

....

Conclusion

....

....

....

....

....

....

2.   To what extent and why did any one single party ruler that you have studied play an important role in international affairs?

NB. In answering this open question, I have chosen the example of Mussolini. Mussolini is not a named individual on the Paper 2 syllabus but can be used in open questions such as this one.

In answering this question, it will be necessary first to explain what Mussolini's main foreign policy aims were, exploring the international role Mussolini had in mind for Italy. Having done this, you need to distinguish between the relatively limited role Italy played in the 1920s and the significantly greater influence Mussolini achieved in the 1930s and early 1940s. Of course, greater influence does not necessarily equate to greater success and Mussolini's more aggressive foreign policy had limited success in the short-term and proved fatal to Fascism in the long-term. It is imperative that you evaluate both the extent to which Mussolini played an important role and the reasons for that. Below I have written an introduction and the first two paragraphs. In addition, I have provided you with the first few sentences of two other sections and then left you space to expand and illustrate them and to write your own conclusion.

There is no doubt that in foreign policy, Mussolini was, above all, keen to increase Italian prestige and his own, *'to make Italy great, respected and feared.'* He wanted Italy to play a much greater role internationally than had been the case under the liberal governments in power since 1861. He aimed to expand Italy's influence in the Balkans, Near East and East Africa and transform her into a great power on a par with Germany, Britain and France. However, in practice, Mussolini was unable to exert the degree of influence he sought, largely because Italy remained relatively weak economically and militarily. Essentially, Italy played a minor role internationally in the 1920s and a significantly larger one in the 1930s and early 1940s, but still nowhere near as great as Mussolini aspired to.

By and large, in the 1920s, Mussolini's foreign policy was peaceful and Italy's diplomatic influence was limited, although Italy had an important role in the League of Nations. Mussolini was for the most part content to co-operate with Britain and France, the strongest European powers in the 1920s who dominated the areas Mussolini was keen to expand in, namely the Mediterranean and North Africa. Nonetheless, in occupying Corfu in 1923, Mussolini did successfully bully Greece in to paying compensation to Italy, undermining the League of Nations in the process, and he was able to negotiate the transfer of Fiume to Italy from Yugoslavia. Mussolini also signed up to both the Locarno Pact (1925) and the Kellog-Briand Pact (1928), both significant international treaties. Mussolini played a restricted and peaceful role at this stage because his priority was extending and then consolidating his political position within Italy. Moreover, a large part of the Italian army was tied up in suppressing rebellion in Libya and, until the mid-1920s, Italy was recovering from the post-war economic crisis.

In the 1930s and early 1940s, Mussolini sought and achieved a greater role for Italy internationally. The main reason for Italy's greater impact in the 1930s, certainly in European affairs, was that more favourable international conditions prevailed. The League of Nations was undermined by the Japanese invasion of Manchuria (1931) and Germany's withdrawal from League membership (1933). Hitler's coming to power in Germany (1933) and his revision of the Versailles Treaty, presented Mussolini with the opportunity to either seek an alliance with the democracies in order to contain Hitler or to achieve an alliance with Germany in order to cash in on Hitler's expansion.

Either way, Mussolini could seek to extend Italy's influence. The potential gains that Italy could make, by means of this diplomatic auction, are shown by the Abyssinian Crisis in which Britain and France sought to appease Mussolini and Hitler looked to strengthen German-Italian relations by continuing to trade with Italy in spite of the League's sanctions. However, 'intentionalist' historians such as MacGregor Knox argue that Mussolini's more aggressive policy in this period was the logical outcome of the Fascist belief in struggle and violence; that Mussolini's foreign policy was ideologically driven and that he was simply waiting was the right opportunities to expand and go to war. According to this view, Mussolini saw an aggressive foreign policy as essential in order to transform the Italian people – to make them into a dynamic, aggressive and united nation.

Having established why Mussolini was able to and wanted to play a greater international role in the 1930s, you need to evaluate the extent of his influence during this period. I have given you the first two sentences below to start off your paragraph on this issue and then left you space to develop and illustrate this.

In the 1930s, Mussolini both diplomatically and militarily had a much greater impact on international affairs. This can be seen in his conclusion of the Stresa Front with Britain and France (1935), his invasion of Abyssinia (1935-36), intervention in the Spanish Civil War (1936-39) and growing ties to Hitler's Germany.

....

....

....

....

....

....

....

....

....

Having evaluated the extent of Mussolini's influence during the 1930s, it is necessary to examine the impact of his intervention in the Second World War. I have given you the first part of a paragraph on this and then left you space to develop and illustrate this.

After agonising in 1939-40 over whether to intervene or not in the Second World War, Mussolini finally committed himself in June 1940 by declaring war on France. Mussolini assumed that Hitler was on the verge of total victory and that Italy could make substantial territorial gains as a German ally. In one sense the role Italy played in the war was minor as Italy's armed forces and industrial strength were very limited and ultimately Italy's poor performance destroyed the Fascist regime. Nonetheless, Mussolini's 'parallel war' in North Africa and the Balkans had a very important role in shaping the Second World War as it extended the scope of the war geographically and undermined Hitler's prospects of victory.

....

....

....

....

....

Your Conclusion:

....

....

....

....

....

....

THE RISE AND RULE OF THE SINGLE PARTY STATE IN GERMANY: 1918-45

Origins of the single-party state

Essay questions are regularly set on the origins of a single party state in Germany (either Germany/Hitler is named in the question or candidates are invited to explore the conditions that gave rise to single party rule in one or two countries that they have studied). In tackling a question like 'Account for the rise to power of Adolf Hitler,' it is necessary to examine both the weaknesses of the Weimar Republic and the strengths of the Nazi Party.

Overview of Germany, 1918-33

There is no doubt that the democratic republic set up in Germany at the end of the First World War faced serious problems from the start. The period 1918-23 saw a series of crises that threatened to overwhelm the Weimar Republic. However, under the guiding hand of Gustav Stresemann (briefly Chancellor and then Foreign Minister), in the years 1924-1929, the Republic appeared to become more stable economically and politically. This recovery was cut short by the Wall Street Crash in October 1929, which led the USA to recall huge loans to Germany, resulting in the collapse of the German economy and large-scale unemployment. Democratic government in Germany began to break down as no chancellor between 1930 and 1932 was able to construct a coalition government that commanded a majority in the Reichstag. Rising unemployment and weak government transformed the fortunes of the Nazi Party (founded in 1919). From a tiny extremist party with just 2% of the seats in the Reichstag in 1928, the Nazis became the largest party in Germany in 1932. In January 1933 the conservative president, Paul von Hindenburg, appointed Adolf Hitler chancellor in a cabinet containing just three Nazis. Hindenburg's assumption that he and his conservative allies would be able to control Hitler was quickly confounded. Within six months Hitler had created a single party dictatorship.

Background

Germany, as a single, unified state, was not created until 1871. Up until 1866 there had been 39 separate states. One of the largest of these states, Prussia, proceeded to absorb the others by means of wars against Austria (1866) and France (1870-71). In 1871 the German Empire was proclaimed. The new Germany, in spite of having an elected Parliament (the Reichstag) had an authoritarian system of government with power chiefly wielded by the Kaiser (emperor). Germany underwent rapid industrialisation, overtaking Britain as Europe's leading industrial country, and developed the most powerful army in Europe.

Kaiser Wilhelm II (1888-1918) pursued an aggressive foreign policy that played a major role in creating the tensions, which sparked off the First World War in 1914. The German government had anticipated a short victorious war, defeating France and Russia by means of the Schlieffen Plan. However, the Schlieffen Plan failed to deliver a quick victory and Germany, and its ally, Austria-Hungary, became locked into a long and costly war of attrition against the Triple Entente (Britain, France and Russia). In 1917 Germany decided to launch a campaign of unrestricted submarine warfare in an attempt to starve Britain into surrender. However, Britain hung on and the gamble backfired as it provoked the USA into declaring war on

Germany. Germany's hopes of victory were not totally extinguished as in 1917 Russia dropped out of the war following a series of defeats and two revolutions, the second of which brought Lenin's Bolsheviks to power. In the spring of 1918 the Germans launched a massive offensive against the French, British and Americans. After initially breaking through the Allies' lines and pushing them back towards Paris, the German attacks lost momentum and from August it was the turn of the Allies to mount a succession of powerful counter-attacks.

By September 1918, the German military leaders, Hindenburg and Ludendorff, accepted that Germany could no longer avoid defeat. In October the Kaiser reluctantly agreed to begin ceasefire talks with the USA and at the same time appointed a cabinet drawn from leading figures in the Reichstag, with the liberal Prince Max of Baden as Chancellor. Wilhelm II seems to have hoped that this concession would enable him to preserve the monarchy in Germany and that it might incline the Allies to treat Germany more generously in the post-war peace negotiations. However, the Kaiser's government quickly began to lose control over the country as a wave of riots, strikes and mutinies broke out. Germany's soldiers, sailors and civilians were angry to find out that Germany was on the verge of defeat after four years of hardship, extreme shortages and two million soldiers killed. For a time it looked as if Germany might follow Russia's recent example and undergo a violent revolution. In an attempt to contain the upheavals, Hindenburg and Prince Max told the Kaiser that he had to abdicate. On November 9th 1918 the Kaiser fled to Holland and Germany was declared a republic. Two days later, the new socialist government, led by Friedrich Ebert, signed a ceasefire with the Allies, bringing World War One to an end.

The new government announced that elections for a constituent National Assembly would be held in January. In these elections, the main parties that supported democracy - the Social Democratic Party (SPD), the Democratic Party (DDP) and the Centre Party (ZP) gained over 70% of the votes cast. In February the Constituent Assembly opened at Weimar (rather than in Berlin where violent disturbances had broken out) and Friedrich Ebert was chosen as Germany's new president. Philipp Scheidemann (SPD) became Chancellor. The Independent Socialists (USPD) refused to join the government so Scheidemann formed a coalition with the Centre and the DDP. The Assembly, after several months of debate, voted in July to adopt the newly drafted constitution.

Q. What long-term problems faced the Weimar Republic?

Without necessarily accepting that the Weimar Republic was doomed to fail from the start, it is clear that it faced serious problems in the years immediately after the First World War. Moreover, although the Republic survived the early crises and became more stable in the mid-1920s, these threats and early weaknesses did not disappear. The world economic crisis of 1929 plunged Germany into renewed crisis and the long-term weaknesses of the Republic were cruelly exposed, contributing to the collapse of democracy in 1933. Therefore any assessment of the rise of a single party state in Germany must examine the long-term problems facing the Weimar Republic.

Q. What early problems and threats did the Republic face?

It was to prove very difficult to establish a democratic system of government in Germany in the wake of military defeat and economic crisis.

The Versailles Treaty (1919)

The new democratic government of Germany was obliged by the Allies to accept peace terms at Versailles in June 1919. Unfortunately for the Weimar Republic, many nationalists blamed the new Socialist government for agreeing to the

Armistice (November 1918) and the Versailles Treaty, claiming that the German army could have fought on, if it had not been stabbed in the back by cowardly, democratic politicians.

Although modern historians are divided about how hard these terms (particularly reparations) hit Germany, there is no doubt that they caused widespread resentment among Germans at the time.

Q. What aspects of the Versailles Treaty did Germans resent?

• The fact that the German government was unable to negotiate the terms of the treaty; Versailles was a *diktat* (dictated peace), which had to be accepted in full or war would resume.

• That Germany lost about 13% of its European territory (plus all of its colonies). What was particularly criticised by Germans was the loss of land in the east; over 2 million Germans ended up living in the new Polish state or in Danzig (under League of Nations' control).

• That the Allies were inconsistent in applying the principle of national self-determination; Poles were united to create a new Poland and Slavs in the Balkans were united in the new Yugolslavia, but Germans living in the Sudetenland (part of the former Austro-Hungarian Empire) were placed under Czech rule and Germany was forbidden to unite with Austria.

• The reparations imposed on their country; the final figure was fixed in 1921 at £6,600 million. The German government claimed that this would cripple Germany; a view shared by the British economist, John Maynard Keynes. However, some recent historians, such as Ruth Henig, challenge this, arguing that the German government exaggerated the burden and that more damage was caused by the way in which Germany chose to pay it off (by increasing the supply of paper money).

• That Germany's armed forces were severely restricted; the army's size was fixed at 100,000; conscription was banned; Germany was not allowed submarines, an airforce or tanks; the Rhineland was to be permanently demilitarized; the German navy could only possess six warships.

Q. What political opposition did the Republic face?

The Weimar Republic (so-called because the Constituent Assembly met there) got off to an extremely difficult start and was dogged by crises over the next four years. There were extreme right and left wing movements in Germany that were opposed to democracy and were committed to overthrowing the Weimar Republic.

Threats from the Left

In January 1919 an extreme left-wing socialist movement known as the Spartacists set up the German Communist Party (KPD). The KPD rejected the new German Republic as insufficiently revolutionary. The KPD was committed to establishing a Bolshevik-style system of government in Germany, involving the confiscation of privately owned factories and land. Over the next four years the Communists organised a series of risings but none of them came close to overthrowing the Republic. From 1920 the KPD contested Reichstag elections and polled between 10 and 15% of the votes cast in the elections of 1928-33. Their continuing hostility to the Republic did undermine its prospects of long-term survival, particularly as it meant that the Left was badly divided between the KPD and SPD who would not work together (except in the case of 1923 in a couple of states). This made it easier for Hitler to come to power in 1933.

The Spartacist Rising, January 1919

In early January 1919 some of the Spartacists staged a rising in Berlin. This was bloodily put down by the freikorps, bands of extreme right-wing ex-soldiers. The Spartacist leaders Karl Liebknecht and Rosa Luxemburg were murdered.

Communist Rising in the Ruhr, March 1920

In March the Communists staged an uprising in the Ruhr, setting up a government at Essen and in April they briefly took over Munich. The Reichswehr (German Army) bloodily restored order, killing hundreds of communists.

'The German October', 1923

The KPD organised street demonstrations and strikes from the summer of 1923 and, in Saxony and Thuringia, the SPD and KPD joined forces to win control of the state governments. The Berlin government used the Army to arrest the KPD ministers and crush the disturbances.

Threats from the Right

Many German nationalists never accepted the Weimar Republic because of the Socialist government's decision to accept the harsh terms imposed at Versailles. The conservative elites (aristocratic landowners, big industrialists and senior army officers, judges and civil servants) who had ruled Germany under the Kaiser largely retained their power after 1918 and they tended to be at best lukewarm in their support for the Republic. More often they were openly hostile to the democratic Republic. Many favoured the restoration of the monarchy or an authoritarian alternative.

The Kapp Putsch, March 1920

In March 1920 Wolfgang Kapp and General von Luttwitz attempted to overthrow the government. Thousands of soldiers who were about to be returned to civilian life joined Freikorps units to seize control of Berlin. Kapp intended to use these 12,000 soldiers to set up a right-wing government with himself as chancellor.

The Defence Minister, Gustav Noske, ordered the Reichswehr (regular army) to restore order. However, the general in charge of the Reichswehr in Berlin, General von Seeckt, refused to order his troops to attack former soldiers. The trade unions organised a general strike which paralysed Berlin. After four days, Kapp realised he could not succeed, lacking sufficient popular support, and fled to Sweden. Over 400 Reichswehr officers were implicated in the putsch but only 48 were dismissed.

The White Terror, 1920-22

1920-22 saw a spate of about 400 political murders, most committed by the extreme right (the "White Terror") but some carried out by the Left. The Freikorps were mainly responsible for this violence. In August 1921 members of the Organisation Consul, a right-wing group, composed mainly of young ex-officers, murdered Matthias Erzeberger, leader of the Centre Party, who had helped negotiate the armistice. In June 1922 Walther Rathenau, the Foreign Minister, was also assassinated by the Organisation Consul.

The "Beerhall Putsch", November 1923

On 8th November Hitler took over a political meeting being addressed by von Kahr, the Bavarian State Commissioner. He announced he was mounting a revolution to overthrow the Weimar Republic. However, Kahr escaped and the Bavarian police and army refused to support the Nazi revolution (Hitler intended to march on Berlin once he had taken control of Bavaria). On 9th November, 2000 SA men marched on the centre of Munich but police opened fire, 16 Nazis were killed and Hitler was arrested later. He was tried in February 1924 and sentenced to 5 years in prison, but only served 9 months.

Q. What problems resulted from the Weimar Constitution?

The Weimar constitution was drawn up between February and July 1919 by the national Constituent Assembly. It established a very advanced democratic system of government, giving all men and women over 20 the vote and strengthened the authority of the Reichstag, the elected house in the German Parliament. Ministers were accountable to the Reichstag, rather than to the Head of the State, the President. However, historians broadly agree that there were certain important weaknesses within the constitution:

1. **The voting system was proportional representation**, meaning that parties gained the same percentage of seats in the Reichstag as the percentage of votes they polled in the elections. This created a number of problems. The system allowed very small parties to gain representation in the Reichstag and, because there were eight major parties in Germany and a score of smaller ones, resulted in the Reichstag's seats being widely distributed among a large number of parties.

    In practice this meant that no party was ever able to gain a majority in the Reichstag, necessitating a series of coalition governments, consisting normally of three or more parties working together.

    These coalition governments did not last long as it proved difficult for the parties involved in them to keep working together. For example, 1919-23 saw eight different government coalitions. The failure to provide stable government was a key factor in explaining why many Germans never supported the Republic and why many other Germans lost faith in the democratic system after 1929, turning to the more authoritarian alternatives promised by either the Nazis or the Communists.

2. **Article 48 of the constitution gave the President extensive emergency powers.** He was able to suspend civil liberties in the event of an emergency, such as the outbreak of civil war. Under President Ebert (1919-25) this did not prove a problem but President Hindenburg (1925-34) used these emergency powers in very controversial ways. Firstly, between 1930 and 1932 he used Article 48 to pass decrees implementing measures that his chancellors could not get passed through the Reichstag. This certainly undermined many Germans' confidence in the democratic system. Secondly, in February 1933 Hindenburg used Article 48 to declare a state of emergency following the Reichstag Fire. Hitler was then able to order the arrest of thousands of his Communist and Socialist opponents and close down their newspapers. This was an important step towards his creation of a one party dictatorship.

Q. What economic problems did the Republic face (1919-23)?

1. **There was high unemployment and low industrial output.** This was largely as a result of the disruption caused by a return to a peacetime economy. Many soldiers could not find work when they came back from the front.

2. **Germany lost valuable mineral resources as a consequence of the Versailles Treaty.** Rich coal and iron-ore deposits were handed over to Poland (Upper Silesia) and to France (Alsace-Lorraine), whilst the Saarland was taken under League of Nations control for 15 years.

3. **Inflation had been a serious problem since the outbreak of the First World War.** The value of the mark had declined greatly by 1919 and the

governments of the period 1919-23 were too inclined to print more paper money to finance the cost of war pensions and reparations. The Allied Reparations Committee in April 1921 had fixed reparations at the sum of 132,000 million gold marks (**£6,600 million**). The £6,600 million was to be paid in yearly instalments of £100 million.

Marks to the £	
1914	20
1919	250
1921	1000
1922	35,000
1923	16,000,000,000,000

The Hyper-Inflation Crisis (1923)

Wilhelm Cuno's government was overwhelmed by a growing crisis over reparations. When the German government failed to hand over its reparations payments in January 1923, France and Belgium decided to send 60,000 troops into the Ruhr. Cuno ordered workers in the Ruhr to engage in passive resistance, to go on strike. German workers sabotaged French attempts to transport raw materials back to France and about 150 were killed in clashes with French and Belgian soldiers. The French then sealed the Ruhr off from the rest of Germany, which had disastrous effects on Germany's economy as the Ruhr produced 80% of Germany's steel and 70% of its coal. The percentage of Germans unemployed rose from 2% to 23%.

Gustav Stresemann, leader of the DVP (German People's Party), became Chancellor in August 1923 and briefly led a "Grand Coalition" comprising the DVP, SPD, Centre and DDP. He brought in the banker Hjalmar Schacht to oversee the currency crisis. Stresemann took the controversial decision to order the workers in the Ruhr to co-operate with the French and he resumed reparations payments. Schacht introduced a new currency, the Rentenmark, to replace the old mark (one rentenmark was exchanged for 10,000,000,000,000 old marks). In 1924 the Rentenmark was replaced by the Reichsmark (which continued until 1945).

Q. **What were the long-term effects of the hyper-inflation crisis?**

1. Many of the middle-class who lost their savings in the hyper-inflation were permanently alienated from the Weimar Republic.

2. Germany suffered from a shortage of domestic investment. Many Germans lost confidence in investing in German industry and businesses following the financial crisis of 1923.

3. Germany became dangerously dependent on US loans, as a result of the Dawes Plan. The Dawes Plan (1924) helped German industry to recover in the years 1924-28 but the Wall Street Crash of October 1929 sent the German economy into crisis as America recalled its loans. Germany suffered more than any other European country from the effects of the ensuing Great Depression in the USA.

The Dawes Plan, August 1924

The Dawes Plan was accepted at the London Conference; Germany was to receive an initial loan of £40 million from the USA. Germany's reparation payments were rescheduled. In total, Germany received £3,000 million in loans from the USA in the period 1924-30. The French promised Germany (but not in public) that they would evacuate the Ruhr within a year (the last troops actually left in July 1925).

1924-29: The 'Best Years of Weimar'

Q. **How stable was Germany in this period?**

Historians are divided in their assessments of the Weimar Republic in the mid to late 1920s. Some argue that the greater prosperity and stability enjoyed by Germany in theses years was very superficial and would not have lasted even if the Wall Street Crash had not occurred. Others argue that the Weimar Republic was well on its way to establishing itself until the economic collapse of 1929.

Q. **What evidence is there of progress?**

Economic

➤ In 1925 Germany entered a period of relative prosperity. The Dawes Plan of 1924 meant that Germany was receiving large loans from the USA.

➤ This money was used to modernise German industry; by 1928 industrial output exceeded the record 1913 figure.

➤ Germany's foreign exports increased by 40% in the years 1925-29.

Social

➤ Industrial workers' wages rose by 21% in 1927-28 alone in real terms, making them the highest paid in Europe.

➤ Government spending on health, education and social services grew enormously; in 1913 these items made up 37% of total government expenditure, by 1932 they comprised 68%.

➤ Two new universities were built at Hamburg and Cologne.

➤ Unemployment insurance was introduced for 17 million workers in 1927.

Cultural

➤ Germany, and, particularly Berlin, became a vibrant cultural centre. In architecture, the Bauhaus design movement founded by Walter Gropius was highly influential. Thomas Mann won the Nobel Prize for Literature in 1929

Political

➤ There were no further attempts to seize power by either the extreme Left or Right.

➤ The 1928 elections saw both the KPD (Communists) and the DNVP (Nationalists) lose support significantly – the KPD's seats fell from 62 to 54; the DNVP's from 95 to 73 – whilst the Nazis (DNVP) remained a tiny political force with just 12 seats.

➤ The moderate parties, which supported the democratic system, either made significant gains or maintained their existing levels of support, e.g. the Social Democrats (SPD) increased their seats from 100 to 153.

➤ From 1928 to 1930, the Grand Coalition, consisting of the SPD (Social Democrats), DDP (Democratic Party), DVP (People's Party) and ZP (Centre), commanded over 60% of the seats in the Reichstag.

➤ The election of the conservative Paul Von Hindenburg as President in 1925 can be seen as a stabilising factor for the Republic as he was regarded by some of those who were hostile to the Republic as a "Kaiser-substitute".

Germany's international position

Gustav Stresemann, leader of the German People's Party, wanted to see Germany make the best possible recovery from her humiliation in 1918, even if that meant first accepting all the terms of the Treaty of Versailles, and then having them changed by international consent. After a brief spell as Chancellor in 1923, he became Foreign Minister until his death in 1929. His policy was unpopular with the Nationalists but he made Germany accepted again diplomatically and won the Nobel Peace Prize in 1926 jointly with Aristide Briand, the French Foreign Minister (as recognition of their efforts to improve Franco-German relations).

Q. What were Stresemann's achievements?

1 Stresemann negotiated the withdrawal of the French and Belgians from the Ruhr in 1924.
2 He helped negotiate the Dawes Plan in 1924.
3 At Stresemann's suggestion, the West European countries agreed to guarantee the frontiers of Western Europe as laid down at Versailles in 1919. This was known as the Locarno Pact (1925).
4 Germany was allowed to join the League of Nations in 1926.
5 He negotiated a partial withdrawal of the Rhineland by the Allies in 1928.
6 In 1929 he negotiated the Young Plan, which reduced the total reparations bill by about two-thirds.
7 At the time of his death in October 1929, Stresemann was negotiating the final withdrawal of Allied troops from the Rhineland. This happened in 1930.

Q. **What evidence is there of continuing problems, which were to contribute to the Republic's collapse in 1933?**

Economic

> ➤ Germany was dangerously reliant on US loans.

> ➤ Unemployment never fell below 1.3 million in this period and had risen to 1.9 million by 1929 (**before** the Wall Street Crash).

> ➤ Agriculture did not share in the economic boom of the mid to late 1920s. World agricultural prices were low during this period and many German farmers were undercut by more efficient competition, particularly from Canada and the USA.

Social

> ➤ German farm workers' wages were only just over half the national average in 1929.

Political

> ➤ The German Nationalist Party (DNVP) opposed the Young Plan because it implied that Germany still accepted her war guilt. At the end of the 1920s, the DNVP moved further to the Right with the appointment of Alfred Hugenburg as their leader.

> ➤ Similarly, the Centre Party also moved to the Right under the leadership of Heinrich Bruning.

> ➤ The "Grand Coalition" was unstable as it contained a range of political parties from right of centre to left; in 1930 it was to collapse after the SPD argued with its Centre Party coalition partners over how to respond to the Great Depression.

The Nazi Party

Adolf Hitler was born in 1889, the son of an Austrian customs official. His aim was to become an architect, but his two applications for a place at the Academy of Fine Arts in Vienna were rejected. From 1905-1913 he earned a living by doing odd jobs and selling his own watercolour paintings. In 1913 he moved to Munich. Whilst in Vienna, Hitler became interested in the writings of racist authors, particularly Lanz von Liebenfels, who wrote about the supremacy of the Aryan race. Hitler was a Nationalist of the racial kind. He believed that the Germans were superior to the other nationalities of the Austro-Hungarian Empire (mainly Slavs) and of the rest of the world. Vienna was full of rich Jewish businessmen, whose wealth Hitler resented. Hitler also noted the fact that many leading Socialists and Communists were Jews. Hitler was also influenced by the writings of Charles Darwin, who had argued that the evolution of species was the result of a battle for survival in which only the fittest survived. Hitler believed that this could be applied to human societies.

Hitler and the First World War

As a keen German Nationalist Hitler had greeted the outbreak of war with enthusiasm. Since he was living in Munich, he enlisted in the German rather than the Austro-Hungarian Army. Like most Germans, Hitler had believed that the war was going well, and the collapse in 1918 came as a great shock. Like the majority of Germans, he jumped to the conclusion that Germany had been betrayed, that the Communists and the Social Democrats had 'stabbed the Fatherland in the back' and that these 'November criminals' were to blame for Germany's defeat.

The early years of the Nazi Party

In January 1919 Anton Drexler set up the German Workers' Party (DAP) in Munich; his idea was to create a party that would be both working class and nationalist. Hitler joined the tiny party in September 1919. He was put in charge of recruitment and propaganda and soon showed organisational ability and a talent for oratory. In 1920 Hitler took over as party leader and the party produced a Twenty-Five Point programme, which combined nationalist and socialist demands. In 1921 Hitler set up the Sturmabteilung (storm-troopers) or SA; the SA's initial role was to protect party meetings against attacks by their enemies. They were largely recruited from former members of the Freikorps. Hitler saw the propaganda value of symbols and adopted the swastika as the party emblem and introduced the raised-arm salute. He also renamed the party the National Socialist German Workers Party (NSDAP).

In the early years of the Nazi movement, Hitler aimed to seize power by force. By 1923, Hitler had forged links with other right-wing groups in Bavaria. Hitler aimed to model his putsch on Mussolini's March on Rome, which had led to Mussolini being appointed Prime Minister in October 1922. Hitler banked on gaining the support of Kahr (Bavarian State Commissioner), and other right-wing officials in Bavaria who were hostile to the government in Berlin. However, their support was not forthcoming when Hitler attempted to take control of Munich in November 1923 and consequently the Munich Putsch failed, with 16 Nazis killed and Hitler arrested. Hitler was sentenced to five years in prison but served just nine months in Landsberg prison; during his imprisonment he dictated the first part of his autobiography, *Mein Kampf*.

Q. **What did Hitler learn from the failure of the *Beerhall Putsch*?**

• Crucially Hitler learned from the failure of the Munich Putsch; he changed his tactics – instead of seeking power through revolution, he decided to achieve power by legal means and then, once in power, establish a dictatorship. It would be necessary, as Hitler put it, "*to hold our noses and enter the Reichstag alongside Marxist and Catholic deputies.*"

• Hitler also decided that the Party needed to broaden its appeal beyond that of the working-class; consequently Hitler moved increasingly away from the socialist ideas contained in the Twenty-Five Points and instead looked to win more middle-class support, with an increased emphasis on the nationalist elements of their programme.

• After 1925 the Fuhrerprinzip was strengthened. During Hitler's absence in prison, the Nazi Party had split into a number of warring factions. In 1926 Hitler successfully reimposed his authority over the Party and reorganised it.

The SA were reorganised and given greater responsibility for distributing propaganda. Hitler divided the Party organisation into 35 Gaue (regions). In 1926 Hitler created the SS (Schutzstaffel), as his bodyguards, and founded the Hitler Youth.

However, Party membership remained small at 35,000 (1926) and in 1928 the Party only gained 12 seats in the Reichstag elections (less than 3% of the votes).

The Wall Street Crash of 1929

Q. How did the Wall Street Crash undermine the Weimar Republic and transform the fortunes of the Nazis?

1. Its impact on the German Economy

In October 1929 the USA was hit by a terrible economic crisis, which soon spread to the rest of the world. The 'Wall Street Crash' of October 1929, which wiped millions off the value of American shares, led US investors to withdraw their money from Germany. Businesses in Germany went bankrupt, banks collapsed and people became unwilling to invest their money. The result was soaring unemployment.

On the eve of the Great Depression there had been just under 2 million unemployed in Germany; this rose to 3.5 million in 1930, to 4.4 million in 1931 and peaked in late 1932 at six million.

The Depression, unlike the crisis of 1923, was a deflationary crisis: prices were going down rather than up. This destroyed profit margins and caused more businesses to go bust. The value of Germany's exports fell from £630 million in 1929 to just £280 million in 1932.

2. Its impact on German Politics

The Depression revived the kind of violent and unstable politics that Germany had experienced in the period 1918-23. There was large-scale street violence as the paramilitary organisations of the various political parties, particularly the Nazi SA and the Communist Red Front, clashed with each other. Extremist parties like the Communists grew in strength and gained more votes because people were disillusioned at the inability of the government to solve the problems of the Depression.

Chancellor Brüning's approach to Germany's economic problems in the years 1930-32 was traditional and cautious. He kept government spending and taxes down, balancing the budget, and waited for economic conditions to improve. To Germany's unemployed, this policy seemed callous and ineffective. Many of the jobless (and also those who were worried that they might become unemployed) turned to the extremist political parties.

In the General Election of 1930 the Nazis won 107 seats and the Communists won 89.

In 1930 the Nazis became the second biggest party in Germany and in 1932 the largest.

Q. How?

✓ At a time of economic crisis, many Germans turned to Hitler as a 'messiah' figure who would save Germany in its darkest hour. Figures for the Nazis' electoral fortunes correlate closely with unemployment levels in the period 1930-32: 1928 saw the Nazis with less than 3% of the seats in the Reichstag when unemployment was below 2 million; in the 1930 elections the Nazis gained 107 seats when unemployment topped 3 million; in July 1932 the Nazis won 230 seats when there were more than 6 million jobless. The Nazis promised to tackle unemployment through job creation schemes. This had broader appeal than Bruning's austerity measures.

✓ At a time of weak, unstable government, Hitler appeared to offer the prospect of strong leadership. None of the democratic parties had a leader with the charisma that Hitler possessed. Hitler's attraction to many Germans was demonstrated in April 1932 when he stood as a candidate against Hindenburg, polling 13 million votes to Hindenburg's 18 million, winning many traditional conservative voters away from Hindenburg.

✓ At a time when many property-owners were worried about the possibility of a communist revolution, the Nazis, with their 700,000 strong SA, seemed to present greater security than the government could provide.

✓ They appealed to small farmers/peasants who were struggling with debts, falling food prices and competition from bigger, more commercial farmers. The Nazis promised to protect them and provide subsidies.

✓ The Nazis gained the votes of many lower middle-class Germans (teachers, shop-keepers, civil servants) who were not necessarily unemployed but feared they might end up so.

✓ Many historians have suggested the Nazis picked up little working-class support and, while it is true that most workers in the big cities continued to vote for the SPD or KPD, the Nazis did win significant working-class converts as shown by their predominance within the SA.

✓ Marxist historians have portrayed Hitler as the puppet of big business, arguing that it was their financial support that made possible Nazi electoral success. It is true that the Nazis did receive money from some leading industrialists from 1930 onwards but this was limited before 1933 as many industrialists were worried by the socialist slogans of the more left-wing members of the NSDAP.

✓ They presented an image of dynamism and youth. Their campaigning tactics were more modern that those of other parties, e.g. Hitler flew to many cities in the 1932 elections. Mass rallies created for many Germans a sense of belonging.

✓ Nazi propaganda, skilfully orchestrated by Goebbels, targeted different groups with different messages offering:

> • subsidies to peasants
> • law and order and a return to traditional values to the middle classes
> • jobs for unemployed workers
> • a defence against communist revolution and the revival of Germany as a great power to conservative nationalists.

At the same time, the Nazis promised to unite the country and get all Germans pulling together.

✓ They provided scapegoats for Germany's problems: the Jews (although some historians suggest that the Nazis played down their anti-Semitic message in the early '30s), the democratic system, the Communists, the victor powers in the First World War.

Q. None of this was new, so why did these messages prove more effective in the 1930s than in the 1920s?

> • Disillusionment with the Weimar Republic and democratic parties was far greater, as was the scale of Germany's economic problems.

> • Hitler had created a more respectable image for the Nazis after his release from prison and was therefore able to win more middle class support.

The Breakdown of Democratic Government (1930-32)

Normal democratic government broke down as no government between 1930 and 1932 could command a majority in the Reichstag. Under Article 48 of the Weimar constitution, the president could declare a state of emergency and govern by decree, without consulting parliament. President Paul von Hindenburg had no sympathy with the Weimar Republic; he was a traditional Nationalist and sympathised with Hugenburg's German National People's Party. He regarded the Nazis as radical thugs, but he hated the Social Democrats and Communists even more and was alarmed at the growing strength of the Communists.

In 1930 Hindenburg dismissed Chancellor Müller's government and appointed Heinrich von Brüning of the Centre Party. Brüning had very limited support in the Reichstag but was able to remain in power in the period 1930-32 because Hindenburg used his emergency powers to pass the laws that Brüning requested. By 1932, Hindenburg was tired of having to support the weak Brüning government and so replaced Brüning with the conservative Franz von Papen. Von Papen, however, commanded even less support in the Reichstag, so Hindenburg agreed to call a General Election in July. The result was a triumph for the Nazis who won 230 seats.

Q. Why did Hindenburg not appoint Hitler as Chancellor in the summer of 1932?

After the July 1932 elections, the Nazis were the biggest single party in the Reichstag and no coalition government could be formed without them. President Hindenburg was anxious to get back to a situation in which the government had a parliamentary majority. Such a government would be better able to resist the Communist threat and would also be able to take firm action on the issues of the Versailles Treaty and the economic crisis.

Hindenburg tried to persuade Hitler to join a coalition but Hitler would only do so if he could be chancellor. Hindenburg, who disliked Hitler and feared the SA, was not yet ready to agree to this. Instead Hindenburg called a second election in November 1932. The Nazis' share of seats dropped to 196, but they remained the largest party. Impatient because von Papen was unable to form a coalition, Hindenburg sacked him in November 1932 and replaced him with General Kurt von Schleicher.

The autumn of 1932: the Nazi Party in crisis?

By the end of 1932 the Nazi morale was low following their loss of seats in the November election. Party funds were exhausted as a result of fighting two parliamentary elections and a presidential election in a single year. Some of Hitler's supporters, especially the SA leadership, were impatient with Hitler's legal approach to gaining power and wanted to stage an armed rising.

Furthermore, General von Schleicher tried to win the support of the more left-wing Nazis and thereby split the Party. Schleicher's overtures to Strasser and other more 'left-wing' Nazis failed and Hitler was able to reassert his leadership over the Party. A Nazi businessman, von Schröder, persuaded a number of his business contacts to make significant contributions to Nazi funds. President Hindenburg quickly fell out with Chancellor von Schleicher, who was unable to command a majority in parliament. Von Papen plotted with Hindenburg against Schleicher.

Q. Why did Hindenburg appoint Hitler as Chancellor on January 30th 1933?

By January 1933 Hindenburg had decided that the only way to achieve a majority coalition was by offering Hitler the chancellorship. In fact, Hindenburg was happier to offer Hitler the chancellorship now that the Nazis' position was somewhat weaker than it had been before November 1932. Hindenburg's offer was based on only three of the eleven cabinet members being Nazis; Von Papen would be vice-chancellor and several members of the conservative Nationalist Party would be ministers. Hindenburg believed that they would be able to control Hitler.

The Establishment of the Single-Party State in Germany

From Chancellor to Dictator, 1933-34

Within six months' of being appointed Chancellor, Hitler had outmanoeuvred his conservative cabinet colleagues and set up a single party state.

<u>1933</u>

January	Hitler appointed Chancellor. 3 Nazi ministers in the Cabinet of 11
February	The Reichstag Fire; the parliament building burnt down. This was blamed on the Communists. Hindenburg declared a state of emergency and Communist and trade union leaders were arrested
March	Reichstag elections - Nazis won 44% of seats, Nationalists won 8%
	The Enabling Act passed - Communist deputies were in prison; the Centre voted in favour of the change to the constitution after Hitler promised to leave the Catholic Church alone. Hitler was now able to by-pass the Reichstag in making laws
	Law to co-ordinate the state parliaments issued; all now had a Nazi majority. In 1934 Hitler abolished all state parliaments
April	Hitler replaced all 18 state governors with Nazis
May	Trade unions were banned – they were replaced by the German Labour Front (a Nazi organisation)
June	All parties except for the Nazis were banned
July	Law passed making the Nazi Party the sole legal party

<u>1934</u>

June	Night of the Long Knives: Ernst Röhm and other SA leaders were arrested and killed; Hitler claimed they had been plotting a putsch. No evidence of this; once in power, Hitler found the SA leaders a liability as they demanded a 'second revolution' which would see big businesses nationalised and the army swallowed up in a people's army led by the SA. Hitler needed to secure his links with the Army and big business in order to further his plans to rearm and expand Germany's borders
August	President Hindenburg died. Hitler made himself Führer, combining the positions of president and chancellor. The Army swore an oath of personal loyalty to Hitler

Q. How appropriate is the term 'totalitarian' to describe the Third Reich?

Carl Friedrich and Zbigniew Brzezinski in their study *Totalitarian Dictatorship and Autocracy (Harvard, 1956)* identified seven characteristics of a totalitarian state:

1. Single party dictatorship
2. Cult of the leader
3. 'An elaborate ideology, consisting of an official body of doctrine covering all vital aspects of man's existence to which everyone living in that society is supposed to adhere'
4. A system of terror...effected through party and secret-police control'
5. A monopoly of control by the party and the government of the media and all cultural activity
6. Control of all aspects of citizens' lives through propaganda, education, mass organisations
7. Centralised control and direction of the entire economy

The Third Reich displayed many of these characteristics, as will become clear from the survey below of its main features. However, it is evident that there were definite limits to totalitarianism in Nazi Germany. This is, at least to a considerable extent, because the Third Reich only survived for 12 years.

The Establishment of Single Party Dictatorship

There were three phases in the establishment of dictatorship:

a) Control at the centre (January-March 1933) – Hermann Goering controlled the Prussian police, brought in 50,000 extra police (mainly SA) and purged many policemen. In February the Reichstag Fire led to the Decree for the Protection of People and State, which suspended civil liberties and led to the virtual destruction of the Communist Party. This culminated in the passing of the Enabling Act, by which Hitler acquired power to bypass the Reichstag.

b) Control beyond the centre (April-July 1933) - destruction of opposition groups. Trade Unions were banned in May, replaced by the German Labour Front. The SPD was banned in June 1933; the KPD had effectively been banned in February 1933. In July 1933, Germany became a one party state. In March/April laws were introduced which brought the state governments under Nazi control.

c) January-August 1934 – state parliaments were abolished and state governments made subordinate to the Reich government in Berlin. In June the Night of the Long Knives brought the SA under control and this, along with the army's oath of allegiance to Hitler following Hindenburg's death, cemented the loyalty of army. In August, following Hindenburg's death, Hitler became Fuhrer.

Q. Were the Party and State fully integrated?

No. Many Nazis wanted the Party to take over state institutions at all levels, but this never happened.

• Hitler did not create a new constitution therefore Weimar institutions remained except for the Reichsrat (upper house of the German Parliament) and the Landtage (state parliaments), which were abolished.

• The civil service was purged in 1933 – under the Law for the Restoration of a Professional Civil Service - but not until 1939 was party membership made compulsory for civil servants. Until 1937 a majority of Reich ministers were non-Nazis e.g. von Neurath (Foreign Minister), von Blomberg (War Minister) - but in 1937/38 most non-Nazis were removed (e.g. Neurath was replaced by Ribbentrop) as Hitler began to accelerate his plans for territorial expansion. By 1936, Himmler controlled all police forces in Germany.

• The Army (*Wehrmacht*) escaped co-ordination by the Nazis; the SA leaders had wanted to create a mass, revolutionary "people's army" resulting from the absorption of the Wehrmacht by the SA. Hitler rejected this and the generals were relieved and grateful when Hitler purged the SA in June 1934. In early 1938 Hitler did remove 18 senior generals, including Blomberg and Fritsch (commander-in-chief) and assumed personal command of the armed forces.

The Führer Cult

A cult of the Führer was established; for example, the book *The Hitler No One Knows* sold 420,000 copies between 1932-40. Hitler's birthday was celebrated with mass rallies and parades. The historian Ian Kershaw argues that Hitler was increasingly a victim of the 'Führer myth' and began to confuse fantasy and reality, especially in foreign policy.

Q. Was Hitler a 'Weak' or 'Strong' Dictator?

Historians have argued about whether Hitler was a 'strong' (e.g. Alan Bullock) or 'weak' (e.g. Martin Broszat) dictator. Certainly Hitler undermined orderly government in Germany by his habit of appointing several people to practically the same job, resulting in officials competing for Hitler's favour (*'working towards the Führer'*). He added to existing institutions rather than destroying them; he created Supreme Reich Authorities whose functions often overlapped with existing ministries, e.g. the Four Year Plan office (under Goering) overlapped with the Todt Organisation (road and defence building) and with the Economics Ministry.

Furthermore, Hitler destroyed cabinet or collective government in Germany; the Cabinet met 72 times in 1933, 19 times in 1934, 4 times in 1936 and not at all after 1938. Because Hitler was the single source of authority, he was in a good position to co-ordinate policy but he failed to do so because he became increasingly lazy and was not interested in the day-to-day government business, particularly in domestic policy. Whether or not the resulting chaos was deliberate (the result of Hitler playing off one minister off against another) or unintended (the result of the 'legal revolution' of 1933/34), it did not prevent Hitler from pursuing his main goals of territorial expansion and the creation of a 'pure' race.

Nazi ideology

National Socialism developed many of the forms of an ideology. However, some historians (e.g. Martin Broszat) have argued that Nazism lacked a distinct ideology and view Nazism as merely a branch of Fascism, sharing a Europe-wide militarism, hatred of communism and stressing centralism within the state. Other historians (Hugh Trevor-Roper, Alan Bullock), whilst accepting that Nazi ideology was not clearly defined, argue that the 'Führer principle' was of particular importance to German fascism; and, above all, stress that Hitler provided Nazism (see *Mein Kampf*) with a unique racial and anti-semitic programme, which was absent in Italian fascism. Yet the Nazis' *Twenty-Five Points* of 1920 were a curious mixture of nationalist and socialist elements. It soon became clear that Hitler was not particularly committed to the socialist element.

In Hitler's eyes, the Volk community was everything, the individual nothing. Hitler's aim was to create a society in which every individual saw the purpose of their life as contributing to the greater good of the German volk; he attacked the idea of individual rights as damaging the national community. However, Hitler's community – Volksgemeinschaft – would be superior to all others, composed of pure Aryan Germans. There was no room for asocials, the disabled, or non-Aryans.

Q **What evidence is there that Hitler attempted to rule in accordance with the ideology outlined above?**

i)   Policy towards Asocials

In 1936 an "asocial colony" Hashude was set up, e.g. for chronic alcoholics. Initially the idea was to re-educate them but in the late 1930s many were sent to concentration camps. About 10,000 tramps were sent to concentration camps and many died in them. 25,000 out of Germany's 30,000 gypsies died in camps during the Second World War.

ii)   Policy towards the Disabled

Eugenics had been increasingly influential in the 1920s in Germany and elsewhere; in 1932 the Prussian Health Council had proposed voluntary sterilisation for certain hereditary illnesses. In July 1933 the Nazi Sterilisation Law made it compulsory for a wide range of hereditary illnesses (some of them were hardly hereditary e.g. alcoholism). 320,000 people were sterilised.

1939-41 saw the Nazis pursue a euthanasia programme against the physically and mentally handicapped. 72,000 were killed. The Nazis tried but failed to keep it secret and a number of individuals protested, notably Cardinal von Galen.

iii)   Anti-semitic policies

- In May 1933 the SA organised a one-day boycott of Jewish businesses.

- Soon after Hitler came to power, Jewish civil servants were sacked.

- In 1935 the Nuremberg Laws deprived Jews of German citizenship.

- In 1938 Kristallnacht, an attack on Jewish properties and synagogues, occurred – 20,000 Jews sent to the camps. Following this, Jewish doctors and lawyers were forbidden to work for Aryans and Jewish children had to be taught in separate schools.

- In 1942 at the Wansee Conference, the Final Solution (the extermination of the Jews) was decided.

The historian Daniel Goldhagen, in his book *Hitler's Willing Executioners*, has sparked a great controversy by arguing that the German people were, and, had been for centuries, virulently and uniquely anti-semitic and that ordinary Germans did not just stand by whilst the Jews were persecuted but took pleasure in attacking the Jews, including their murder in World War Two. Many historians have criticised Goldhagen for selective use of evidence and argue that Germans pre-1933 had not been particularly anti-semitic. Certainly in 1933 Hitler turned down SA demands for more than a one day boycott of Jewish shops for fear of a hostile response inside and outside Germany.

The evidence suggests that though many Germans had a vague dislike of Jews in general they got on well wit their Jewish neighbours and failed to respond to Nazi propaganda aimed at inciting hatred of the Jews.

Q. What were the main features of The Terror State?

The Third Reich was certainly a police state with the Gestapo, SD, SS, a purged police and legal system, 18 concentration camps and a vicious punishment code.

- The Decree for the Protection of People and State (February 1933) allowed indefinite detention without trial.

- Dachau, the first concentration camp, opened in March 1933. There were never fewer than 10,000 prisoners in the camps and, in total, probably about 225,000 Germans were imprisoned for political crimes in the years 1933-39 (a fraction of the figures for Stalin's camp system).

- Hermann Goering set up the Gestapo in Prussia in 1933; Heinrich Himmler took control of the Gestapo after 1933. From 1936 Himmler was in control of all police. The Gestapo was heavily dependent on denunciations by ordinary Germans, e.g. in Wurzberg 54% of all race-related charges were initiated by private citizens.

- The SS was created in 1925 (under Himmler's control from 1929) and became immensely powerful after the Night of the Long Knives. It had 200,000 members by 1935. Their main duties were to run the concentration camps (from 1934) and to enforce racial policies.

- The SD was set up in 1931 by Himmler; increasingly they were given the task of gathering intelligence and monitoring public opinion.

- After 1933, judges could be removed for their political beliefs; special courts were set up for political crimes, including a People's Court for treason offences; judges were ordered to interpret the law according to 'the will of the Führer.'

Control of the media and culture

The media and arts were controlled. In March 1933, the Ministry for Popular Enlightenment and Propaganda was set up by Josef Goebbels. Goebbels regarded radio as the most important medium; the Reich Radio Company brought all broadcasting under Nazi control. A cheap radio, the Volksepfanger, was mass-produced; in 1932 less than 25% households had a radio, by 1939 more than 70% did. In 1933 there were 4700 daily papers in Germany, by 1944 only 1000. Eher Verlag (Nazi publishing house) controlled 66% of the Press by 1939. The sole news agency permitted was run by the Nazis. All films had to pass censors and about half of Germany's best-known film stars emigrated.

Nazi rituals were created to celebrate the Nazi state: the Nuremberg rallies, celebrations of the Munich Putsch, of Hitler's birthday.

Control of all aspects of citizens' lives

Leisure and work were controlled through party organisations. The German Labour Front was run by Robert Ley; Strength Through Joy organised recreational opportunities for workers whilst the Beauty of Labour's task was to improve work-place amenities for workers. Non-Nazi recreational clubs were often closed down, even chess clubs.

Two examples of Nazi attempts to control the lives of individuals in line with Nazi ideology are their policies towards a) women and b) young people.

a) Nazi policies towards Women

The Nazi slogan *'Kinder, Kirche und Kuche'* (Children, Church, Kitchen), defined the spheres of activity the Nazis wanted to confine women to. The Nazis took much further Weimar policies (from 1930) to restrict female employment. Married women were often excluded from the civil service and other professions. Restrictions were placed on the numbers of women at university. From 1933, women who left work to marry (an Aryan) received an interest free marriage loan; the amount to be repaid fell by 25% with each child born. The Women's Enterprise (DFW) organised training for women in domestic skills; by 1939, 3.5 million women had attended such courses.

The Nazis were very anxious to increase the birth-rate; it had been falling across Europe in the 1920s but most severely in Germany and this had potentially serious consequences for the Nazis' expansionist aims. In the 1930s the Nazis tried a number of policies to increase the birth-rate, including awarding medals for prolific mothers (bronze for 4/5 children, silver for 6/7 and gold for 8 or more). Women were encouraged to lead healthy lifestyles and divorce was made easier for those in childless marriages.

The birth-rate did rise from 990,000 in 1932 to 1.28 million in 1937, but this was well short of the 1.6 million births of 1920 and probably was more the result of improved economic conditions.

However, from 1936 the Nazis had to modify their employment policies because of labour shortages; from this point, growing numbers of women were recruited into jobs. By 1939 more women were in employment than in 1933 and by 1943 women were conscripted into war work.

b) Youth in Nazi Germany

Young people were of particular importance to the Nazis as they were Gemany's future and were also more susceptible to indoctrination. The Hitler Youth (*Hitler Jugend*) was set up 1925; by 1933 there were only 55,000 members, whereas total youth groups in Germany numbered 5 to 6 million members.

In 1933 all other youth groups, except for those run by the Catholic Church, were closed down and absorbed into the Hitler Youth (HJ). In 1936 all youth groups were incorporated into the HJ. By 1939, 82% of all 11-18 year olds were in the HJ or League of German Maidens (the equivalent for girls). In 1939 membership became compulsory.

Boys were trained for war, women for motherhood. The HJ became less popular in the late 1930s as activities and discipline became more militarised and membership became compulsory. Consequently, alternative youth groups, illegal after 1936, attracted growing numbers. The most popular group were the Edelweiss Pirates (included a number of regional groups, e.g. the Navajos of Cologne) who were working class and refused to join the HJ. They organised their own activities and often beat up HJ members. They were rarely involved in political activities but a few joined resistance groups in the war. The Nazis found them difficult to deal with, partly because there was no organised leadership that they could target. In 1944 the Nazis did hang the leaders of the Cologne Pirates.

There were also middle/upper class youth groups who rejected the HJ; these became known as the Swing Movement. They, unlike the Edelweiss pirates, did not meet in parks or on the streets but tended to do so in night clubs or their parents' homes; they angered the Nazis by dancing to American, black music and wearing English style clothing. These alternative groups reveal the limit to Nazi controls.

Education

The main aim of Nazi educational policy was to develop loyalty to the regime; there was no emphasis on developing the individual's abilities. In 1933 the Law for Restoration of a Professional Civil Service led to a purge of teachers; by 1937 the Nazi Teachers' League represented 97% of all teachers. Lessons, particularly History and Biology, became politicised; there was a much greater emphasis on Physical Education in schools and eugenics was introduced. Teachers increasingly became disillusioned because of constant Party interference and as a result of being undermined by the HJ.

Q. What were relations between the Nazis and the Christian Churches like?

1.   The Catholic Church

The Nazis lacked the confidence to destroy the established churches though they did undermine them. In the case of the Catholic Church, Hitler signed an agreement, the Concordat, with the Pope in 1933, under which Catholic bishops had to take an oath of loyalty to the Nazi state. In 1936 the Nazis broke the Concordat by closing down Catholic youth organisations and by beginning to close monasteries. This led to the Pope denouncing the Nazi regime in his 1937 encyclical *'With Burning Concern'*. In 1941 the Catholic press was closed down. However, the Church survived and some individual Catholic clergy spoke out against the Nazis, particularly Cardinal Galen who in 1941 denounced the murder of the handicapped; his sermon was printed and widely distributed.

2.   The Protestant Churches

The Nazis tried a different strategy with the Protestant church, trying to infiltrate it and control it from within. Already in 1933, there existed a nationalist movement within the Protestant church, known as the 'German Christians'. In 1933 they won 75% of the votes in church elections and their leader, Ludwig Muller, was made Reich Bishop. However, in 1934 dissenting clergy set up the 'Confessional Church' in opposition to Nazi attempts to Nazify the Church; Pastor Niemoller was their leader and a majority of clergy joined them. Niemoller was imprisoned in 1938.

Therefore, the Churches to some extent continued to provide sources of values and information different from the Nazi regime.

The Economy in Nazi Germany

Q. What were the main features of Hitler's economic policy?

When Hitler became Chancellor in January 1933, he knew that his continuing popularity depended on his being able to tackle Germany's economic problems, particularly unemployment, successfully. At the same time he was determined to rearm Germany and to prepare for war. For both these reasons he wanted to rebuild the German economy.

Hitler needed the support of industrialists and so used Hjalmar Schacht as Reichsbank President and Reich Economics Minister, 1934-7. Hitler ignored the socialist elements in the Nazis' Twenty-Five Points and rejected SA calls for nationalisation of big businesses in a 'second revolution'. Many industrialists became very closely identified with the regime, e.g. Krupp (steel/arms manufacturer) and I. G. Farben (chemicals).

Hitler had no coherent economic plan in January 1933; he adopted three approaches:

a) Autarky
b) Deficit financing – spending money on job creation, large-scale borrowing
c) *Wehrwirtschaft* – an economy geared to the demands of war.

Until 1936 Hitler followed fairly orthodox financial policies – the New Plan (September 1934) involved government control of foreign exchange and bilateral trade agreements, particularly with Balkan countries. Peasant farmers were protected by tariffs on imported food, and helped by cheap loans and tax exemptions. Hitler addressed the problem of high unemployment by a variety of methods. He was aided by the fact that, by 1933, world trade was starting to recover but nonetheless his success in creating new jobs and reviving industry was substantial, as these figures show:

Numbers of Unemployed in Germany (in millions)

1932	5.6	1934	2.3	1937	0.9	1938	0.2

Q. How was unemployment tackled?

Unemployment was beginning to fall before the Nazis came to power (it peaked in 1932), but Hitler, once in power, certainly accelerated the process. **This was achieved by:**

- Spending money on public works programmes, schemes to build new houses, plant forests and reclaim land. Total government spending rose from RM 8.6 billion in 1932 to RM 29.3 billion by 1938.

- Encouraging the expansion of the car industry by removing the luxury tax on cars, cutting the tax on petrol and beginning a programme of autobahn building which gave Germany a new motorway network.

- Offering cash incentives to persuade women to give up their jobs.

- After 1935, instituting a massive re-armament programme created hundreds of thousands of new jobs in industry.

- Re-introducing conscription in 1935. This also helped to bring unemployment down by taking young men between the ages of 18 and 20 out of the job market.

By 1937 there was a shortage of skilled labour. All this government spending helped stimulate economic growth and to restore confidence.

Industrial output
In 1933 industrial production was only 66% of its pre-Depression level, but by 1937 Germany was producing more than she had in the most prosperous Weimar years.

Gross National Product
Germany's GNP in 1928 was 72 billion Reichsmarks; by 1933 it had fallen to 44 billion; by 1938 it had risen to 80 billion.

Wage Levels
Wages recovered to a large extent too: in 1933, average wages in Germany were only 77% of their 1928 level but by 1939 they were 89% of the 1928 level. Overall, German workers benefited from falling unemployment and rising wages but, in real terms, wages were not quite as high as in the best years of the Weimar Republic.

The Four Year Plan (1936)

Hitler's achievements in tackling unemployment and stimulating economic growth were offset by a serious problem. To rearm, Germany Hitler needed to import more fuel and raw materials such as rubber, bauxite and iron ore. This worsened Germany's balance of payment problem (Germany was importing much more than it was exporting). By the end of 1935, Hitler's advisers told him that Germany could not afford both to import all the food she was importing and to import all the industrial raw materials. This is often referred to as the 'Guns or Butter?' crisis. Hitler felt that he could not risk cutting down on the availability to food because this might make his government unpopular, so he decided instead to try to make Germany self-sufficient in industrial raw materials.

Hermann Goering was put in charge of The Four Year Plan, which began in 1936. The plan was intended to make synthetic substitutes for imported oil and rubber and to devise ways of using Germany's poor quality coal and iron ore. This marked a departure from traditional economic policy and was opposed by Hjalmar Schacht, Hitler's Economics Minister, who resigned in 1937.

Hitler, in a secret 'Four Year Plan Memorandum', outlined the need to gear the economy for war within 4 years. Overall, the Plan was not a success. The scheme to produce artificial rubber ('BUNA') worked, and production of synthetic fuel doubled, but in most other categories of production, targets were not met; by the time the war broke out Germany was still dependent on imported fuel and raw materials, particularly on iron-ore from Sweden. Furthermore, the subsidising of inefficient small peasant farmers by the Nazi regime, meant that by 1939 Germany was still importing 19% of its food requirements.

Rearmament

Government spending in armaments in billions of Reichsmarks

1932	0.8	1933	1.9	1935	6.0	1938	17.2

> In 1933 Germany had an army of 100,000 men, no tanks, no warplanes and a navy of limited tonnage.

> By 1939 the Germans had 1200 bombers and 98 divisions in their Army, though about a third of these were untrained and unorganised. The Navy comprised 2 battleships, 2 armoured cruisers, 17 destroyers and 47 U-boats.

The period 1936-39 saw a massive increase in arms spending; 66% of German industrial investment was devoted to war production.

Q. Was Hitler preparing for total war or limited war?

Despite this huge increase in armaments expenditure, Germany would not be ready for total war (the total mobilisation of the economy to support a long war) until the mid-1940s. Historians are divided over whether Hitler had planned to get Germany prepared for total war prior to 1939. Some historians argue that Hitler never intended to achieve full mobilisation of the economy because he aimed to wage a series of short, blitzkrieg campaigns, which would allow Germany to exploit the economic resources of conquered countries before launching another attack. According to this interpretation, Hitler's strategy failed when he became trapped in a long war of attrition with the USSR from June 1941, which ultimately led to the USSR (and its allies) wearing Germany down.

However, other historians, notably Richard Overy, suggest that Hitler was planning for total war, rather than blitzkrieg campaigns, but miscalculated in 1939 as he did not think his invasion of Poland would provoke a general European war.

Q. Was Hitler forced by a growing economic crisis to go to war in 1939?

The historian Tim Mason has argued precisely this: that growing inflationary pressures - Schacht's resignation as President of the Reichsbank in January 1939 was partly because of concerns over this - and increasing working class discontent with the limited supply of consumer goods (consumer good production rose by 69% in the period 1933-38 compared to a 389% increase in industrial goods over the same period) and the failure of wages in the late 1930s to rise in real terms, shaped Hitler's decision to go to war in 1939. Mason suggests that Hitler was seeking to escape from these growing economic problems by going to war.

However, most historians have rejected Mason's thesis. Mason's critics argue that firstly, growing economic difficulties did not amount to a crisis and, secondly, that it was diplomatic and military considerations, rather than economic factors, which influenced Hitler's decision over the timing of war.

Opposition to the Nazis

Opposition to the Nazis has received more attention from historians over the past 25 years; as historians have come to realise that the Nazi system was less efficient than was traditionally believed, they have become increasingly aware of opposition to the Nazis. Grumbling and minor dissent, especially over lack of wage rises and increases in working hours, were quite widespread. SOPADE (the SPD in exile) reports indicate that most grumbling was the result of economic conditions.

The working class posed a real challenge to the Nazis in that they made up 45% of the population and had tended to support the SPD and KPD before 1933; the SPD had 1 million members in 1933 and 4 million associate members within the trade unions. The Nazis arrested many socialists in 1933 but some of the SPD leaders operated from exile (SOPADE), first from Prague and, from 1938, from Paris. SOPADE's activities were mainly intelligence gathering and its policy after 1933 was to wait for the collapse of the Nazi regime.

The KPD were more active in their opposition; by 1939 KPD organisations existed in 89 Berlin factories. There was rising working class dissatisfaction in the period 1937-39 because of the failure to win substantial pay rises. The KPD tried to undermine the Nazi regime by distributing leaflets. Both the SPD and KPD smuggled pamphlets into Germany; 1.6 million were seized at the border in 1935 and in 1934-36 200,000 people in Germany were able to read each edition of 'Socialist Action' (SPD). However, their leadership had been seriously hit by the mass arrests following the Reichstag Fire. 10,000 communists had been arrested and thereafter the KPD operated in very small cells and concerted action was, therefore, very difficult. Left-wing opposition to the Nazis continued to be hampered by the ongoing conflict between the SPD and KPD.

The Churches clashed with the Nazi regime on three occasions:

a)   Pastor Niemoller's opposition to the centralisation of the Protestant churches into a single Reich Church in 1933.

b)   Catholic protests against the order to replace crucifixes by portraits of Hitler in Catholic schools.

c)   Cardinal von Galen's protest against the euthanasia programme.

Opposition from within the Army

Many officers welcomed Nazi rearmament policies but some senior officers had serious misgivings about Hitler's foreign policy. Before the outbreak of war the only significant opposition to emerge within the Army was that centring on Ludwig Beck, Chief of Staff, who, in 1938, conspired to bring down Hitler during the Sudeten crisis. This proved ineffective and opposition disappeared until defeat in World War Two seemed inevitable; the Stauffenberg Bomb Plot of July 1944 had significant backing from senior officers who sought to bring about a negotiated peace with the Allies.

Opposition after 1939

During World War Two, a variety of resistance groups emerged; notably the White Rose at Munich University, led by Sophie and Hans Scholl, who were executed in 1943 for distributing anti-Nazi leaflets and the Kreisau Circle, a group of conservative opponents, who met at the home of Count von Moltke . The Kreisau Circle aimed to draw up plans for the period after Hitler's downfall rather than trying to bring it about. Moltke was arrested in 1944 and other members of the group then linked up with Stauffenberg. 5000 people were executed after the Bomb Plot. By 1945 500,000 Germans were in concentration camps.

Q. **Why was opposition to the Nazi regime so limited?**

1. Because there was much positive support for the regime, and, especially for Hitler himself. This was partly the result of Goebbels' propaganda machine but mainly because the regime delivered results particularly in terms of tackling unemployment and in foreign policy. Hitler was seen as a moderate who would tame radical Nazis like Ernst Röhm and in his early years in power Hitler constantly stressed in his speeches that he sought peace.

2. Because organised centres of opposition were destroyed in 1933 - rival political parties, trade unions etc

3. Because opposition was illegal and because of the fear inspired by the SS and Gestapo. Terror was effective because, although it affected only a minority, it made the majority unwilling to speak out about issues that they did not feel immediately affected them.

Hitler's Foreign Policy

The aims of Hitler's foreign policy

Q. **What are the main sources of evidence for Hitler's foreign policy aims?**

- The Twenty-Five Points (1920)
- Mein Kampf (1924/25)
- Hitler's 'Second Book' (1928) – written but not published
- Four Year Plan Memorandum (1936)
- Hossbach Memorandum (1937)

The historian AJP Taylor argued that when Hitler came to power he had no precise goals, just a desire for expansion and that his foreign policy thereafter was shaped purely by opportunism. Most historians (e.g. Hugh Trevor-Roper) reject this view, arguing that from 1924-25 onwards, when Hitler wrote *Mein Kampf*, clear objectives are evident, which Hitler then put into effect in the 1930s. Hitler did not have a detailed blueprint or timetable for expansion but what stands out is that that he had decisively rejected more traditional German nationalists' goal of a return to the borders of 1914. Instead, driven by his racialist theories, Hitler sought *lebensraum* (living-space) in the east as his main aim. Fritz Fischer has argued for continuity between German foreign policy pre-1914 and pre-1939, but other historians point to the unique racial element in Nazi foreign policy.

Foreign policy was of primary importance to Hitler. His main priority from 1934, once he had established his dictatorship, was to rearm Germany.

- Revising the Versailles Treaty was for Hitler not the ultimate goal but a means towards the larger aim of winning lebensraum; breaking the restrictions that Versailles had imposed on Germany's armed forces was a prerequisite for expansion.

- Hitler's racist ideas meant that he was committed to the creation of a Greater German Reich, incorporating all German-speakers. However, he wanted to go much further than that; he sought *lebensraum* for the German 'master race' and also to seize areas which had the resources that Germany needed (*Grosswirtschaftsraum*: 'Greater Economic space'). Hitler envisaged a Germany which would include the whole of Eastern Europe and the western part of the USSR. The native peoples of the area, mainly Slavs and regarded by the Nazis as '*untermenschen*' (sub-human), would work for the Germans as slaves.

Early successes

Initially Hitler had to proceed cautiously because in 1933 Germany's armed forces were considerably weaker than those of its neighbours such as France and Poland. However, from 1936 onwards, the pace of Hitler's foreign policy accelerated sharply, causing his cautious generals great anxiety.

In 1933 Hitler withdrew Germany from the League of Nations and from the League's Disarmament Conference, using France's refusal to allow German rearmament as an excuse. Hitler sought to win British support by claiming that he was prepared to accept a limit of 200,000 for the German Army. By this time many British politicians were arguing that the Versailles Treaty had been too harsh and that revisions should be made.

Before seriously starting on rearmament, Hitler signed a friendship treaty with Poland in 1934, thus reassuring the Poles. Hitler certainly remained committed to winning back Germany's lost lands from Poland but it is possible that he saw in Poland a potential client-state that might act as an ally against the USSR.

A reminder to Hitler of the need for caution: The Dollfuss Putsch (July 1934)

In July 1934 Austrian Nazis tried to seize power in Vienna in order to achieve the Anschluss (union with Germany), and murdered the Austrian Chancellor, Engelbert Dollfuss. The putsch failed and Kurt Schuschnigg, an opponent of the Nazis, became chancellor. The incident alarmed Mussolini, who had had close relations with Dollfuss, so much that he mobilised Italian troops at the Brenner Pass, on the Austro-Italian border. Most contemporaries believed that Hitler was behind the attempted Austrian Nazi putsch but historians are divided over this question.

Revisions of the Versailles Treaty (1935):

➢ **Reunion with the Saar**

In January, the inhabitants of the Saar, run by the League of Nations since 1920, voted by a vast majority in favour of reunion with Germany.

> The reintroduction of conscription and Hitler's announcement of rearmament

In March, Hitler announced that he was reintroducing military conscription and that he intended to create an army of 550,000 men. He also revealed that German already had begun to build, in breach of Versailles, an airforce. These announcements alarmed Britain, France and Italy. Although Mussolini was a Fascist, he was concerned about Hitler's declared aim of achieving the Anschluss. This was because Italy had gained the South Tyrol, a German-speaking area, in the Treaty of St Germain and Mussolini feared that if Hitler took over Austria, he would then demand the South Tyrol. Furthermore, if Germany took over Austria, Mussolini suspected that Hitler might look to expand into the Balkans where Mussolini had his own ambitions.

A brief show of concerted opposition to Nazi expansion: the Stresa Front (April 1935)

Immediately after Hitler's reintroduction of conscription, he was faced with what was potentially a serious obstacle to his expansionist plans; the leaders of Britain, France and Italy met at Stresa and agreed that they would take collective action in the event of further German breaches of Versailles.

However, the Stresa Front quickly broke down:

- Britain angered France and Italy by signing the Anglo-German Naval Agreement in June 1935, allowing Germany to have a navy with a tonnage of 35% that of Britain.

- In October 1935 Mussolini launched an attack on Abyssinia, which angered Britain and France and completed the collapse of the Stresa Front, after Britain and France had unsuccessfully (and rather half-heartedly) tried to get Mussolini to withdraw.

Q. Why did Britain and France choose to appease Hitler between 1936 and 1938?

> The British Government had decided that some of the Versailles Treaty's restrictions on Germany were unreasonably harsh, and that making concessions to Hitler would make Hitler behave more reasonably and thus maintain peace in Europe. This assumption was the basis of British foreign policy for the next four years, and that policy came to be known as Appeasement.

> Memories of the horrific slaughter of the First World War meant that many people in France and Britain were committed to the prevention of another war. This sentiment was reinforced by knowledge of the effects of bombing of civilians during the Spanish Civil War.

> Appeasement was also the consequence of the British government's determination to avoid a war in Europe at a time when Japanese expansion (e.g. the invasion of Manchuria in 1931) seemed to threaten British interests in the Far East.

> French leaders were opposed to German breaches of the Versailles Treaty but believed France was too weak to prevent them unless Britain took joint action alongside her. British politicians, on the other hand, were more favourably disposed towards German revisions of the treaty as long as this was done through negotiation.

> ➤ France was politically very divided in the 1930s; many on the Right in France were more concerned about the French Communist Party and the threat of Soviet expansion than about Hitler.

> ➤ Britain and France were preoccupied with resolving the economic problems caused by the Wall Street Crash.

> ➤ France and Britain were reluctant to confront Germany because they could not count on support from the USA, which was following an isolationist foreign policy during the 1930s.

Re-militarising the Rhineland (March 1936)

Hitler generally proved adept at reading how his opponents were likely to respond. Encouraged by the collapse of the Stresa Front, and by the international community's preoccupation with the Abyssinian crisis, he felt confident enough to remilitarize the Rhineland, a breach of both the Versailles Treaty and the Locarno Pact (1925). Although the League of Nations condemned this action, France and Britain did nothing about it. Hitler's generals were astonished; they had advised against the move, believing it would provoke a war with the much larger French Army.

Gaining Allies

During 1936 and 1937 Hitler worked to build up a system of alliances. He and Mussolini both sent troops and planes to fight alongside the forces of the rebel Nationalist General, Francisco Franco in the Spanish Civil War (1936-39). During the Abyssinian crisis (1935-36), Germany continued to trade with Italy in spite of League imposed sanctions on Italy, which damaged Italy's relations with Britain and France. In October 1936 Hitler and Mussolini signed the Rome-Berlin Axis, a friendship treaty. Hitler also found that the Japanese Government shared his dislike of Soviet Russia. In November 1936 Germany and Japan signed the Anti-Comintern Pact, an agreement to co-operate to prevent the spread of Communism.

The Hossbach Memorandum (November 1937)

In November 1937, Hitler held a meeting with key military and diplomatic personnel, at which he outlined his plans for 'Lebensraum', which he said needed to be achieved by 1943-45. Hitler spoke about the need to achieve Anschluss with Austria and to destroy Czecholslovakia. Some of Hitler's more cautious generals and diplomatic officials, who were non-Nazis, expressed their concerns at his expansionist plans. Over the next few months, Hitler removed these doubters, including Neurath, the Foreign Minister, and Blomberg, the War Minister. In addition, 18 generals were obliged to retire. Hitler had now very largely cut his links with the military and diplomatic personnel he had inherited from the Weimar Republic.

Achieving the Anschluss (March 1938)

At the beginning of 1938 Hitler had no plans for an immediate takeover of Austria and yet in March the Anschluss was achieved. This demonstrates that while Hitler had certain consistent aims (in this case, union with Austria), he was an opportunist when it came to timing and methods. By 1938, Hitler was seeking to bring closer the union of Germany and Austria (with a view to eventual Anschluss); so, in February 1938, he summoned Austria's Chancellor, Kurt Schuschnigg to a meeting at Berchtesgaden and bullied him into making concessions including the appointment of a leading Austrian Nazi, Artur Seyss-Inquart, as Interior Minister.

Once he returned to Vienna, Schuschnigg tried to regain the initiative by announcing a plebiscite (referendum) would be held in which the Austrian people would be given the chance to vote on whether they wanted Austria to remain *'a free and German, independent, Christian and united'* country. Hitler, fearing that an unsupervised plebiscite might go against him, used the threat of force to compel President Miklas to sack Schuschnigg in favour of Seyss-Inquart, who immediately invited the German Army into Austria. Following a virtually bloodless invasion on March 12th the Anschluss was proclaimed. In a Nazi-supervised plebiscite, 99% of those who voted expressed their approval of the Anschluss.

Neither Britain nor France had the will to resist Hitler, partly because there were many in both countries who regarded Hitler's desire for a greater Germany as reasonable.

The Sudeten Crisis, September 1938

It seems clear that Hitler sought to pick a quarrel with the Czech government over the Sudetenland in order to provide an excuse for invading Czechoslovakia and destroying it.

Q. Why did Hitler seek the destruction of Czechoslovakia?

❖ He saw the Czechs as an inferior race and had resented them since his time growing up within the old Austro-Hungarian Empire.

❖ Czechoslovakia had been created by the hated 1919-20 Peace Settlement and included over 3 million Sudeten Germans who had, in Hitler's eyes, been denied the right of self-determination.

❖ Czechoslovakia was a democratic state.

❖ Czechoslovakia was an ally of both France and the USSR and had an efficient army; it constituted an obstacle to Hitler's expansion eastwards.

The Anschluss had left Czechoslovakia, Hitler's next target, in a vulnerable position, with German troops along its southern as well as its northern border. In seeking to gain control of Czechoslovakia and its strong armaments industry, Hitler carefully built up links with the Sudeten German Party led by Henlein. Hitler encouraged Henlein to keep on raising his demands in order to prevent an agreement between the Czech government and the Sudeten Germans.

Britain's Prime Minister Neville Chamberlain still believed that Hitler wanted nothing more than a Greater German Reich and that peace could be maintained by appeasing him.

➔ On September 15th he visited Hitler at Berchtesgaden and during the next week he and French Prime Minister Daladier devised a plan under which Czechoslovakia would be made to hand over any territory where more than 50% of the inhabitants were German to Germany. The Czechs were not consulted about this but they had little choice but to agree since France was their main ally.

➔ On September 22nd Chamberlain met Hitler again at Bad Godesberg. Hitler then raised his demands by asking for immediate occupation of the Sudetenland. War seemed imminent, and the Czechs and their French allies began to mobilise. The Poles and the Hungarians, encouraged by Hitler, also began to demand that parts of Czechoslovakia should be handed over to them.

➔ Chamberlain, in a last bid to preserve the peace, appealed to Mussolini who persuaded Hitler to attend a conference, along with Daladier of France, at Munich on September 29th. The Czechs were not consulted and their other ally, the USSR, was not invited. It was agreed that Hitler should occupy the Sudetenland in stages rather than all at once. Since France, the USSR, and Britain were not prepared to support them and they could not win a single-handed war against Germany, the Czechs were forced to agree to this.

In return Hitler signed a non-committal document expressing a desire for a lasting Anglo-German peace. For the Czechs the loss of the Sudetenland was a disaster, which deprived them not only of much of the country's vital industrial base but also all of its strongest frontier defences. Poland and Hungary were given Teschen and Ruthenia respectively.

The hollowness of appeasement revealed: Hitler seized the rest of Czechoslovakia and Memel (March 1939)

Chamberlain and Daladier soon discovered that appeasement was based on a fundamental misunderstanding of Hitler's aims: he was not going to be content with the union of all German-speakers. Hitler began to encourage the separatist feelings of the Slovaks. When the new Czech President, Hacha, was confronted with the demand that his country should be further divided up and that the Czech part of it should become part of the Reich, he gave in.

On March 15th the Czech provinces of Bohemia and Moravia were occupied by German troops and became part of Germany. Slovakia was to be an independent state, though the Slovaks had to conduct their foreign policy along lines laid down by Berlin. A week later Hitler demanded that Lithuania hand back Memel, a city with German inhabitants, which Germany had lost as a result of the Versailles Treaty.

The Polish Crisis

After March 1939 it was obvious to Britain and France that the only way to stop Hitler was by fighting him.

➔ Britain signed a treaty on 31st March 1939 in which they promised to defend Poland if Poland was attacked.

➔ In April Britain also announced the introduction of conscription for 20-21 year olds, the first time Britain had had peacetime conscription.

➔ In order to undermine Britain's will to fight in defence of Poland, Hitler began by demanding just the return of Danzig, a mainly German-speaking city, and for rail and road access across the 'Polish Corridor' (separating East Prussia from the main part of Germany). It is possible that perhaps Hitler hoped that the Poles would agree to hand over Danzig and then become allies in Germany's planned war against the USSR.

➔ The Poles, encouraged by Britain's guarantee, decided to refuse Hitler's demand for Danzig and, in late March, ordered partial mobilisation, which angered Hitler.

➔ In April Hitler ordered his generals draw up plans for an attack on Poland ("Case White").

➔ Then in August Hitler secretly approached the Soviet Government for an alliance. This followed on lukewarm and ultimately abortive negotiations between the British and French, on the one hand, and, the USSR, on the other, for collective military action to defend Poland.

The Nazi-Soviet Pact, August 1939

This agreement, published on August 23rd 1939, came as a great shock to the British and French. Stalin was seeking to buy time in which to strengthen his armed forces for the war with Germany, which he believed to be inevitable. The Pact also contained a secret agreement in which Russia and Germany divided up Poland between them and Russia was given permission to seize Estonia, Latvia and Lithuania and certain territories from Finland and Rumania. Hitler may well have thought that the pact would deter Britain and France from defending Poland. If it did not deter them, then the Pact would ensure that a war between Germany and Poland did not escalate into a war between Germany and Russia.

The Outbreak of World War Two

On September 1st, Germany invaded Poland, and on September 3rd Britain and France declared war on Germany. They were unable to offer any practical aid to the Poles, who were swiftly defeated by the Germans and by the Russians, who attacked Poland on September 17th. In October the Poles surrendered. However, Britain and France refused to accept Germany's occupation of Poland and so Hitler was now committed to a major European war earlier than he had intended. He had probably assumed that France and Britain's guarantees to Poland were just a bluff.

Blitzkrieg in the West

Hitler's main aim remained a war of conquest against the USSR and he therefore tried to get a negotiated peace with Britain and France in the autumn of 1939. When this failed, Hitler decided that before he attacked the Soviet Union he must achieve control over Western Europe.

In April 1940 German forces rapidly overran Denmark and Norway, a disaster that led to Neville Chamberlain's resignation as British Prime Minister. On May 10th, the day that Winston Churchill took over as Prime Minister, the Germans attacked Holland, Belgium, Luxembourg and France. By June, the first three countries had fallen and German troops were sweeping through France. The French surrendered on June 22nd. Only on June 10th had Mussolini decided to join in the war on Hitler's side and Italian troops had then invaded France.

The Battle of Britain (July-September 1940)

Hitler's spectacular victories were extremely popular in Germany but left Britain undefeated, although Britain had been forced to evacuate its expeditionary force at Dunkirk. Hitler still hoped for a negotiated peace but Churchill was defiant and Britain fought on. Hitler, therefore, decided that he must invade Britain in order to knock her out of the war before turning his attention to the USSR. However, the Luftwaffe failed to win control of the skies in the Battle of Britain.

Allies and Liabilities

Hitler soon discovered that his ally, Mussolini, was more of a liability than an asset. Mussolini launched unsuccessful campaigns in the Balkans and North Africa and Hitler felt obliged to help Italy both in conquering Yugoslavia and Greece and in maintaining his position in North Africa. These campaigns delayed Hitler's invasion of the USSR until late June 1941, a delay that was arguably fatal to its success. Meanwhile the German Navy, especially its U-boat (submarine) force, was given the job of starving Britain into surrender by sinking supply ships in the Atlantic. However, the campaign failed and Britain was able to hold out until the USA entered the war.

Operation Barbarossa (June 1941)

On June 22nd 1941, 3 million Axis troops invaded the USSR. The Russians, caught unprepared, retreated rapidly. By winter, the Germans were at the outskirts of Leningrad and were within 40 kilometres of Moscow, but the early onset of harsh winter conditions, for which they were ill-equipped, and a brilliant counter-attack planned by Marshal Zhukov, using Russian troops transferred from the Far East, meant that Moscow did not fall. Hitler did not achieve the quick blitzkrieg victory he had hoped for. From 1942, the war in Russia became a long drawn-out slogging match, which the German economy was not geared to support.

On December 11th 1941, four days after the Japanese attack on Pearl Harbour, Hitler declared war on America, which was already supplying Britain and Russia.

1942

In many ways 1942 marked the point at which the pendulum of war began to swing against Germany. In North Africa, Hitler's Afrika Korps drove the British out of Libya, which they had conquered from the Italians, and advanced into Egypt. In October, the British, led by General Montgomery, scored a decisive victory at El Alamein. By May 1943, North Africa was fully under Allied control.

In Russia, Hitler ordered an offensive southwards towards the oil fields of Transcaucasia. This advance was held up at Stalingrad, which the Red Army defended heroically. Late in 1942, the Russians launched a great counter-offensive, trapping the German Sixth Army and forcing its surrender on 31st January 1943. Hitler could have withdrawn the Sixth Army from Stalingrad before it became encircled but he became obsessed with capturing the city. About 100,000 Germans had died in the battle and 93,000 were taken prisoner Stalingrad was a great material and psychological blow for the Germans, and showed how much Russian military leadership and capability had improved since 1941.

1943

In the summer of 1943 US and British forces invaded Sicily and Italy successfully. Mussolini was overthrown and his successor, Marshal Badoglio, surrendered to the British and Americans. However, German forces in Italy fought to delay the Allied advance up the peninsula, which was not completed until spring 1945. German commandos rescued Mussolini in September 1943 and Hitler set him up as puppet ruler of the Salo Republic. In the spring of 1945, Mussolini and his mistress were executed by Communist partisans.

On the Eastern Front, in July 1943, the Red Army won a crushing victory at Kursk and then began to drive the Germans westwards.

1944

In 1944 the Red Army drove the Germans completely out of the USSR and most of Eastern Europe as they advanced towards Berlin. In the West, Britain and America launched the largest amphibious invasion in history on the Normandy coast on D-Day, June 6th 1944. Paris was liberated in August. Hitler's last offensive in the West, the 'Battle of the Bulge' of December 1944–January 1945, temporarily pushed the Allies back but failed to alter the course of the war.

1945

In February 1945, Russian troops invaded Germany and, in the West, the British and Americans had crossed the Rhine and were advancing on Berlin. By April, Berlin was besieged by the Red Army. On April 30th, Hitler committed suicide in his bunker in Berlin. On May 8th Germany surrendered. Goering and other leading Nazis were tried at Nuremburg for war crimes.

Q. Why did Hitler lose the War?

⇒ 1939-41 saw a huge increase in Germany's investment in rearmament but this was inefficiently managed. Only under Albert Speer (from 1942) was there efficient co-ordination of war production. He trebled weapons production in two years. Rivalries between different Nazi leaders and agencies, and, military interference in rearmament production, had prevented them from efficiently exploiting Germany's industry and raw materials and those of the countries that she occupied.

⇒ The Nazis only introduced 'Total War' measures in 1943; only then did Germany adopt mass production techniques. However, strategic bombing limited its expansion. In Britain, 'total war' was launched much earlier.

⇒ German production failed to keep pace with the demands of total war. German armoured divisions in 1939 had 328 tanks each; by 1943, 73 each and, by 1945, only 54 each. The Red Army had the reverse experience; by 1943 Russia was out-producing Germany in tanks and planes. Marshal Zhukov was a genius at deploying millions of men, which Soviet generals were unable to do properly in 1941. The USSR was aided by Lend-Lease from the USA from June 1942 ($ 11 billion in total).

⇒ Hitler underestimated the USSR and did not prepare for a winter campaign in 1941. Russia's vast size, the severity of the winter weather and the toughness of its people defeated the Germans. The Red Army, in Churchill's phrase, *"tore the guts out of the German Army"*. Nazi atrocities in the USSR led to a powerful Russian partisan movement emerging.

⇒ Declaring war on the USA was a mistake; if Hitler had not done so in December 1941, it is conceivable that the USA would then have prioritised the Pacific War over Europe even though it was extremely likely that war between the USA and Germany would have broken out quite soon in any case. America was beyond the range of German bombers and was the world's leading industrial power. In a war of attrition, the USA was certain to out-produce Germany and therefore beat her.

⇒ The German navy lost the Battle of the Atlantic (1940-43): between June 1940 and June 1944 Britain essentially fought a naval war, supported increasingly by aircraft. The navy was vital to keep Britain and its empire supplied. In 1941-42 U-boats reduced British trade to less than 33% of its 1939 volume. Disaster was only avoided by Britain expanding agricultural output, e.g. establishing the Land Army, and by stockpiling goods in the 1930s. In 1942, 1,662 British ships were sunk but, in 1942, a new centemetric radar system was introduced, which was much more effective in hunting U-boats, and better anti-submarine torpedoes were fitted to aircraft. In 1943, 237 German U-boats were sunk.

⇒ Until 1943, British night bombing and USAF day bombing proved very costly to the Allies and, towards the end of 1943, both were on the point of abandoning it. However, the development of the 'strategic fighter' - the Mustang - enabled the USAF to eliminate the Luftwaffe threat. Allied bombing in 1944-45 diverted German resources away from the war on land and sea; 33% of Germany's heavy guns and radar equipment were used for anti-aircraft defence. It also prevented the expansion of industrial output by Germany.

⇒ Hitler diverted vital resources away from the war-effort to the Final Solution.

Hitler's Foreign Policy 1933-39

1933
January   Hitler appointed Chancellor

September   Germany left the Disarmament Conference &
                    the League of Nations

1934
July   Chancellor Dolfuss of Austria assassinated

1935
January   Saar plebiscite
March   Conscription introduced; Hitler announced that he
                    would create an army of 550,000
April   Stresa Front signed by GB, France & Italy

June   Anglo-German Naval Treaty
October   Abyssinia invaded by Mussolini

1936
March   Rhineland reoccupied by German troops
July   Spanish Civil War began
October   Rome-Berlin Axis signed
November   Anti-Comintern Pact signed by Germany & Japan

1937
May   Bombing of Guernica by Luftwaffe in Spanish Civil War

November   British Foreign Secretary Lord Halifax visited Berlin
                    Hossbach Memorandum

1938
12 March   Anschluss – Austria united with Germany
September
12th   Nuremberg rally – Hitler demanded the Sudetenland
15th   Chamberlain visited Hitler at Berchtesgaden
18th   French Premier Daladier visited London
22nd   Chamberlain met Hitler again at Bad Godesberg
29th   Munich Conference – Mussolini, Hitler, Chamberlain & Hitler
                    agreed to hand the Sudetenland to Germany
October   The Sudetenland occupied

1939
March   Rest of Czechoslovakia occupied by Germany;
                    Memel seized by Germany
May   Pact of Steel – military alliance between Germany & Italy
August   Nazi-Soviet Pact
1st September   Poland invaded by Germany
3rd September Britain and France declared war on Germany

Revision and essay writing activities on the Rise and Rule of the Nazi Party

Below, you will find two essay questions, which cover most of the issues that I have dealt with in the Germany section of the Revision Guide. By examining these questions, you will be able to test your understanding and recall of that material and, in addition, practise your essay writing skills. I have given you some ideas about how they could be tackled and then provided you with space to add examples and further points.

1. How did Hitler exploit conditions in Germany to create a single party state?

Firstly, you need to take the question apart and see that you are being asked to analyse both the conditions which prevailed in the Weimar Republic which made possible Hitler's creation of a Nazi regime and the methods he used to take advantage of those conditions. Secondly, you should see that the question requires you to consider developments up to July 1933 (rather than just January 1933, when Hitler became chancellor) when the Nazi Party became the sole legal party.

In terms of analysing 'conditions' which gave rise to the Third Reich, you might either group these into short (1929-33) and long-term (since 1918) or, alternatively, adopt a thematic approach (probably better, less likely to lead you in to a narrative which becomes unfocused) in which you look at 'political', 'economic' and 'social' conditions. In order to write a really good answer, you should look to establish links between these conditions. With reference to the methods by which Hitler exploited these conditions, you need to ensure that you link methods to conditions, rather than simply describing what Hitler's methods were.

Below this paragraph, you will see some points relating to different types of condition, which played a part in the creation of a single party state in Germany. I have left space so you can add more points and examples to illustrate the key points.

Political conditions
Long-term
• The Republic was handicapped because of its association with the hated Versailles Treaty. Nationalist hostility towards the Republic was shown by the Kapp Putsch (1920).
• The Weimar constitution contained weaknesses; proportional representation, given the existence of a large number of parties, made for a series of short-lived coalition governments. The constitution also gave the President enormous power, particularly through Article 48.

Other long-term political conditions:

....

....

....

....

....

....

Short-term
• Collapse of the "Grand Coalition" in 1930 after the SPD walked out because of an argument with the Centre over cutting unemployment benefit.
• Growing political polarisation in 1930-33, saw the rise of both the NSDAP and the KPD (the latter gained 17% of the votes cast in Nov 1932 elections).
• The Reichstag Fire (February 1933) increased the propertied classes' fear of a communist revolution.

Other short-term political conditions:

....

....

....

Economic conditions
• Early economic crisis 1919-23; many of the middle-class were permanently alienated by a loss of savings during the hyper-inflation.
• Germany was hit particularly hard by the effects of the Wall Street Crash (1929), causing soaring unemployment.

More points about economic conditions:

....

....

....

....

....

....

How was Hitler able to exploit the above conditions?

• Hitler - charismatic leadership, oratory
• Hitler saw after the Munich Putsch (1923) that the way to power had to be by means of 'legal revolution'. Hitler committed the NSDAP to becoming the largest party in the Reichstag.
• By forming an alliance with Hugenberg and the DNVP from 1929.
• As a result of the Reichstag Fire, Hitler was able to persuade Hindenburg to declare a state of emergency.
• The Enabling Act (March 1933) gave Hitler the power to make law without the Reichstag; he used this power to dismantle democracy and create a single party state.

Other points about how Hitler was able to exploit conditions:

....

....

....

....

....

....

Conclusion:

....

....

....

....

....

....

....

....

....

....

....

2. How far was the single party regime in Germany successful by 1940 in achieving its aims?

In answering this question, first it is necessary to identify what the Nazis' aims were. The question does not specify foreign or domestic policy (the reference to 'in Germany' is to the regime, not to its policies in Germany), so both areas of policy should be considered. Below I have started by pointing to the debate among historians about the nature of the Nazis' aims and then listed their main aims. Following this, I have created a detailed plan, which examines the Nazis' success in certain areas of policy. I have also just indicated certain other aims that would merit assessment in this essay and I have left space for you to provide your own points and examples/evidence you might use in answering this question.

The historiographical debate - was Hitler an 'intentionalist' (according to Bullock, Trevor-Roper) with a set agenda or was the Nazi regime opportunist/functionalist (according to Broszat, Mommsen) which lacked clearly formulated aims and instead responded to circumstances in a chaotic fashion (Hitler as "weak dictator")?

How do we know what the Nazis' aims were? – The Twenty-Five Points (1920), Mein Kampf (1925), Four Year Plan Memorandum (1936), Hossbach Memorandum (1937).

What were the Nazis' aims?

The Nazis were not united, especially over the socialist elements of the Twenty-Five Point programme; Gregor Strasser and many of the SA leaders sought a "second revolution" involving the creation of a people's army and the nationalisation of big businesses. By 1933, Hitler had rejected these demands.

Foreign policy
To rip up the Versailles Treaty; rearmament; unite all German speakers; win Lebensraum in the East. The German historian Fritz Fischer has argued that there is a continuity between German foreign policy pre-1914 and pre-1939 but other historians point to the unique racial element in Nazi foreign policy.

Domestic policy
- **Economic**: to revive the German economy in order to **(a)** maintain domestic support by reducing unemployment, **(b)** to support rearmament; achieve autarky (economic self-sufficiency).
- **To destroy/suppress opposition & maintain a monopoly of political power**.
- **To create a totalitarian state** in which all aspects of Germans' lives were controlled and to indoctrinate the population with Nazi ideology.
- **To create a master race**

How successful were these aims?

1.   In Economic policy?

• Mopped up unemployment very successfully (only 0.2 million by 1938) by means of deficit financing, public works schemes, and rearmament.
• Industrial output reached record levels; by 1939 GNP was 33% higher than in 1929.
• Huge rearmament - 66% of investment went on rearmament in the period 1936-39.
But there were limits to this success and serious problems emerged -
• Nazi officials and economics experts/businessmen were divided over the 'Guns or Butter Crisis' in 1936. Hitler responded with the Four Year Plan.
• The economy was not geared for total war by the end of 1939 (some historians question whether this was Hitler's aim, Richard Overy argues that it was).
• 1939-41 saw a huge increase in investment in rearmament but this was

inefficiently managed. Only under Albert Speer (from 1942) was there efficient co-ordination of war production. He trebled weapons production in two years.
• Inflationary pressures began to build from 1937, this was partly why Schacht resigned as Economics Minister. Tim Mason argued that Hitler went to war in 1939 in order to escape a growing economic crisis; however, this view is not generally shared by historians.
• Autarky failed; Germany was still dependent on imports, particularly food (importing 19% of its requirements in 1939) and Swedish iron-ore.
• Real wages in the late 1930s were below the 1928 level and consumer good production lagged far behind that of industrial goods; this reflects Hitler's priorities (i.e. rearmament paramount after 1936).

2. In terms of destroying/suppressing opposition and maintaining a monopoly of political power?

(a) Very successful application of terror state
• Hitler quickly established a single party state in 1933; Law for the Protection of the German People and State (February 1933) used to arrest thousands of Communists; Enabling Act (March 1933) allowed Hitler to make law without the Reichstag; trade unions banned (May 1933); all other parties outlawed (June 1933); state parliaments abolished (January 1934).

• Purge of the SA in Night of the Long Knives (June 1934); Hitler became Fuhrer after Hindenburg's death (August 1934) and army swore oath of personal loyalty to him.

• Creation of a police state: Gestapo, SD, SS (expanded to 200,000 by 1935), 18 concentration camps - 225,000 people imprisoned 1933-39.

However, opposition was not totally eliminated, e.g. activities of SOPADE (200,000 people read *Socialist Action* in mid-1930s), conspiracy by General Beck in 1938.

• Nevertheless, opposition was driven underground and it was very ineffective.

(b) The regime also generated considerable positive support:

....

....

....

....

....

....

3.   In creating a totalitarian society?

....

....

....

....

....

....

....

4.   In creating a master race?

....

....

....

....

....

....

....

....

....

....

....

....

5.   In Foreign policy/rearmament?

....

....

....

....

....

....

....

....

....

....

....

....

Conclusion:

....

....

....

....

....

....

....

....

....

Suggested Reading

Listed below are just a few suggestions for useful reading on the four topics covered in this guide.

Russia

Peter Oxley, *Russia, From Tsars to Commissars*, OUP, Oxford, 2001. This is an excellent survey of Russian history from 1855 to 1991. It summarises in a very accessible way the key historical debates on Communist Russia.

Kevin McDermott, *Stalin: Revolutionary in an Era of War*, Palgrave, 2006. A more sophisticated book, but excellent on the historical debates surrounding Stalin.

David Christian, *Power and Privilege: Russia and the Soviet Union in the Nineteenth and Twentieth Centuries*, Pitman, 1986. Superb overview of Russian history, with very interesting sources dispersed throughout.

China

Geoff Stewart, *China 1900-76*, Heinemann, 2006. In my view, the best school textbook on the period. Clear, well written and with a good level of detail.

Edwin Moise, *Modern China*, Longman, London, 1994. A detailed survey of modern Chinese history. It provides a thorough account of the prescribed period (1946-64). The author's text is interesting but is quite sophisticated.

JAG Roberts, *A History of China*, Macmillan, London, 1999. Its chapters on China 1911-76 are clearly laid out and detailed. There is extensive discussion of different historical interpretations of the key issues.

Italy

John Hite & Chris Hinton, *Fascist Italy*, John Murray, 1998. Interestingly laid out and comprehensive textbook, with plenty on historical interpretations and key debates.

Christopher Duggan, *A Concise History of Italy*, Cambridge University Press, 1994. An excellent summary of Fascist Italy in Chapters 7 and 8.

Martin Clark, *Modern Italy 1871-1995*, Longman, 1996. Authoritative and interesting account of Fascist Italy in Chapters 10-14.

Germany

Ian Kershaw, *Hitler*, Longman, 1991. Best short biography of Hitler by the leading British expert on Nazism.

David Evans and Jane Jenkins, *Years of Weimar and the Third Reich*, Hodder and Stoughton, 1999. Thorough and well laid out survey, with excellent sources and clear coverage of the key historical debates.

Peter Pulzer, *Germany 1870-1945*, Oxford University Press, 1997. Concise and very well written overview of German history (Chapters 5-7 for rise and rule of the Nazis).